MICROSOFT® EXCEL

Yvonne Johnson
Pamela R. Toliver

ADDISON-WESLEY

An imprint of Addison Wesley Longman, Inc.

Reading, Massachusetts • Menlo Park, California • New York • Harlow, England
Don Mills, Ontario • Sydney • Mexico City • Madrid • Amsterdam

Senior Editor: Carol Crowell
Production Supervision: Patty Mahtani/Diane Freed
Copyeditor: Robin Drake/Barb Terry
Proofreader: Holly McLean-Aldis
Technical Editors: Martha Johnson, Deborah Minyard, Robin Edwards
Indexer: Mark Kmetzko
Composition: Compset, Inc.
Cover Illustration: © Frederic Joos/SIS
Cover Designer: Anthony Saizon
Cover Design Supervisor: Gina Hagen
Marketing Manager: Michelle Hudson
Manufacturing Manager: Hugh Crawford

ISBN 0-201-31119-4

Ordering from the SELECT System
For more information on ordering and pricing policies for the SELECT Lab Series and supplements, please contact your Addison Wesley Longman sales representative or call 1-800-552-2499.

Addison-Wesley Publishing Company
One Jacob Way
Reading, MA 01867
http://www.awl.com/he/is/
is@awl.com

4 5 6 7 8 9 10-DOW-009998

Preface to the Instructor

Welcome to the *Select Lab Series*. This applications series is designed specifically to make learning easy and enjoyable, a natural outcome of thoughtful, meaningful activity. The goal for the series is to create a learning environment in which students can explore the essentials of software applications, use critical thinking, and gain confidence and proficiency.

Greater access to ideas and information is changing the way people work. With Office 97 applications, you have greater integration capabilities and easier access to Internet resources than ever before. The *Select Lab Series* helps you take advantage of these valuable resources, with special assignments devoted to the Internet and with additional connectivity resources that can be accessed through our Web site, **http://www.awl.com/he/is/**.

The *Select Lab Series* offers dozens of proven and class-tested materials, from the latest operating systems and browsers, to the most popular applications software for word processing, spreadsheets, databases, presentation graphics, desktop publishing, and integrated packages, to HTML, to programming. For your lab course, you can choose what you want to combine; your choice of lab manuals will be sent to the bookstore, combined in a TechSuite, allowing students to purchase all books in one convenient package at a discount.

In addition to the individually bound books for each application for Office 97, you also may choose the complete *Select*: *Office 97 Professional*, which covers in one combined text Windows 95, Outlook, Internet Explorer 3.0, Word 97, Excel 97, Access 97, and PowerPoint 97.

Your Addison Wesley Longman representative will be happy to work with you and your bookstore manager to provide the most current menu of *Select Lab Series* offerings, outline the ordering process, and provide pricing, ISBNs, and delivery information. Or call 1-800-447-2226 or visit our Web site at http://www.awl.com/he/is/.

Organization

The "Overview of Windows 95" familiarizes students with Windows 95 before launching into the application. Students learn the basics of starting Windows 95, using a mouse, using the essential features of Windows 95, getting help, and exiting Windows 95.

Each Office 97 application is then covered in depth in five or six projects that teach beginning to intermediate skills. An overview introduces the basic concepts of the application and provides hands-on instructions to put students to work using the application immediately. Students learn problem-solving techniques while working through projects that provide practical, real-life scenarios that they can relate to.

Web assignments appear throughout the text at the end of each project, giving students practice using the Internet.

Approach

The *Select Lab Series* uses a document-centered approach to learning. Each project begins with a list of measurable objectives, a realistic scenario called the Challenge, a well-defined plan called the Solution, and an illustration of the final product. The Setup enables students to verify that the settings on the computer match those needed for the project. The project is arranged in carefully divided, highly visual objective-based tasks that foster confidence and self-reliance. Each project closes with a wrap-up of the project called The Conclusion, followed by summary questions, exercises, and assignments geared to reinforcing the information taught through the project.

Other Features

In addition to the document-centered, visual approach of each project, this book contains the following features:

- An overview of Windows 95 and Excel 97, so that students feel comfortable and confident as they function in the working environment.
- Keycaps and toolbar button icons within each step so that the student can quickly perform the required action.
- A comprehensive and well-organized end-of-the-project Summary and Exercises section for reviewing, integrating, and applying new skills.
- An illustration or description of the results of each step so that students know they're on the right track all the time.
- Nearly all the topics in this book were designed to match the guidelines for the Microsoft Office 97 User Certification program, which certifies individuals as Proficient or Expert users. The performance-based tests, developed by an independent company and endorsed by Microsoft, test the skills that employers expect and require of employees. Since author Yvonne Johnson is on the certification test review panel, she has provided much guidance for the topical content of this book to help users prepare for certification. To view the complete list of guidelines, go to http://www.awl.com/is/select/.

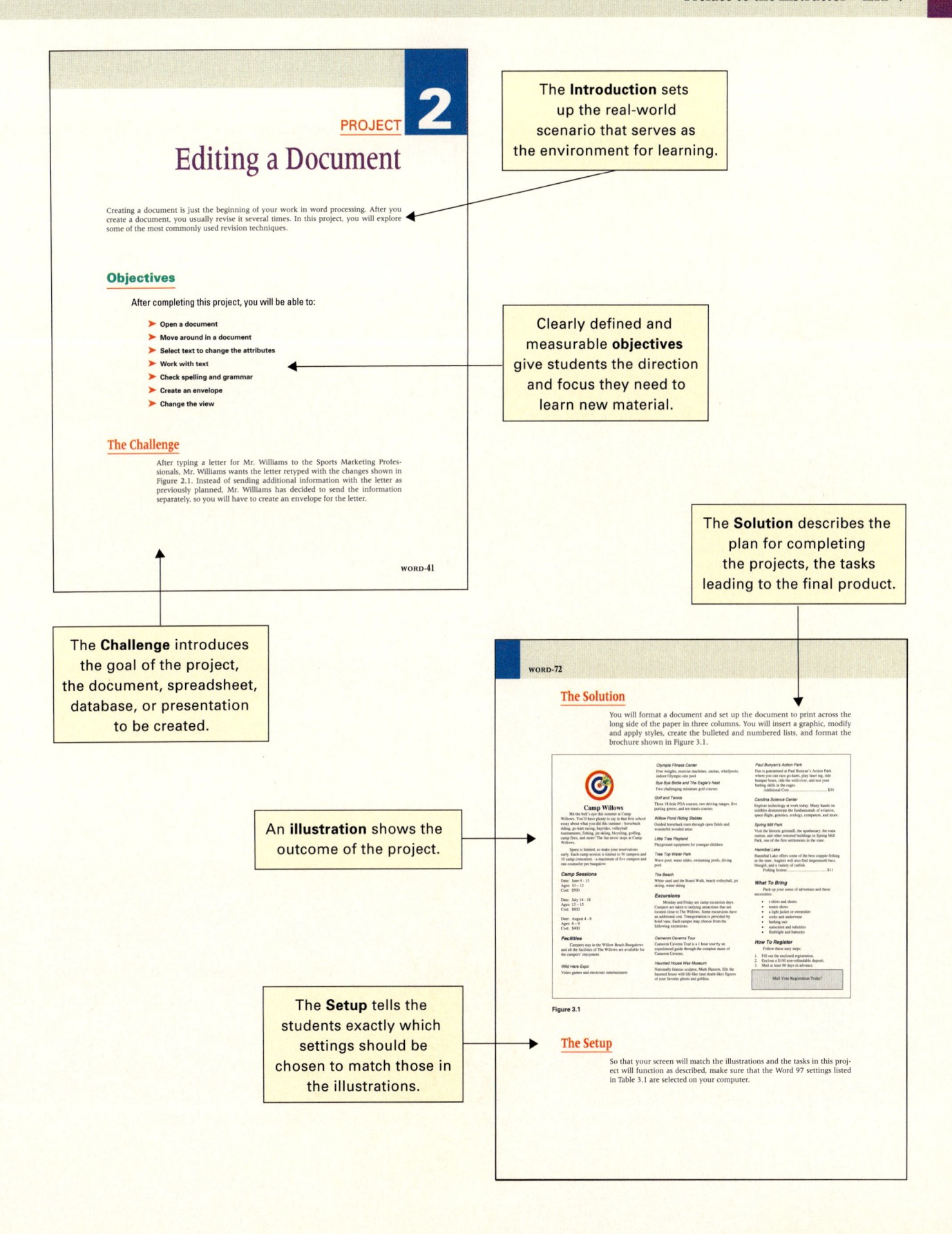

The **Introduction** sets up the real-world scenario that serves as the environment for learning.

Clearly defined and measurable **objectives** give students the direction and focus they need to learn new material.

The **Challenge** introduces the goal of the project, the document, spreadsheet, database, or presentation to be created.

The **Solution** describes the plan for completing the projects, the tasks leading to the final product.

An **illustration** shows the outcome of the project.

The **Setup** tells the students exactly which settings should be chosen to match those in the illustrations.

PROJECT **2**

Editing a Document

Creating a document is just the beginning of your work in word processing. After you create a document, you usually revise it several times. In this project, you will explore some of the most commonly used revision techniques.

Objectives

After completing this project, you will be able to:

- ➤ Open a document
- ➤ Move around in a document
- ➤ Select text to change the attributes
- ➤ Work with text
- ➤ Check spelling and grammar
- ➤ Create an envelope
- ➤ Change the view

The Challenge

After typing a letter for Mr. Williams to the Sports Marketing Professionals, Mr. Williams wants the letter retyped with the changes shown in Figure 2.1. Instead of sending additional information with the letter as previously planned, Mr. Williams has decided to send the information separately, so you will have to create an envelope for the letter.

WORD-41

WORD-72

The Solution

You will format a document and set up the document to print across the long side of the paper in three columns. You will insert a graphic, modify and apply styles, create the bulleted and numbered lists, and format the brochure shown in Figure 3.1.

Figure 3.1

The Setup

So that your screen will match the illustrations and the tasks in this project will function as described, make sure that the Word 97 settings listed in Table 3.1 are selected on your computer.

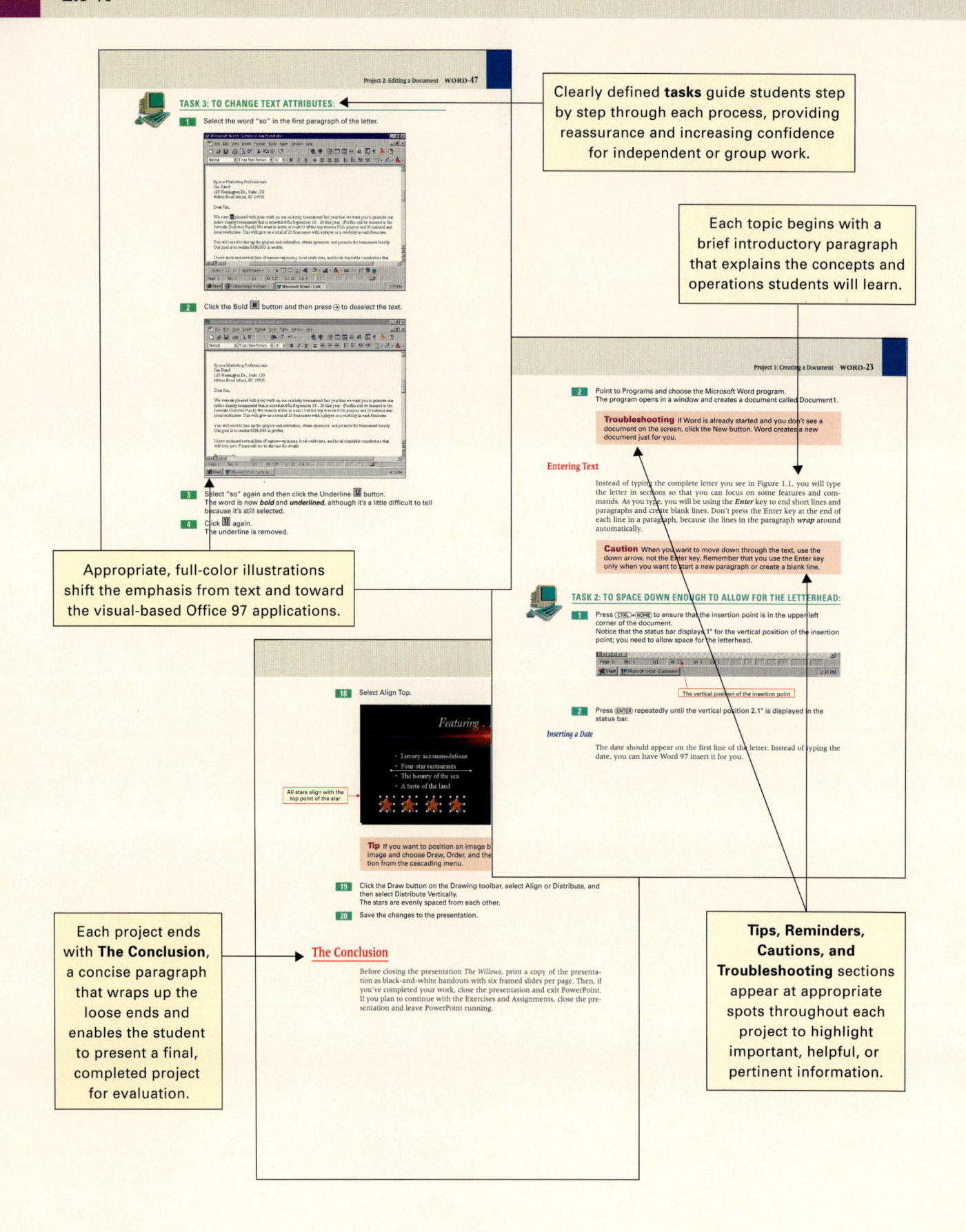

Clearly defined tasks guide students step by step through each process, providing reassurance and increasing confidence for independent or group work.

Each topic begins with a brief introductory paragraph that explains the concepts and operations students will learn.

Appropriate, full-color illustrations shift the emphasis from text and toward the visual-based Office 97 applications.

Each project ends with **The Conclusion**, a concise paragraph that wraps up the loose ends and enables the student to present a final, completed project for evaluation.

Tips, Reminders, Cautions, and Troubleshooting sections appear at appropriate spots throughout each project to highlight important, helpful, or pertinent information.

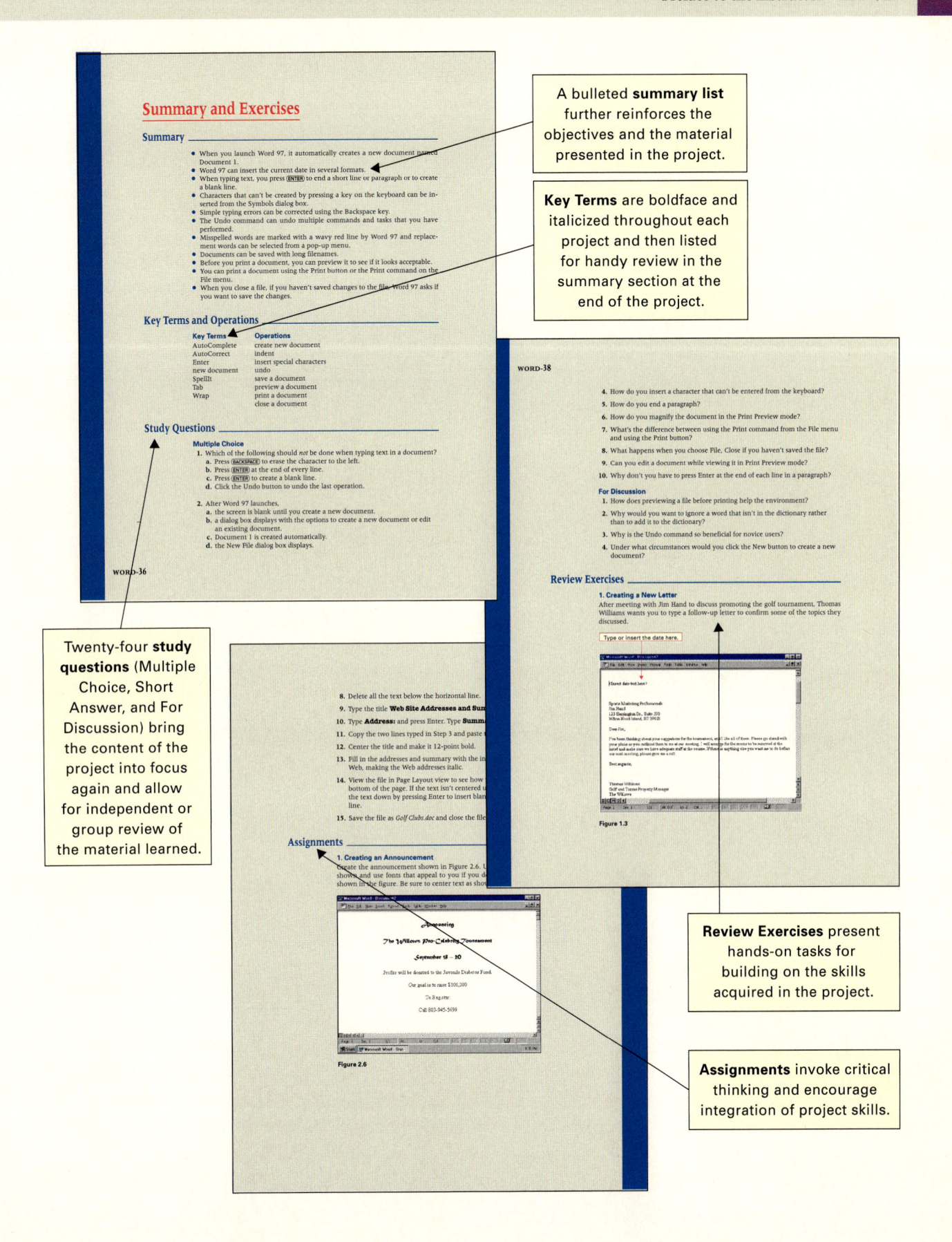

A bulleted **summary list** further reinforces the objectives and the material presented in the project.

Key Terms are boldface and italicized throughout each project and then listed for handy review in the summary section at the end of the project.

Twenty-four **study questions** (Multiple Choice, Short Answer, and For Discussion) bring the content of the project into focus again and allow for independent or group review of the material learned.

Review Exercises present hands-on tasks for building on the skills acquired in the project.

Assignments invoke critical thinking and encourage integration of project skills.

Supplements

You get extra support for this text from supplemental materials, including the *Instructor's Manual* and the Instructor's Data Disk.

The *Instructor's Manual* includes a Test Bank and Transparency Masters for each project in the student text, as well as Expanded Student Objectives, Answers to Study Questions, and Additional Assessment Techniques. The Test Bank contains two separate tests with answers and consists of multiple-choice, true/false, and fill-in questions referenced to pages in the student text. Transparency Masters illustrate over one hundred key concepts and screen captures from the text.

The Instructor's Data Disk contains student data files, completed data files for Review Exercises and assignments, and the test files from the *Instructor's Manual* in ASCII format.

Thanks to . . .

When team members combine their knowledge and skills to produce a work designed to meet the needs of students and professors across the country, they take on an unenviable challenge.

To **Carol Crowell** and **Barb Terry,** thanks for the steady focus and refocus needed to get this project off the ground.

Thanks to **Martha Johnson, Robin Edwards,** and **Deborah Minyard,** who were more than just technical editors, but who also made sure things worked the way we said they would. Thanks to **Robin Drake**—without your great help and comments during development, nothing in this book would match; and to **Chuck Hutchinson,** for excellent editing. To those in production, especially to **Pat Mahtani,** your design efforts have paid off in a highly user friendly book!

To **Michelle Hudson,** thanks for your strong marketing insights for this book.

And, finally, thanks to everyone at Addison Wesley Longman who has followed this project from start to finish.

P. T.
Y. J.

Acknowledgments

Addison-Wesley Publishing Company would like to thank the following reviewers for their valuable contributions to the *SELECT Lab Series*.

James Agnew
Northern Virginia
Community College

Joseph Aieta
Babson College

Dr. Muzaffar Ali
Bellarmine College

Tom Ashby
Oklahoma CC

Bob Barber
Lane CC

Robert Caruso
Santa Rosa Junior
College

Robert Chi
California State
Long Beach

Jill Davis
State University of New
York at Stony Brook

Fredia Dillard
Samford University

Peter Drexel
Plymouth State College

David Egle
University of Texas, Pan
American

Linda Ericksen
Lane Community College

Jonathan Frank
Suffolk University

Patrick Gilbert
University of Hawaii

Maureen Greenbaum
Union County College

Sally Ann Hanson
Mercer County CC

Sunil Hazari
East Carolina University

Gloria Henderson
Victor Valley College

Bruce Herniter
University of Hartford

Rick Homkes
Purdue University

Lisa Jackson
Henderson CC

Martha Johnson
(technical reviewer)
Delta State University

Cynthia Kachik
Santa Fe CC

Bennett Kramer
Massasoit CC

Charles Lake
Faulkner State Junior
College

Ron Leake
Johnson County CC

Randy Marak
Hill College

Charles Mattox, Jr.
St. Mary's University

Jim McCullough
Porter and Chester
Institute

Gail Miles
Lenoir-Rhyne College

Steve Moore
University of South
Florida

Anthony Nowakowski
Buffalo State College

Gloria Oman
Portland State University

John Passafiume
Clemson University

Leonard Presby
William Paterson
College

Louis Pryor
Garland County CC

Michael Reilly
University of Denver

Dick Ricketts
Lane CC

Dennis Santomauro
Kean College of
New Jersey

Pamela Schmidt
Oakton CC

Gary Schubert
Alderson-Broaddus
College

T. Michael Smith
Austin CC

Cynthia Thompson
Carl Sandburg College

Marion Tucker
Northern Oklahoma
College

JoAnn Weatherwax
Saddleback College

David Whitney
San Francisco State
University

James Wood
Tri-County Technical
College

Minnie Yen
University of Alaska
Anchorage

Allen Zilbert
Long Island University

Contents

Overview of Windows 95

Overview of Windows 95

Microsoft Windows 95 is an *operating system,* a special kind of computer program that performs three major functions. First, an operating system controls the actual *hardware* of the computer (the screen, the keyboard, the disk drives, and so on). Second, an operating system enables other software programs such as word processing or spreadsheet *applications* to run. Finally, an operating system determines how the user operates the computer and its programs or applications.

As an operating system, Windows 95 and all other programs written to run under it provide *graphics* (or pictures) called *icons* to carry out commands and run programs. For this reason, Windows 95 is referred to as a *Graphical User Interface* or GUI (pronounced *gooey*). You can use the keyboard or a device called a *mouse* to activate the icons.

This overview explains the basics of Windows 95 so that you can begin using your computer quickly and easily.

Objectives

After completing this project, you will be able to:

- ➤ **Launch Windows 95**
- ➤ **Identify the desktop elements**
- ➤ **Use a mouse**
- ➤ **Use the basic features of Windows 95**
- ➤ **Organize your computer**
- ➤ **Work with multiple programs**
- ➤ **Get help**
- ➤ **Exit Windows 95**

Launching Windows 95

Because Windows 95 is an operating system, it launches immediately when you turn on the computer. Depending on the way your computer is set up, you may have to type your user name and password to log on — to get permission to begin using the program. After Windows 95 launches, the working environment, called the *desktop,* displays on the screen.

Identifying the Desktop Elements

Figure W.1 shows the Windows 95 desktop with several icons that represent the hardware and the software installed on the computer. *My Computer* enables you to organize your work. The *Recycle Bin* is a temporary storage area for files deleted from the hard disk. At the bottom of the desktop is the *Taskbar* for starting programs, accessing various areas of Windows 95, and switching among programs.

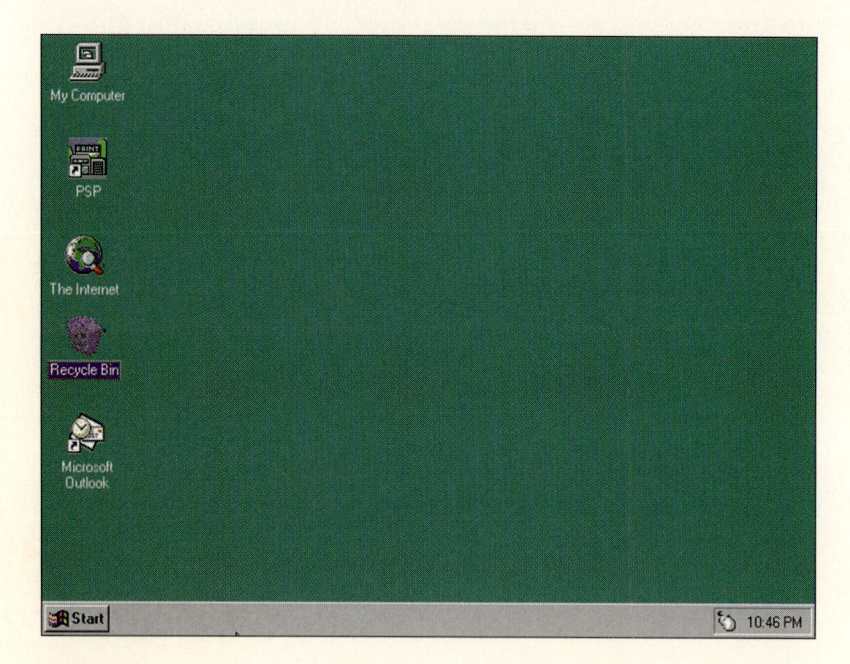

Figure W.1

Note The desktop can be customized, so the desktop on the computer you're using will not look exactly like the one shown in the illustrations in this overview.

Using a Mouse

A pointing device is almost an indispensable tool for using Windows 95. Although you can use the keyboard to navigate and make selections, using a mouse is often more convenient and efficient.

When you move the mouse on your desk, a pointer moves on the screen. When the pointer is on the object you want to use, you can take one of the actions described in Table W.1 to give Windows 95 an instruction.

Table W.1   Mouse Actions

Action	Description
Point	Slide the mouse across a smooth surface (preferably a mouse pad) until the pointer on the screen is on the object.
Click	Press and release the left mouse button once.
Drag	Press and hold down the left mouse button while you move the mouse, and then release the mouse button to complete the action.
Right-click	Press and release the right mouse button once. Right-clicking usually displays a shortcut menu.
Double-click	Press and release the left mouse button twice in rapid succession.

TASK 1: TO PRACTICE USING THE MOUSE:

1 Point to the My Computer [icon] icon, press and hold down the left mouse button, and then drag the mouse across the desk.
The icon moves.

2 Drag the My Computer icon back to its original location.

3 Right-click the icon.

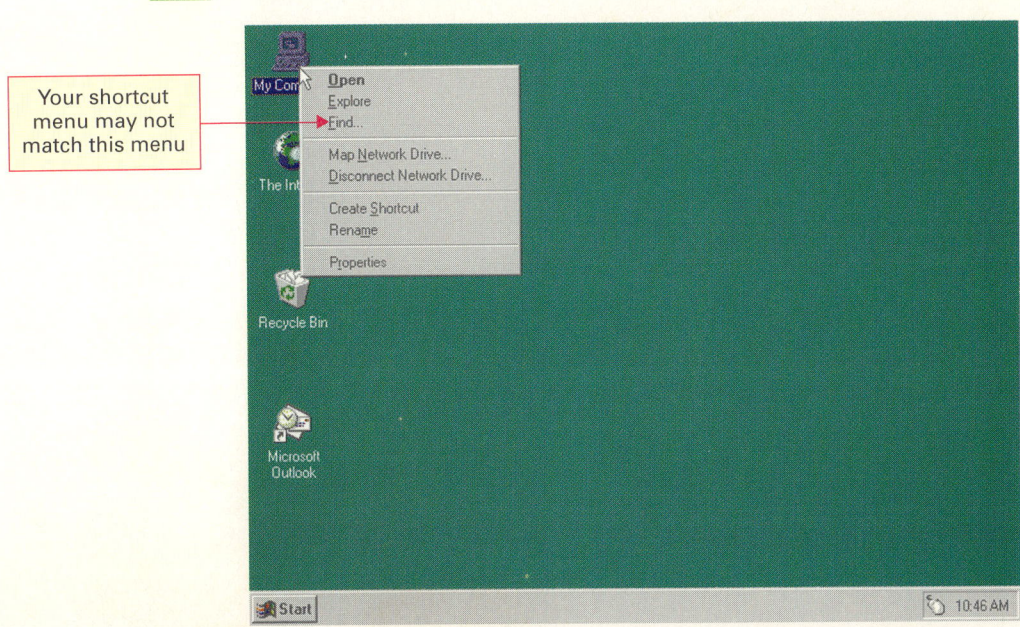

Your shortcut menu may not match this menu

4 Click a blank space on the screen. The shortcut menu closes.

5 Double-click the My Computer icon.

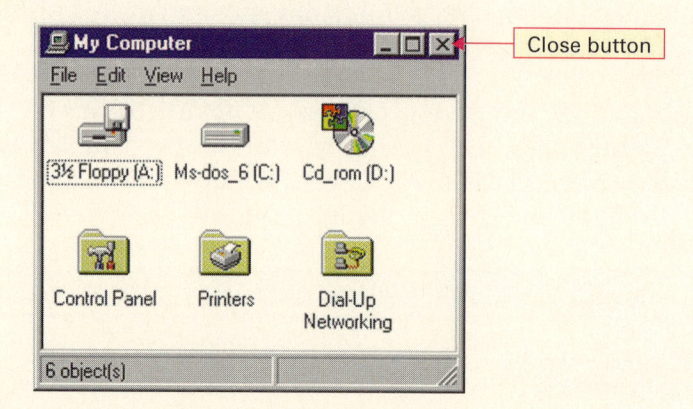

6 Click the Close ☒ button to close the My Computer window.

Using the Basic Features of Windows 95

The basic features of Windows 95 are menus, windows, menu bars, dialog boxes, and toolbars. These features are used in all programs that are written to run under Windows 95.

Using the Start Menu

Menus contain the commands you use to perform tasks. In Windows 95, you can use the Start menu shown in Figure W.2 to start programs and to access other Windows options.

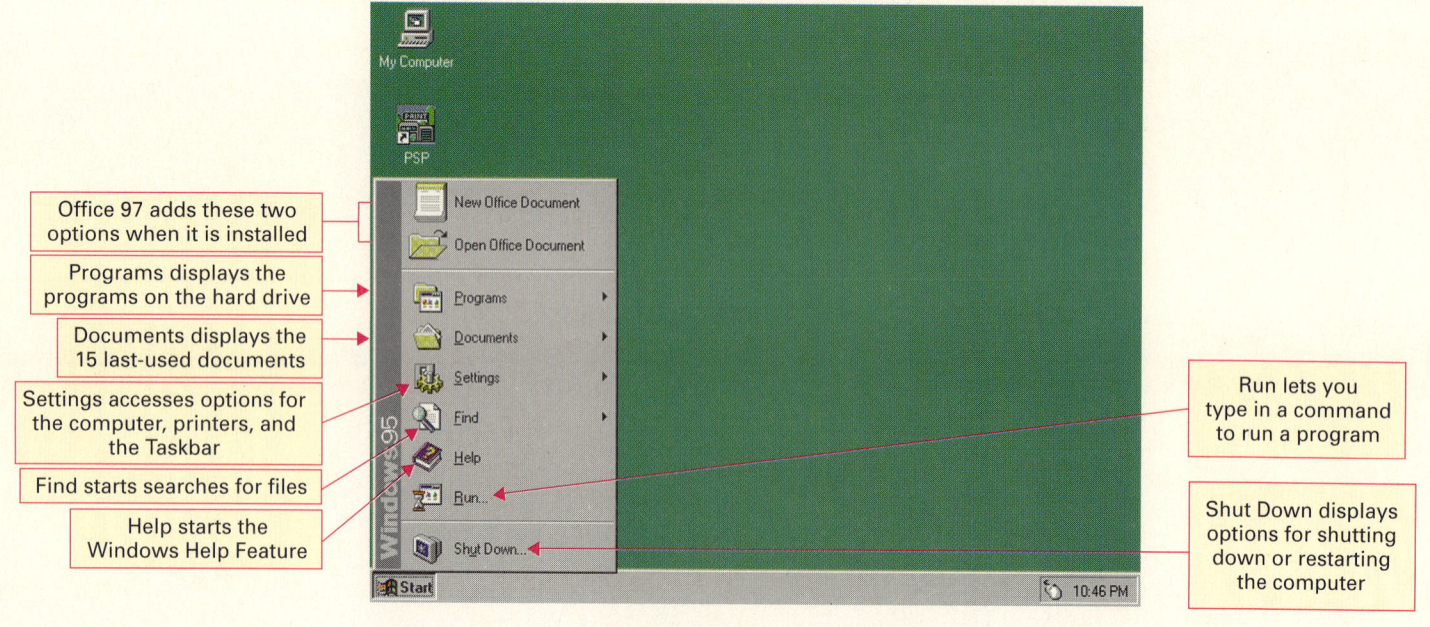

Figure W.2

TASK 2: TO USE THE START MENU TO LAUNCH A PROGRAM:

1 Click the Start button.
The triangles beside several of the menu options indicate that the options will display another menu.

2 Point to Programs and click the Windows Explorer icon.
The Exploring window opens (see Figure W.3). You can use this feature of Windows 95 to manage files.

Using Windows

Clicking on the Windows Explorer icon opened a *window*, a Windows 95 feature that you saw earlier when you opened the My Computer window. Figure W.3 shows the common elements that most windows contain.

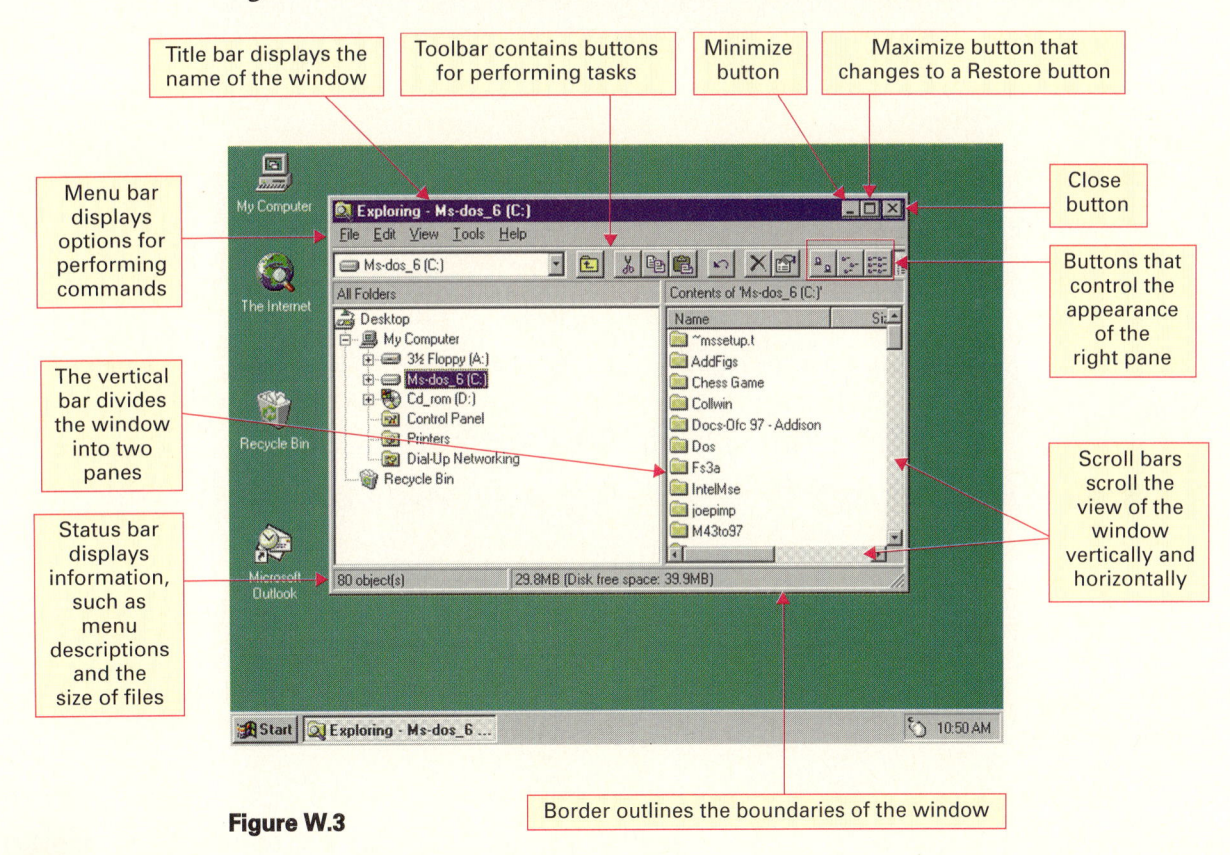

Figure W.3

- Title bar displays the name of the window
- Toolbar contains buttons for performing tasks
- Minimize button
- Maximize button that changes to a Restore button
- Menu bar displays options for performing commands
- Close button
- Buttons that control the appearance of the right pane
- The vertical bar divides the window into two panes
- Scroll bars scroll the view of the window vertically and horizontally
- Status bar displays information, such as menu descriptions and the size of files
- Border outlines the boundaries of the window

TASK 3: TO WORK WITH A WINDOW:

1 Click the Maximize ☐ button if it is displayed. If it is not displayed, click the Restore ⬚ button, and then click the Maximize button.
The Maximize button changes to a Restore ⬚ button.

2 Click the Minimize ☐ button.

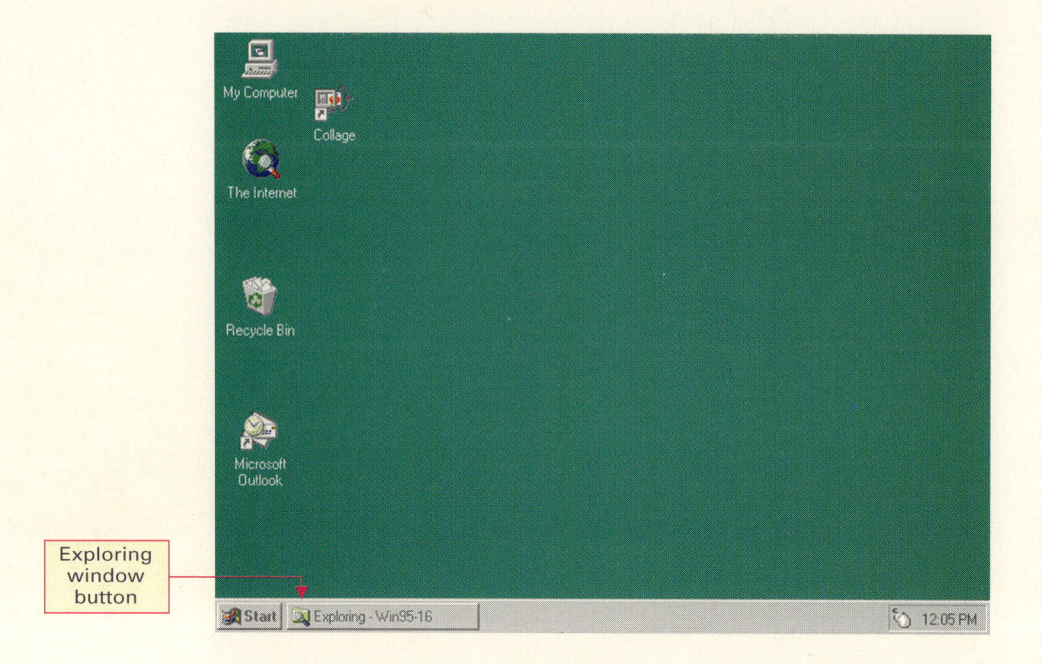

Exploring window button

3 Click the Exploring button on the Taskbar and then click 🗗.

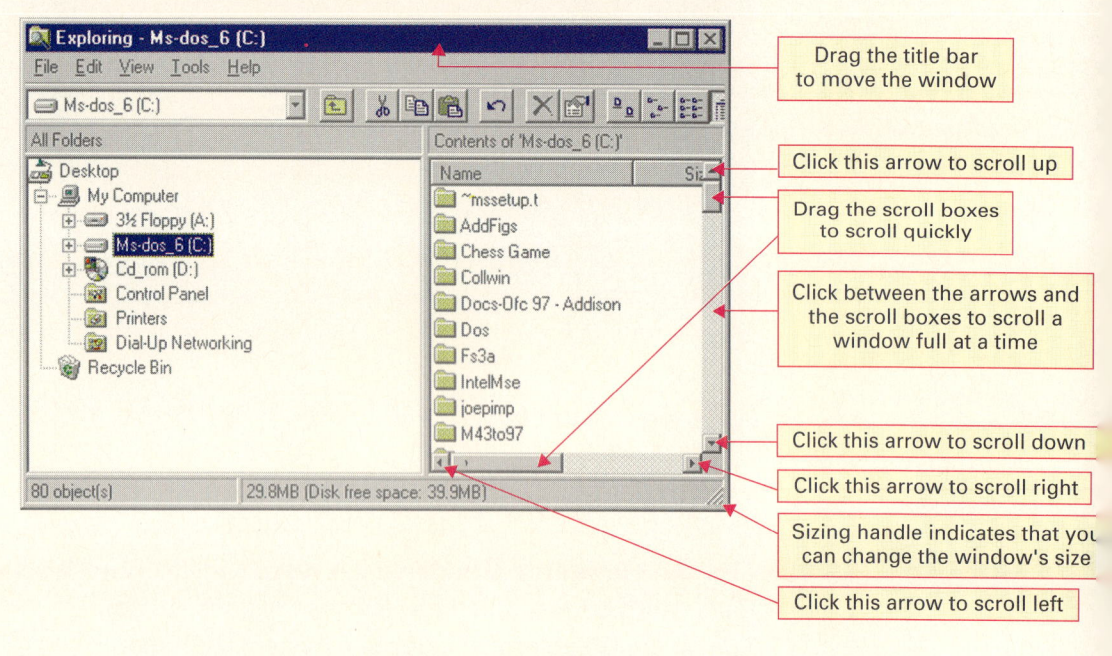

Drag the title bar to move the window

Click this arrow to scroll up

Drag the scroll boxes to scroll quickly

Click between the arrows and the scroll boxes to scroll a window full at a time

Click this arrow to scroll down

Click this arrow to scroll right

Sizing handle indicates that you can change the window's size

Click this arrow to scroll left

4 Point to the border of the Exploring window until the pointer changes to a double-headed black arrow, and then drag the border to make the window wider. (Be sure that all the buttons in the toolbar are visible.)

5 Practice scrolling.

6 When you are comfortable with your scrolling expertise, click 🗖.

Using Menu Bars and Toolbars

Menu bars and toolbars are generally located at the top of a window. You can select a menu option in a menu bar by clicking the option or by pressing ⏎ALT and then typing the underlined letter for the option. When you select an option, a drop-down menu appears. Figure W.4 shows a menu with many of the elements common to menus.

> **Note** Because you can select menu commands in two ways, the steps with instructions to select a menu command will use the word choose instead of dictating the method of selection.

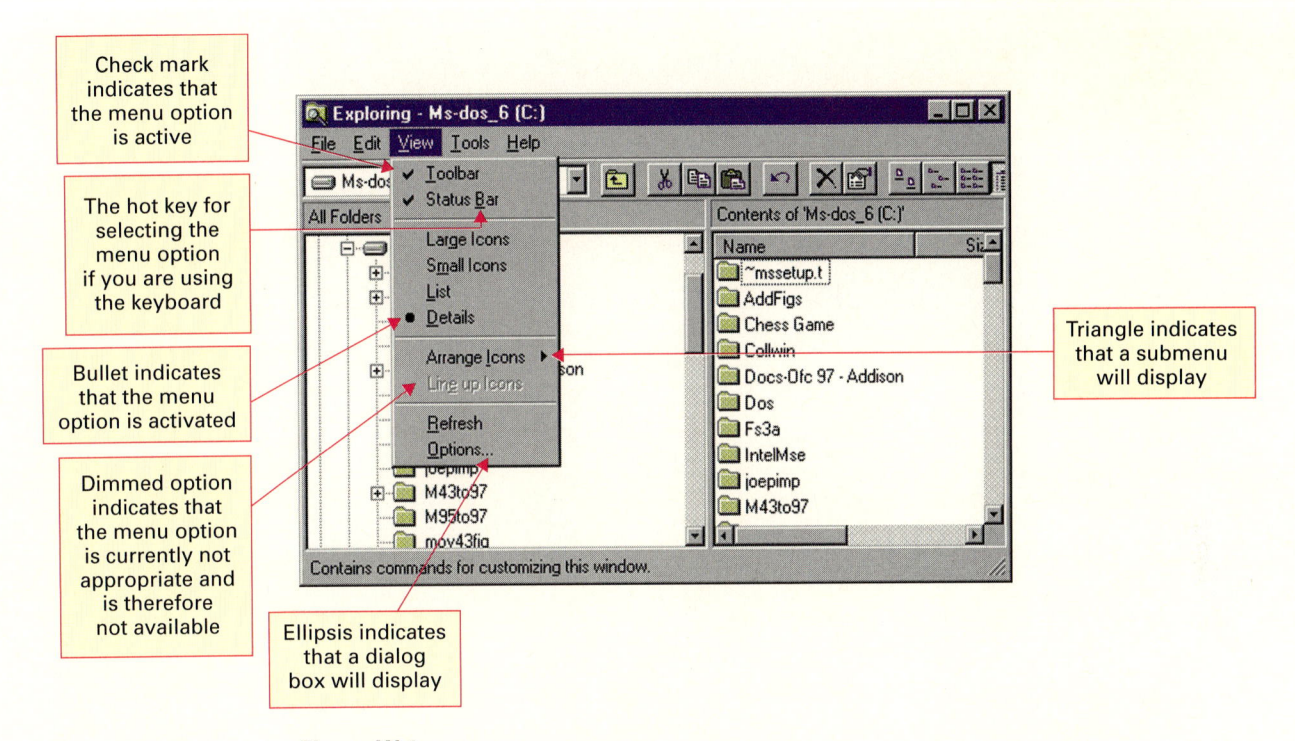

Check mark indicates that the menu option is active

The hot key for selecting the menu option if you are using the keyboard

Bullet indicates that the menu option is activated

Dimmed option indicates that the menu option is currently not appropriate and is therefore not available

Ellipsis indicates that a dialog box will display

Triangle indicates that a submenu will display

Figure W.4

Toolbars contain buttons that perform many of the same commands found on menus. To use a toolbar button, click the button; Windows 95 takes an immediate action, depending on the button's function.

> **Tip** If you don't know what a button on the toolbar does, point to the button; a ToolTip, a brief description of the button, appears near the button.

TASK 4: TO USE MENUS AND TOOLBARS:

1   Choose View in the Exploring window.
The View menu shown in Figure W.4 displays.

2   Choose Large Icons.

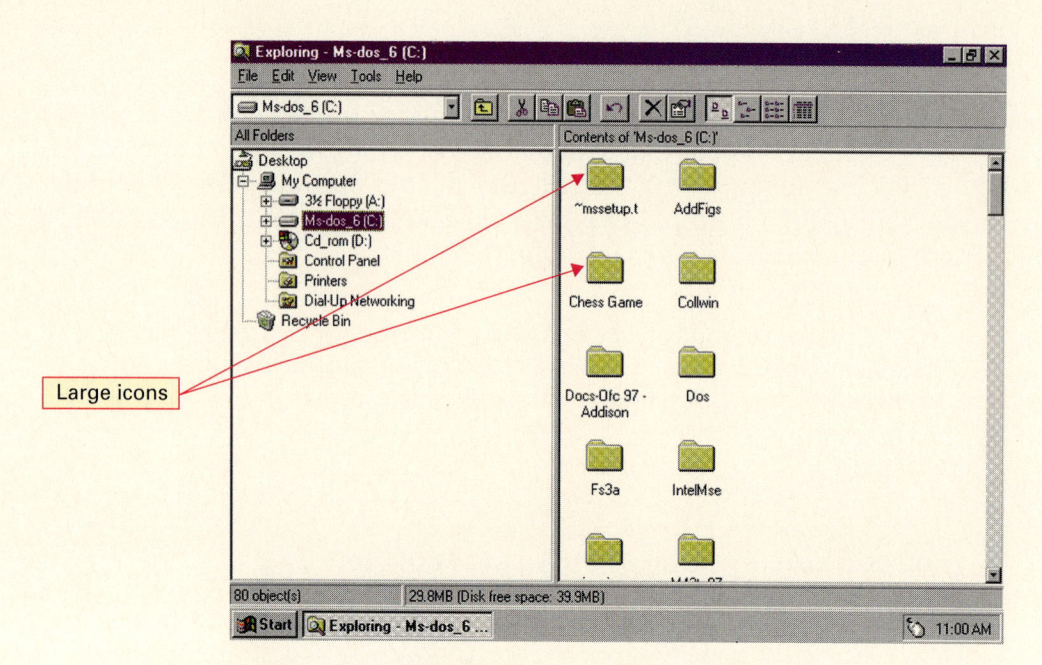

Large icons

3   **Click the Details 🖩 button on the toolbar.**

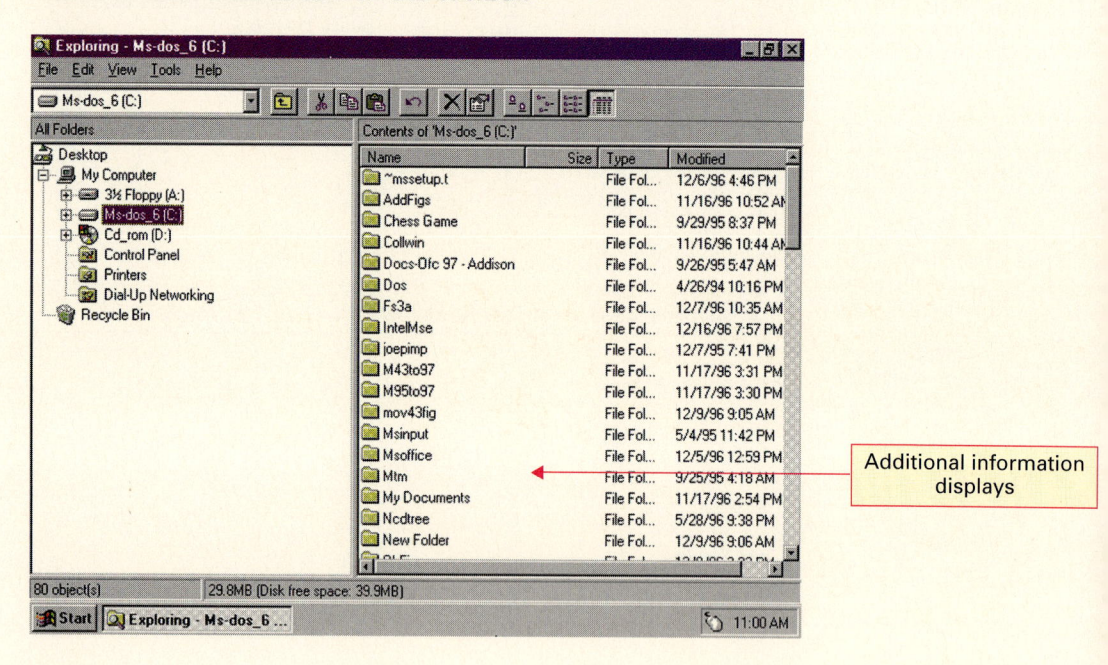

Additional information displays

Using Dialog Boxes

When many options are available for a single task, Windows 95 conveniently groups the options in one place, called a ***dialog box.*** Some functions have so many options that Windows 95 divides them further into groups and places them on separate pages in the dialog box. Figures W.5 and W.6 show dialog boxes with different types of options. Throughout the remainder of this project, you practice using dialog boxes.

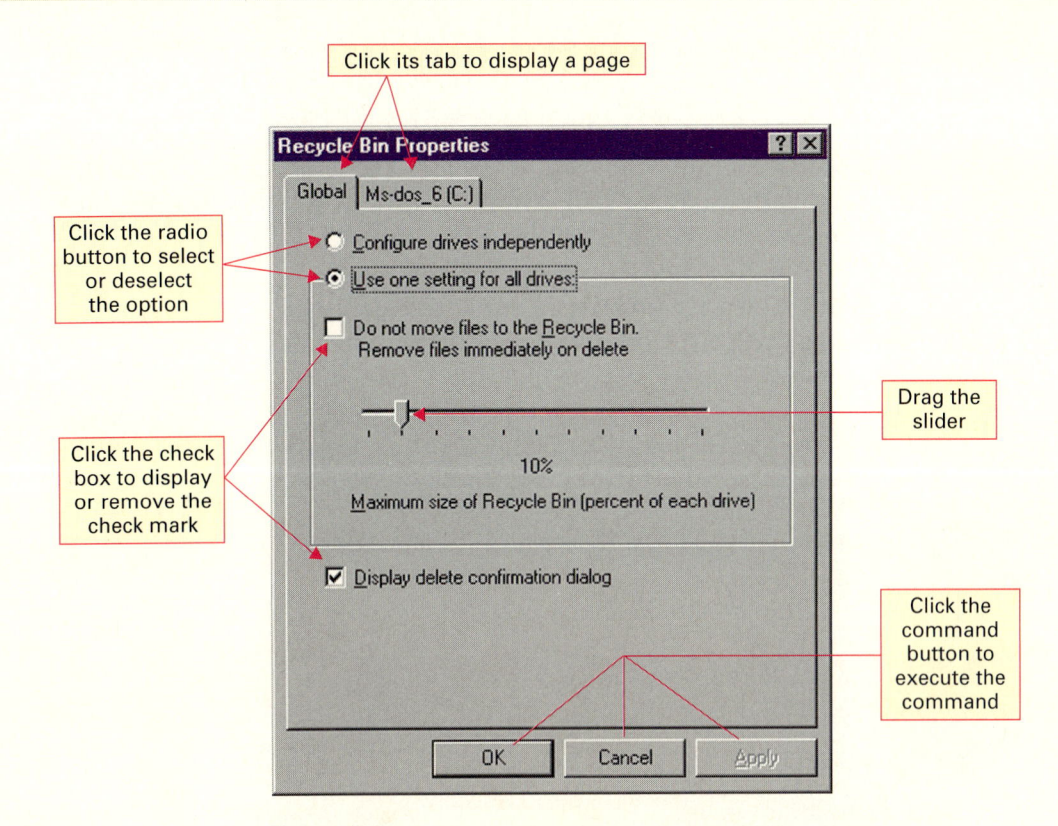

Click its tab to display a page

Click the radio button to select or deselect the option

Click the check box to display or remove the check mark

Drag the slider

Click the command button to execute the command

Figure W.5

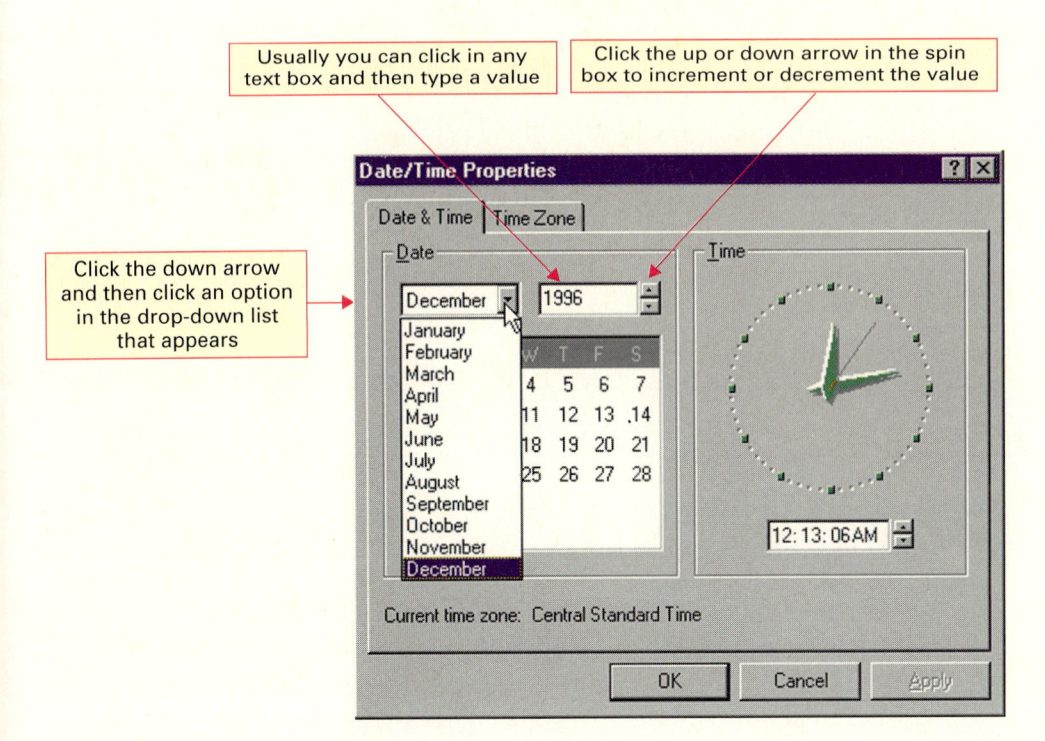

Usually you can click in any text box and then type a value

Click the up or down arrow in the spin box to increment or decrement the value

Click the down arrow and then click an option in the drop-down list that appears

Figure W.6

Getting Help

Windows 95 provides you with three methods of accessing help information: You can look up information in a table of contents; you can search for information in an index; or you can find a specific word or phrase in a database maintained by the Find feature.

Additionally, Windows 95 provides *context-sensitive help,* called *What's This?* for the topic you are working on. This type of help is generally found in dialog boxes.

After you learn to use Help in Windows 95, you can use help in any Windows program because all programs use the same help format.

TASK 12: TO USE HELP CONTENTS, INDEX, AND FIND:

1 Click the Start button on the Taskbar and click Help.

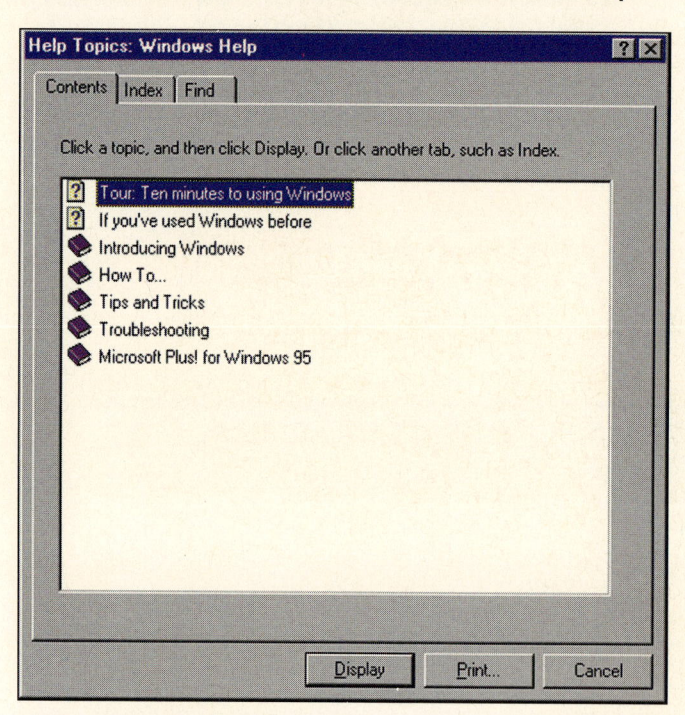

2 Click the Contents tab if a different page is displayed. The Contents page displays.

3   **Double-click Tips and Tricks.**

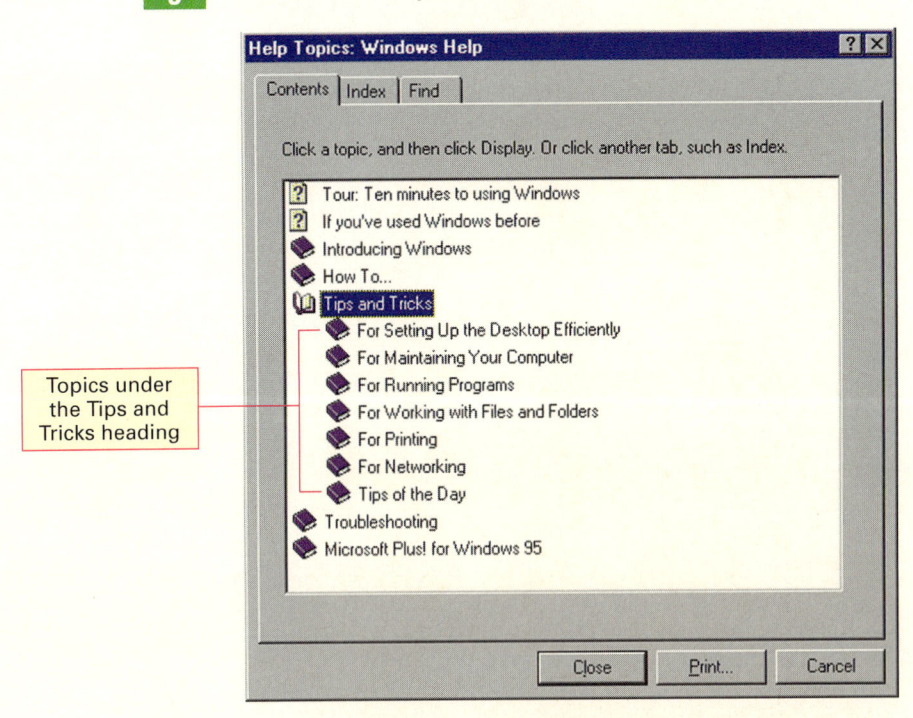

Topics under the Tips and Tricks heading

4   **Double-click Tips of the Day.**

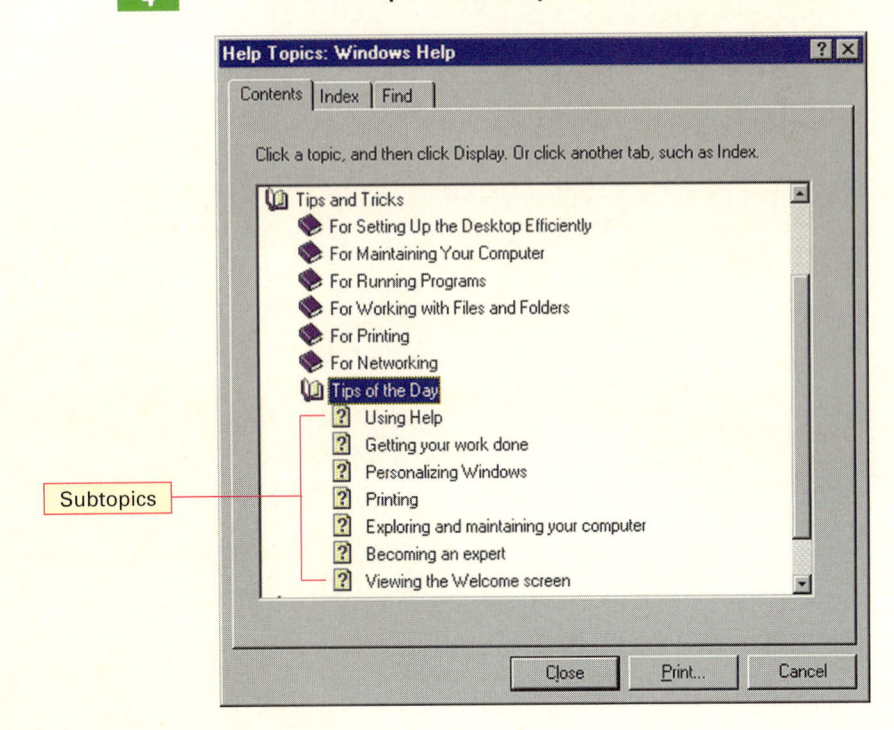

Subtopics

5 Double-click Using Help.

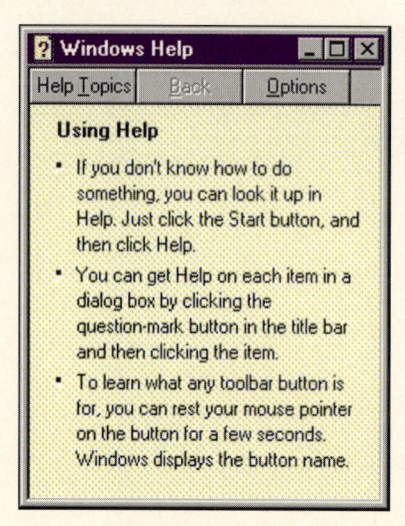

6 Read the information, click the Help Topics button, and then click the Index tab.

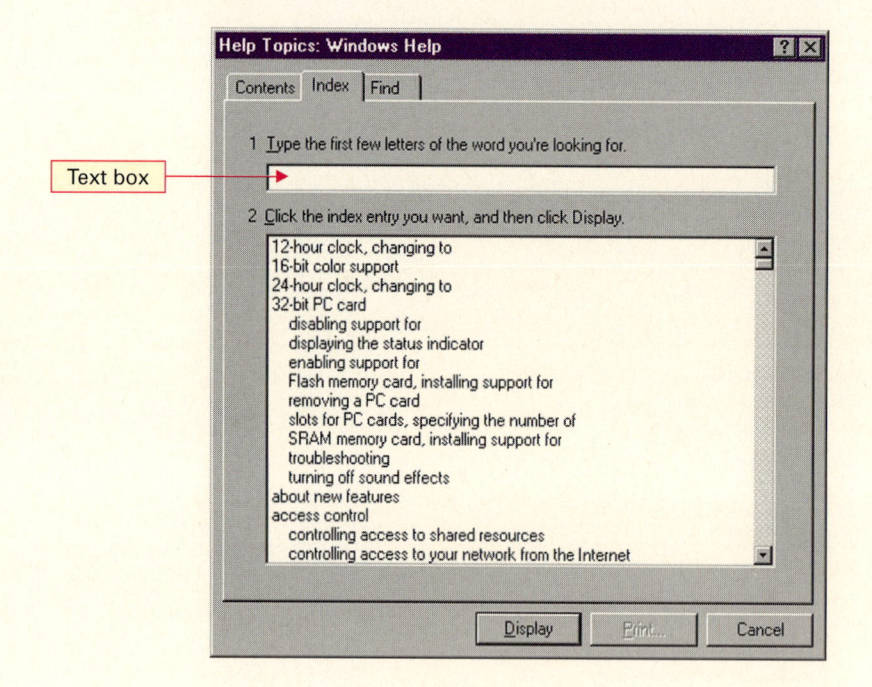

7 Type **shortcut** in the textbox.

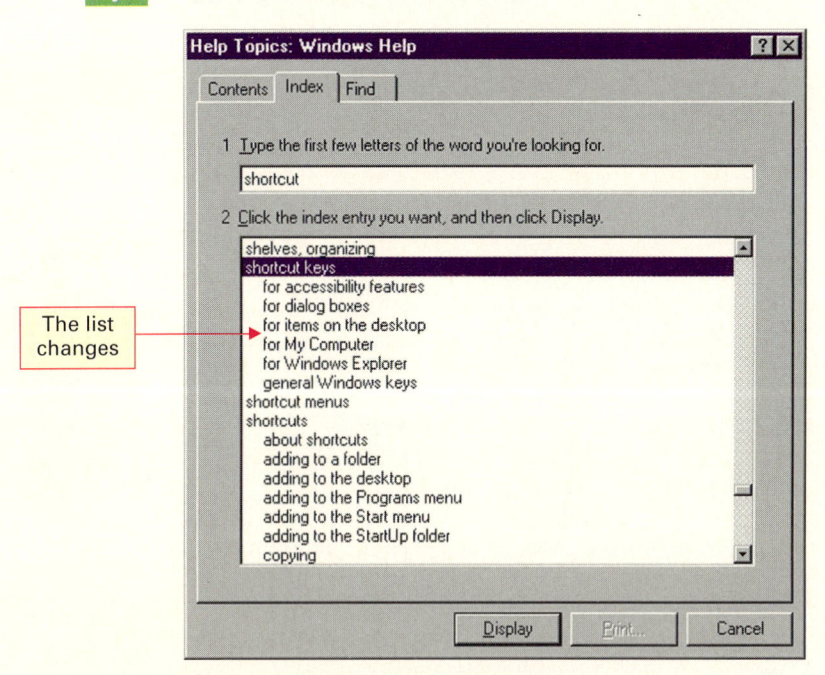

8 Double-click "shortcut menus" in the list.

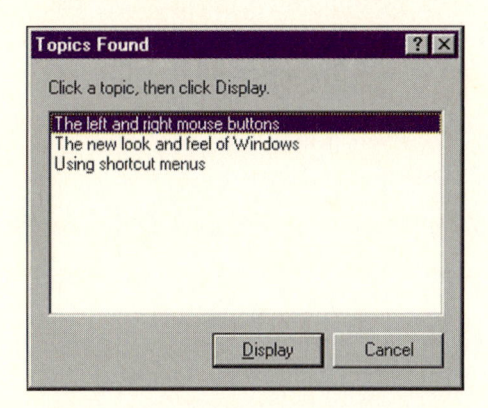

9 Double-click "Using shortcut menus."

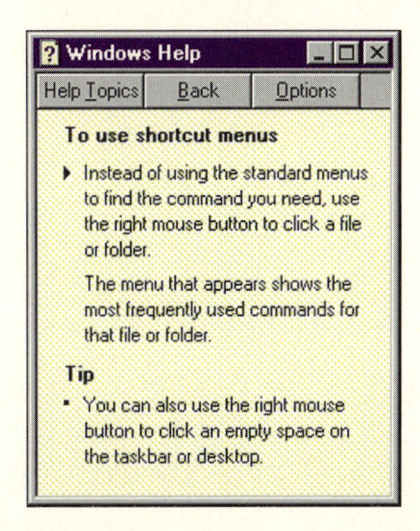

10 Read the information, click the Help Topics button, and then click the Find tab.

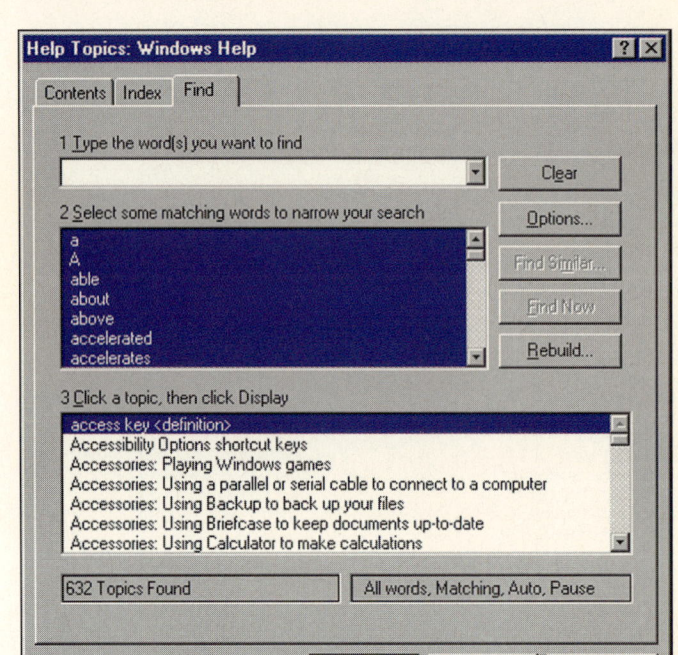

11 Click the What's This ? button in the Help Topics title bar. A question mark is attached to the mouse pointer.

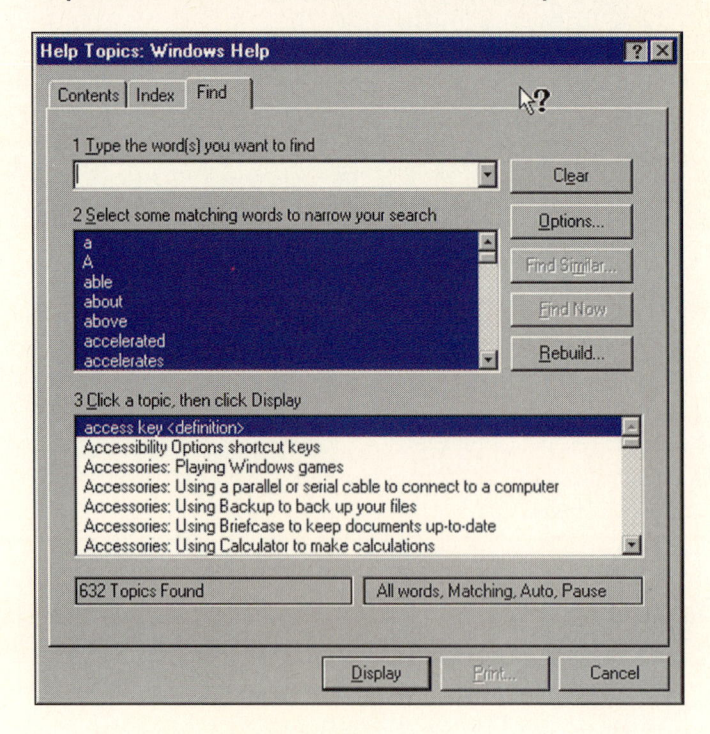

12 Click the Options button.

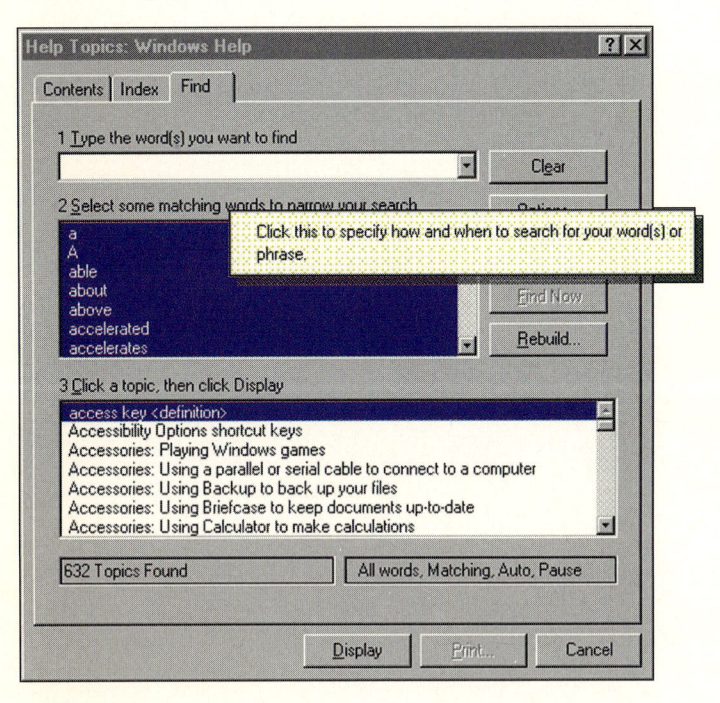

13 Read the pop-up message and then click it.
The message closes.

14 Type **printing help.** (If the list at the bottom of the screen doesn't change, click the Find Now button.)

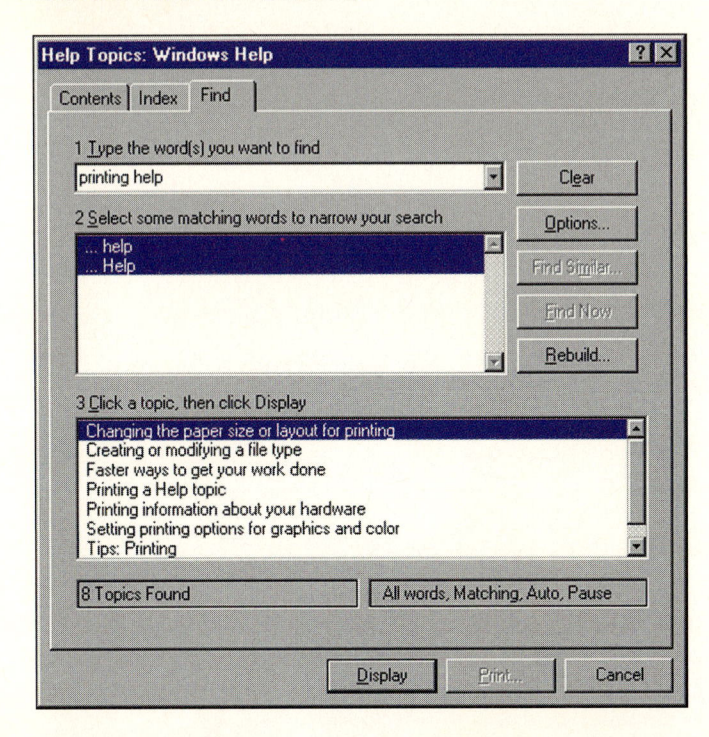

15 If necessary, scroll to "Printing a Help topic" in the list that displays and then double-click it.

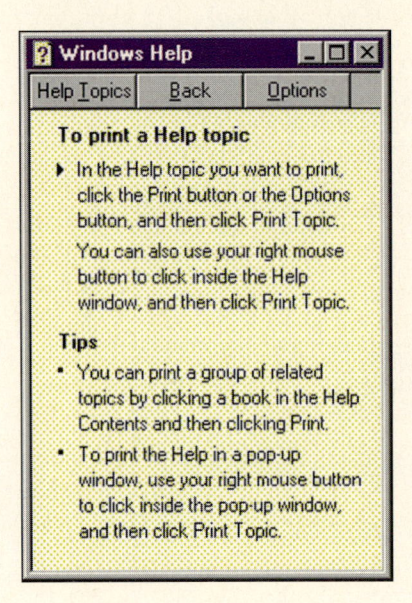

16 Click ⊠. The Help dialog box closes.

Tip You can print any help article by right-clicking anywhere in the article and choosing Print Topic.

Exiting Windows 95

When you are ready to turn off the computer, you must exit Windows 95 first. You should never turn off the computer without following the proper exit procedure because Windows 95 has to do some utility tasks before it shuts down. Unlike most of us, Windows 95 likes to put everything away when it's finished. When you shut down improperly, you can cause serious problems in Windows 95.

TASK 13: TO EXIT WINDOWS 95:

1 Click the Start button and then click Shut Down.

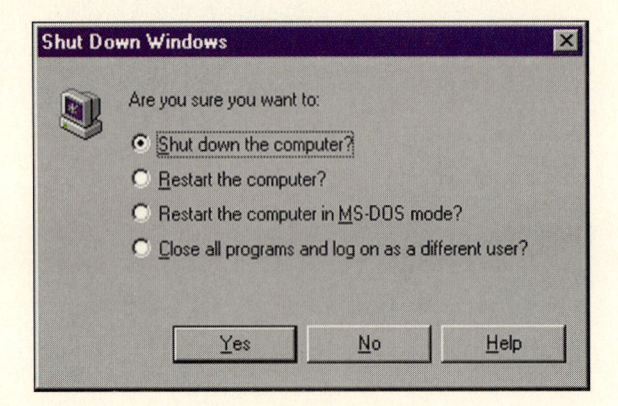

2 Click Shut down the computer? and then click Yes.

3 When the message "It's now safe to turn off your computer" appears, turn off the computer.

Spreadsheets
Using Microsoft Excel 97

Overview

Excel is a tool you can use for organizing, calculating, and displaying numerical data. You might use Excel to record your checking account transactions, plan a budget, prepare a bid, control inventory, track sales, or create an expense report. Before you can become proficient with Excel 97, however, you need to get acquainted with the program and learn how to perform some of the most basic functions. Then you will be ready to start working on the projects in this part of the book.

Objectives

After completing this project, you will be able to:

➤ **Identify Excel 97 Features**

➤ **Launch Excel 97**

➤ **Identify Excel 97 Screen Elements**

➤ **Get help**

➤ **Close a workbook**

➤ **Exit Excel 97**

Identifying Excel 97 Features

Excel 97 is the electronic equivalent of one of those green (or buff color) columnar pads that bookkeepers and accountants use. Excel calls the area in which you work a *worksheet* — other programs call this a spreadsheet. An Excel worksheet has 256 *columns* and 65,536 *rows*, for a whopping total of 16,777,216 cells. Is that big or what?

Note A *cell* is the intersection of a column and a row.

An Excel worksheet is actually a page in a **workbook** file. By default, a new workbook file has three worksheets, but you can add additional worksheets if you need them — as many as your computer memory allows.

You can do more than store numbers with Excel 97; you can use it to perform calculations, recalculate formulas when numbers are changed, analyze data, and create charts and maps from the data that you enter. Many of the same text features available in a word processing program are also available in Excel. For example, you can check the spelling of words, use text styles, add headers and footers, and insert graphics and other objects. Figure 0.1 shows a worksheet with numbers, calculations, text formatted with styles, a graphic, and a chart.

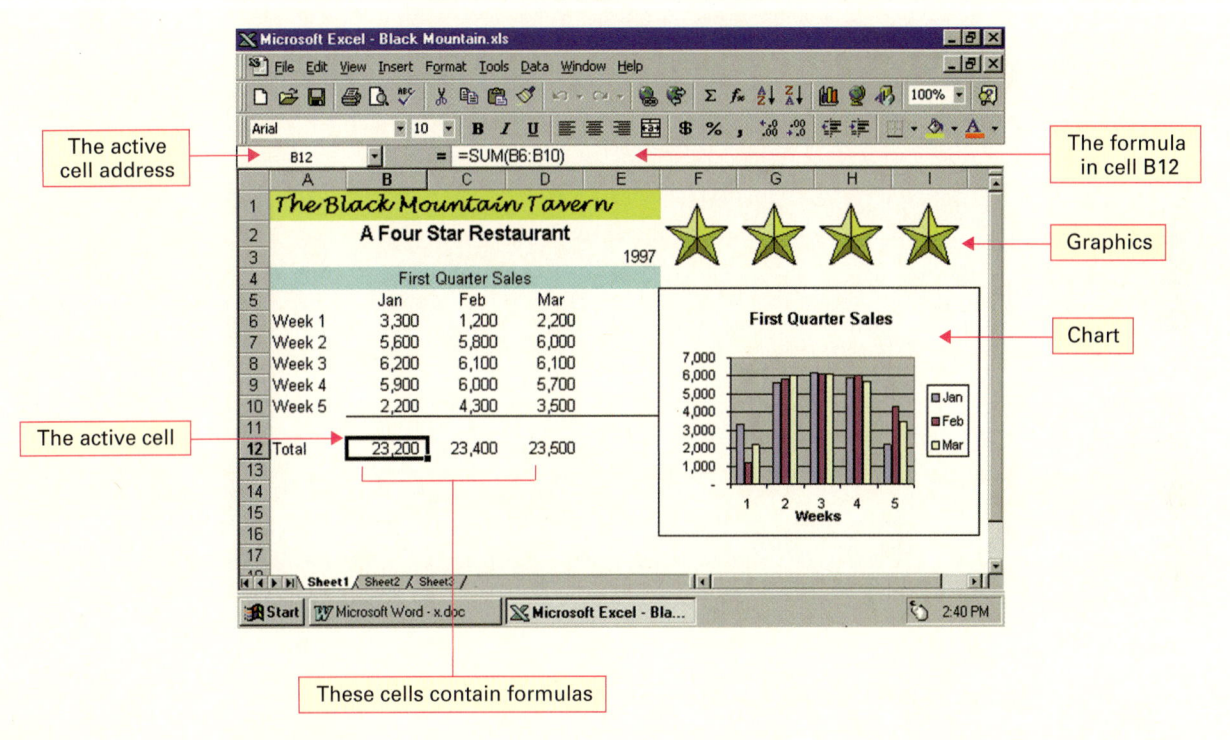

Figure O.1

Launching Excel 97

When you start your computer, you may have to log on to a network or perform some other steps before Windows 95 starts. After the Windows 95 desktop displays on the screen, you're ready to launch Excel 97.

TASK 1: TO LAUNCH EXCEL 97:

1 Click the Start [Start] button and point to Programs.

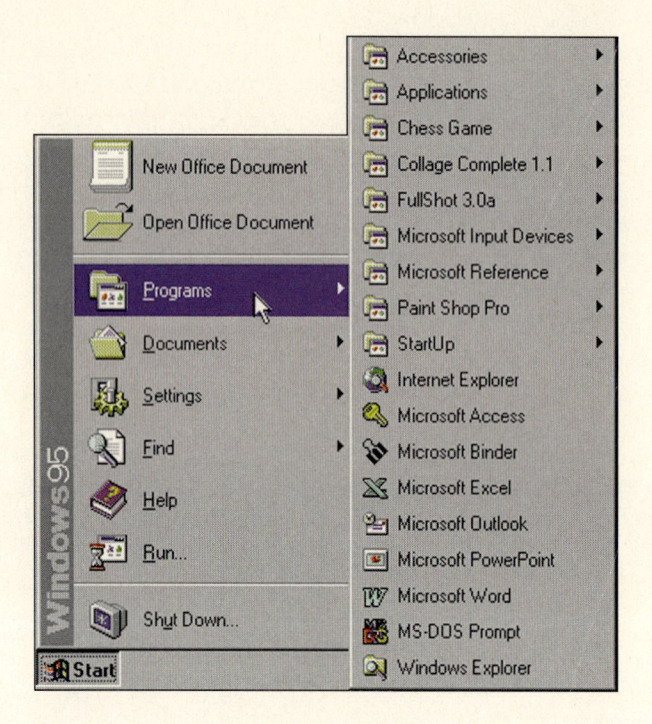

2 Point to Microsoft Excel and click.
The program opens in a window and creates a workbook called *Book1*.

Identifying Excel 97 Screen Elements

When you create a new workbook, the screen should look similar to the one shown in Figure O.2. The Excel 97 screen has many of the common elements of a Windows 95 screen as well as some elements that are unique to the Excel 97 program.

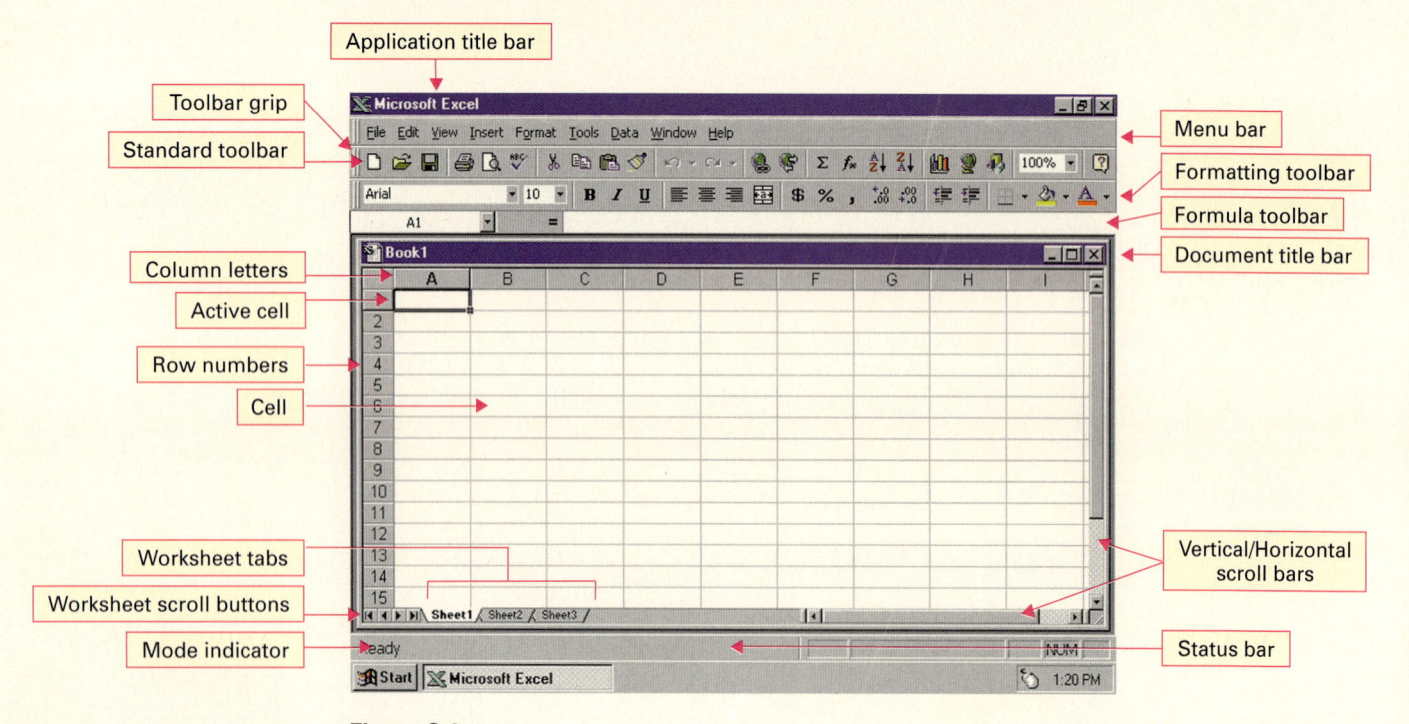

Figure O.2

Note The screen displays two Close buttons. The button in the Application title bar closes Excel 97; the button in the document title bar closes the current workbook. If the document window is maximized, the Close button appears in the menu bar.

Table 0.1 lists the elements of the Excel 97 screen.

Table O.1   Elements of the Excel 97 Screen

Element	Description
Application title bar	Displays the name of the application and the Minimize, Maximize/Restore, and Close buttons. If the document window is maximized, the name of the workbook also displays in the application title bar.
Document title bar	Displays the name of the workbook file and the Minimize, Maximize/Restore, and Close buttons. If the window is maximized, there is no document title bar and the document buttons display in the menu bar.
Menu bar	Contains menu options. To use the menu, click an option to display a drop-down menu, and then click a command on the drop-down menu to perform the command, view another menu, or view a dialog box.
Standard toolbar	Contains buttons for accomplishing commands. To use the toolbar, click the button for the command you want to perform.
Formatting toolbar	Contains buttons and controls for formatting. To use the toolbar, click the button for the command you want to perform or click a drop-down list arrow to make a selection.
Formula bar	Displays the cell address and the contents of the active cell. Also used to enter and edit formulas.
Active cell	Marks the cell where data will be entered with a black border.
Scroll bars	Vertical and horizontal Scroll bars scroll the screen vertically and horizontally.
Worksheet tabs	Display the names of worksheets in the current workbook. Clicking a tab displays the worksheet.
Worksheet scroll buttons	Scroll the worksheet tabs (if you have too many worksheets to display all the tabs).
Status bar	Displays information about the current workbook. The Mode indicator displays on the far left side of the status bar.
Row numbers	Indicate the numbers associated with the rows.
Column letters	Indicate the letters associated with the columns.
Cell	The intersection of a column and a row, referred to with an address that combines the column letter(s) with the row number, such as A1, AA223, and so on.
Mode	Displays on the left side of the status bar and shows a word that describes the current working condition of the workbook. For example, the word *"Ready"* means that the worksheet is ready to receive data or execute a command. Other modes include *Edit, Enter, Point, Error,* and *Wait.*

Note Although you can turn off the display of certain screen elements (toolbars, the Formula bar, and the Status bar), generally all the screen elements are displayed in Excel 97 because they are used so often.

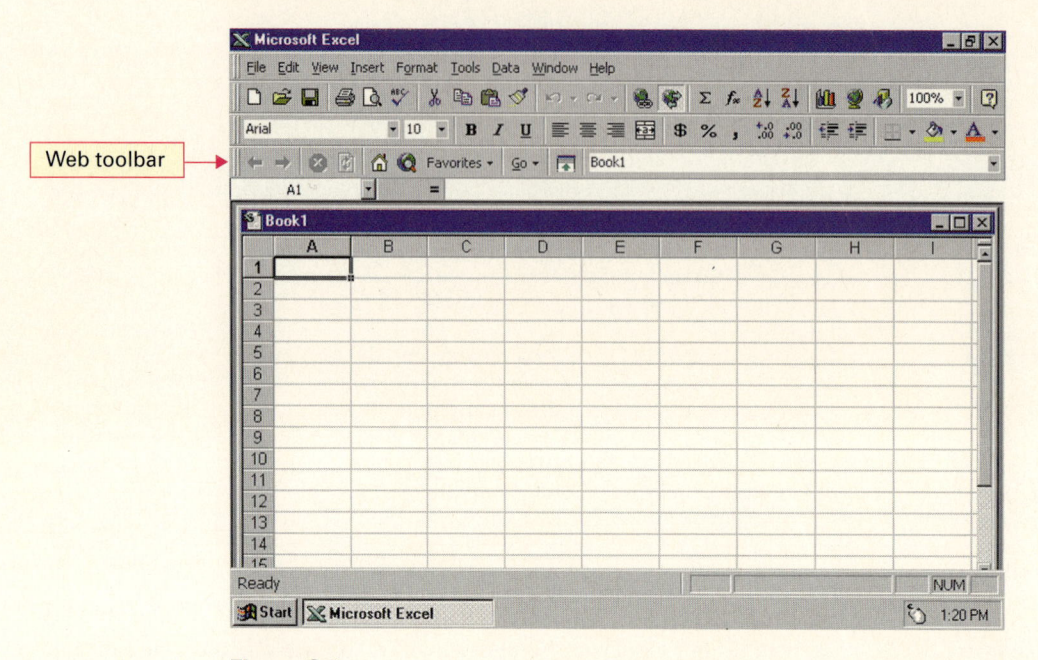

Web toolbar

Figure O.3

Working with Toolbars

Toolbars contain buttons that perform functions. Usually the tools grouped together on a toolbar perform tasks that are all related. For example, the buttons on the Chart toolbar all perform tasks related to creating and modifying charts.

The Standard toolbar and the Formatting toolbar are the default toolbars, the ones that Excel 97 automatically displays. You can display or hide as many toolbars as desired. You also can move toolbars to different locations on the screen. When a toolbar is displayed, Excel places it where it was last located.

If you use the Internet frequently, you may want to display the **Web toolbar** by clicking the Web Toolbar button in the Standard toolbar. With the Web toolbar displayed, your screen should look like Figure O.3. To hide the Web toolbar, click the Web Toolbar button again.

TASK 2: TO WORK WITH TOOLBARS:

1 Choose View, Toolbars.

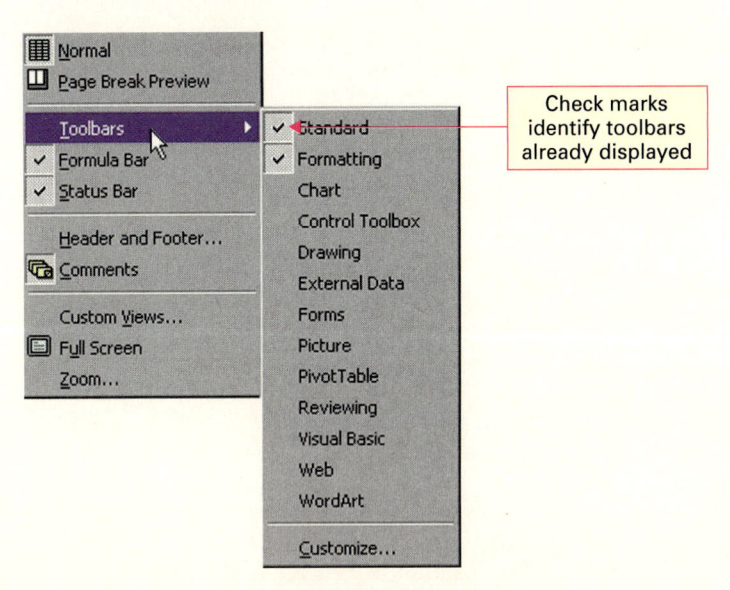

Check marks identify toolbars already displayed

2 Choose Chart.

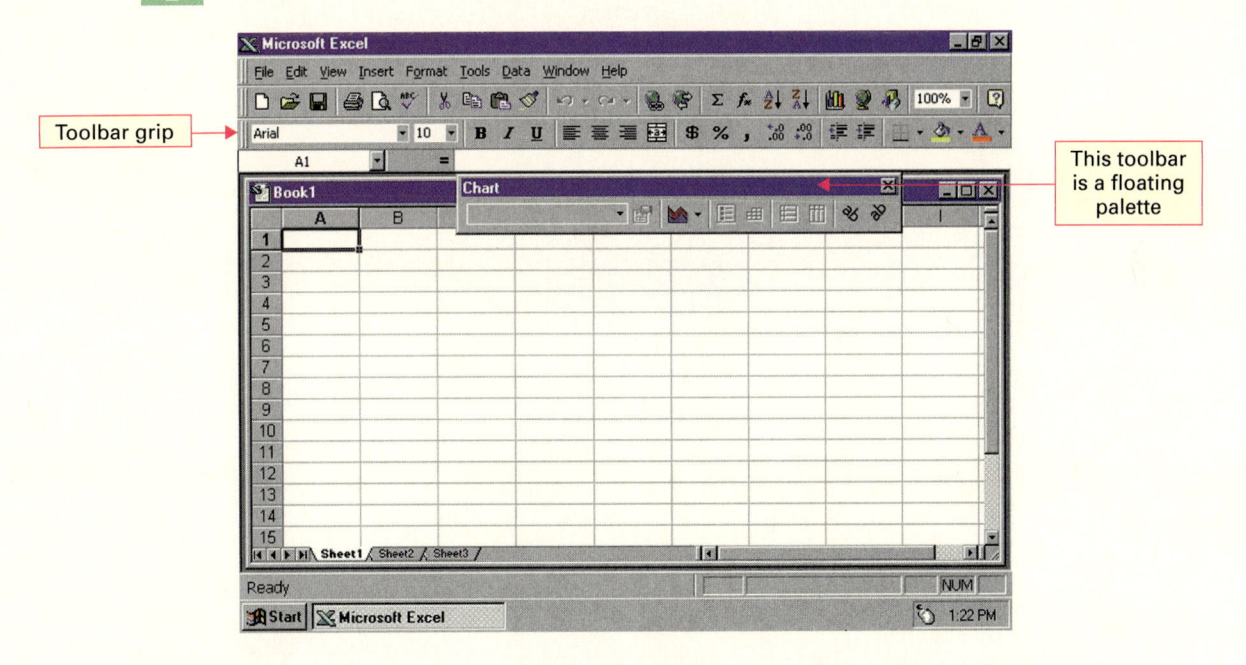

Toolbar grip

This toolbar is a floating palette

3 Point to the title bar of the Chart toolbar and drag the toolbar to a new location. If the toolbar doesn't appear as a palette, drag the toolbar by grabbing the grip. The toolbar moves.

4 Choose View, Toolbars, Chart.
The toolbar no longer displays.

Getting Help

Excel 97 provides several ways to get help. You can use the standard Windows 95 help dialog box that contains the Contents, Index, and Find pages and the What's This Help feature. Additionally, you can use the Office Assistant and Microsoft on the Web, both help features unique to Office 97.

Using the Office Assistant

The Office Assistant offers help on the task you are performing, often referred to as *context-sensitive help*. If the Office Assistant doesn't display the help you want, you can type a question to obtain the desired help.

TASK 3: TO USE THE OFFICE ASSISTANT:

1   Click the Office Assistant 🔲 button if you don't see the Office Assistant.

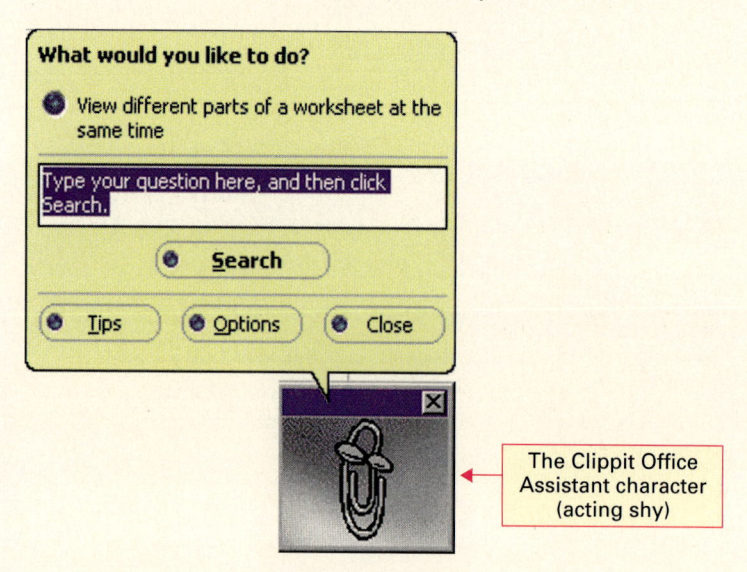

The Clippit Office Assistant character (acting shy)

2 Type **How do you enter a formula?**

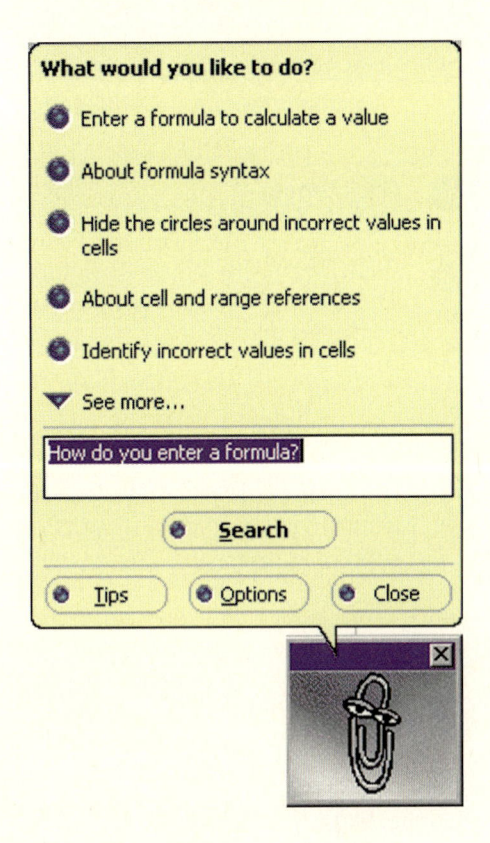

3 Click Search and then click About formula syntax.

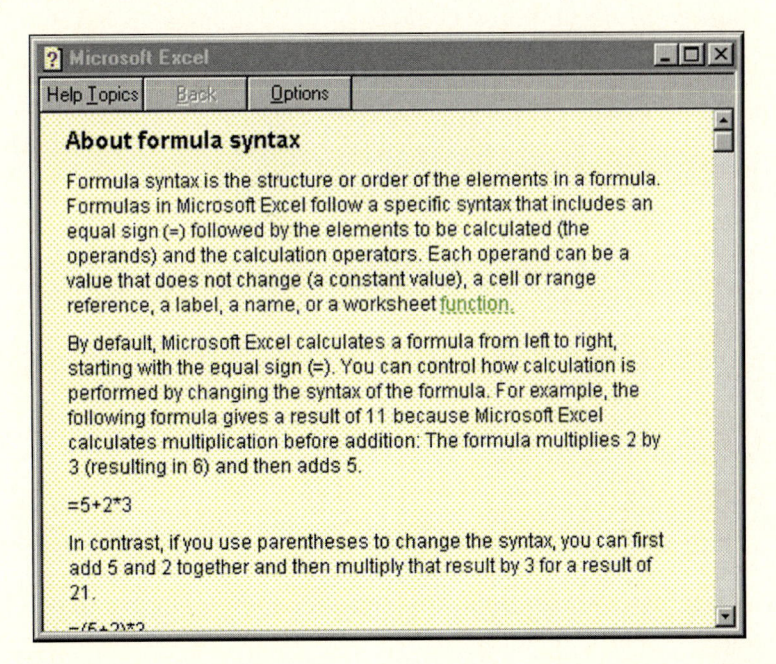

4 Read the Help dialog box and then click ☒ on the Help title bar.
The Help dialog box closes, but the Office Assistant window remains open.

5 Click the Office Assistant character in the Office Assistant window.
The Office Assistant asks what you want to do.

> **Note** The default Office Assistant is a paper clip named Clippit. Other assistants include Shakespeare, a robot, and a cat — to name a few.

6   Click Close.
The "bubble" closes.

7   Click ⊠ on the Office Assistant title bar.
The Office Assistant window closes.

Getting Help from the World Wide Web

Microsoft maintains several sites on the Web that have useful information, user support, product news, and free programs and files that you can download. If your system is connected to the Internet, you can access this type of help easily. The Microsoft sites are open to all users.

> **Note** When Microsoft is beta testing a program, the company maintains "closed sites" open only to beta testers with a valid password.

TASK 4: TO READ ANSWERS TO FREQUENTLY ASKED QUESTIONS:

1   Choose Help, Microsoft on the Web.

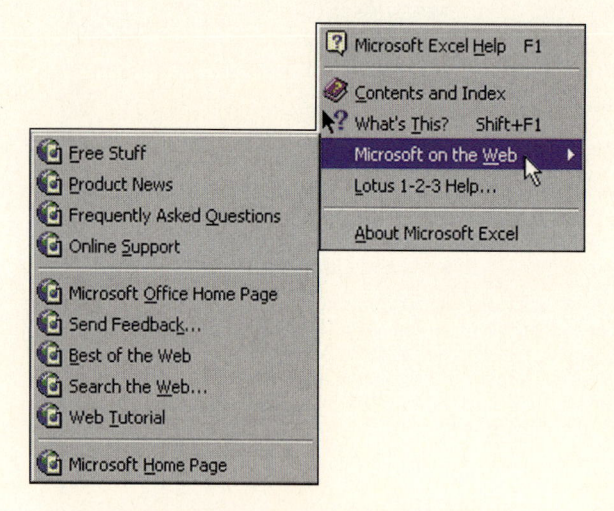

2   Choose Frequently Asked Questions.
The Internet browser program Internet Explorer starts and connects to the appropriate Web site.

3   When you finish browsing the Web, click ⊠ in the browser window. (I know you're tempted to start browsing around, but you can do that later.)

Closing a Workbook and Exiting Excel 97

Before you exit Excel, you should always save any work that you want to keep and then close any open workbooks. When you exit Excel 97, the program closes, and the Windows 95 desktop is visible unless you have another program running in a maximized window, however, the program will be visible, not the desktop.

> **Tip** If you forget to save and close a changed file before you try to exit, Excel 97 asks whether you want to save changes. You can choose Yes to save the changed file, No to exit without saving, or Cancel to cancel the exit request.

TASK 5: TO CLOSE THE WORKBOOK AND EXIT EXCEL 97:

1 Click the Close ⊠ button in the document title bar.

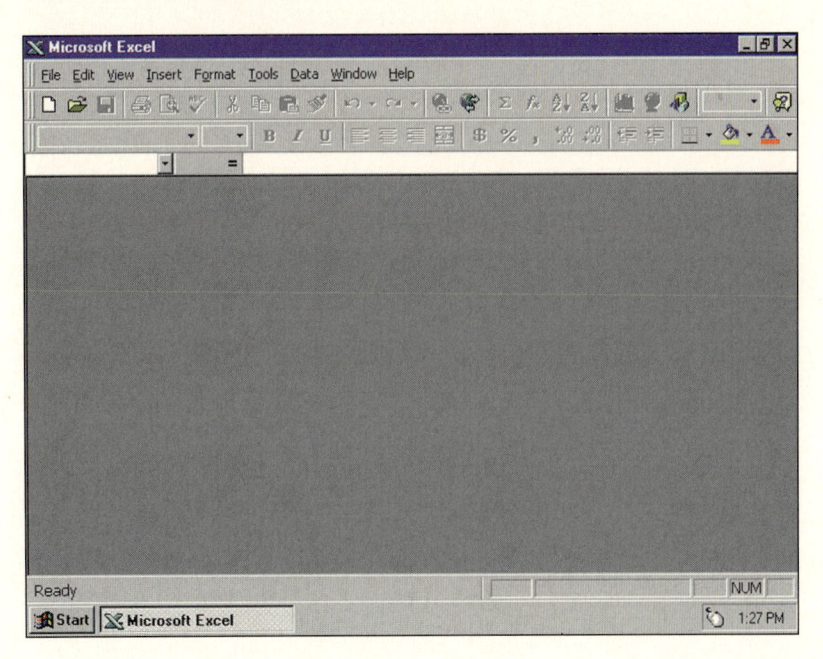

2 Click ⊠ in the application title bar.
The Excel 97 program closes.

Summary and Exercises

Summary

- Excel 97 is a full-featured spreadsheet program that's easy to use.
- An Excel workbook includes three worksheets by default.
- Worksheets enable you to store numbers, perform calculations and recalculations, analyze data, and create charts and maps.
- Many features found in Word processing are also available in Excel 97.
- Excel 97 provides a variety of Help features.
- Excel 97 warns you if you try to exit the program without saving your work.

Key Terms and Operations

Key Terms	Operations
active cell	exit Excel 97
cell	get help from the Web
column	start Excel 97
column indicators	use Office Assistant
Edit mode	
Enter mode	
Error mode	
Formatting toolbar	
formula bar	
menu bar	
mode indicator	
Office Assistant	
Point mode	
Ready mode	
row	
row indicators	
scroll bars	
Standard toolbar	
status bar	
title bar	
toolbar	
Wait mode	
Web toolbar	
What's This?	
workbook	
worksheet	
worksheet scroll buttons	
worksheet tab	

Study Questions

Multiple Choice

1. Another name for a columnar worksheet is a
   a. workbook.
   b. spreadsheet.
   c. cell.
   d. booksheet.

2. The intersection of a column and a row is
   a. a worksheet tab.
   b. a cell.
   c. an active cell.
   d. an indicator.

3. The number of worksheets in a workbook is limited
   a. by default.
   b. to three.
   c. by memory.
   d. to 256.

4. The size of an Excel worksheet is
   a. 128 columns by 9,999 rows.
   b. 65,536 columns by 256 rows.
   c. over 256 million cells.
   d. 256 columns by 65,536 rows.

5. The name of a worksheet displays
   a. in the column letters.
   b. on the worksheet tab.
   c. in the row number.
   d. in the status bar.

6. Which of the following applications would most likely be created in Excel?
   a. a letter
   b. a budget
   c. a memo
   d. a meeting report

7. The standard Windows 95 help features used in Excel include all of the following except
   a. What's This?
   b. Contents.
   c. Index.
   d. Office Assistant.

8. Before exiting Excel 97, you should
   a. save and close all files.
   b. close all files, saving those that you want to keep.
   c. close all files without saving because Excel saves them automatically.
   d. close the Office Assistant.

9. Which of the following statements are false?
   a. The Office Assistant gives context-sensitive help and unsolicited help.
   b. The Office Assistant is an animated character.
   c. The Office Assistant can not be turned off.
   d. The Office Assistant displays help in a bubble.

10. Which of the following are false statements?
   a. The formula bar displays the cell address and the cell contents of the active cell.
   b. The formula bar is a floating palette.
   c. The formula bar is used for typing formulas.
   d. The formula bar can be hidden.

Short Answer

1. How do you start Excel?

2. What is a cell address? Give examples.

3. How are columns and rows identified?

4. How do you display the Web toolbar?

5. Why are screen elements not usually hidden in Excel?

6. Name some of the things that Excel can do.

7. Name some of the word processing features that are found in Excel.

8. Name and describe the different help features in Excel.

9. Name some of the mode indicators in Excel.

10. How many cells are in a worksheet?

For Discussion

1. Name some tasks that you could perform in Excel for your own personal use.

2. Discuss the advantages of using a program like Excel over keeping columnar records manually.

3. Name examples of situations that would benefit from having multiple worksheets in the same file.

4. Discuss the value of a chart in a worksheet.

Review Exercises

1. Starting Excel and Exploring the Workbook

In this exercise, you will start Excel 97 and move around in the workbook.

1. Start Excel 97.

2. Turn on the Web toolbar if it isn't displayed.

3. What text is displayed in the status bar?

4. What text is displayed in the formula bar?

5. Click the tab that says Sheet2.

6. Is there any change in the status bar and in the formula bar?

7. Turn the Web toolbar on if necessary and then turn it off.

2. Getting Help on the Web

In this exercise, you will explore the help feature on the World Wide Web.

1. Choose Help, Microsoft on the Web.

2. Choose Product News.

3. Print the initial Web page that displays.

4. Disconnect from the Internet and exit Internet Explorer.

Assignments

1. Getting Online Help

Start Excel 97 and use the Office Assistant to find a help topic about the Text Import Wizard. Choose Options and print the topic. When finished, close the Help dialog box.

2. Using the Web Toolbar

Start Excel 97 and display the Web toolbar in the new workbook if it isn't already displayed. Go to this address: http://www.dominis.com/Zines/ and explore the site. Give a brief description of what you find. When finished, close Internet Explorer, disconnect from the Internet, and exit Excel 97.

Creating a Workbook

In order to use Excel 97 effectively, you must know how to create, save, and print workbooks. In this project, you will enter text and numbers and calculate the numbers with formulas and functions to create a simple worksheet. (This might sound like a lot, but I promise you won't have to use all 16,777,216 cells!)

Objectives

After completing this project, you will be able to:

- ➤ **Create a new workbook**
- ➤ **Move around in a worksheet and a workbook**
- ➤ **Name worksheets**
- ➤ **Enter data**
- ➤ **Enter simple formulas and functions**
- ➤ **Save a workbook**
- ➤ **Preview and print a worksheet**
- ➤ **Close a worksheet**

The Challenge

Mr. Gilmore, manager of The Grande Hotel, wants a down-and-dirty worksheet to compare the January receipts to the February receipts for both restaurants in the hotel (the Atrium Café and the Willow Top Restaurant). Since the worksheet is just for him, you won't have to worry about formatting right now.

The Solution

You will create a workbook with a page for the Atrium Café and a page for the Willow Top Restaurant as shown in Figure 1.1. (For now, don't worry about aligning headings such as Jan and Feb. You'll learn this in a later project.)

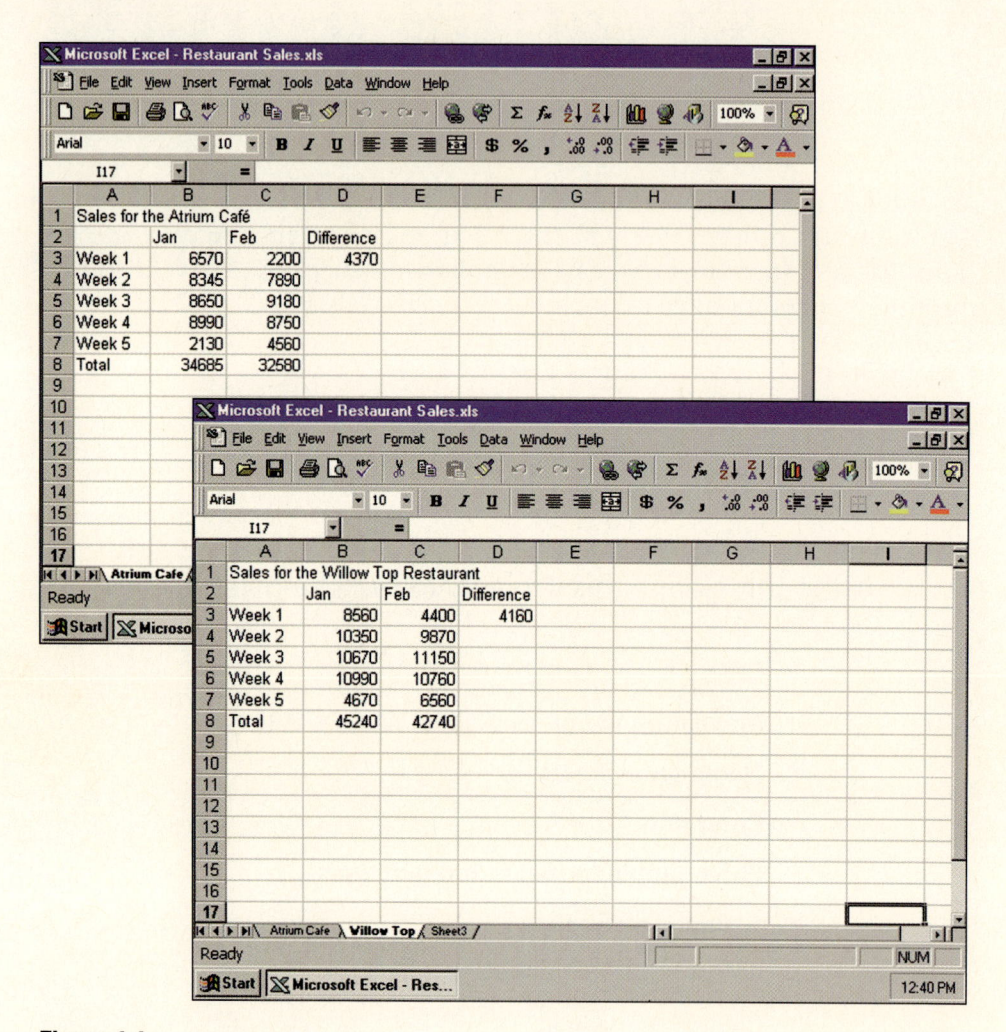

Figure 1.1

The Setup

So that your screen will match the illustrations in this chapter and to ensure that all the tasks in this project will function as described, you should set up Excel as described in Table 1.1. Because these are the default settings for the toolbars and view, you may not need to make any changes to your setup.

Table 1.1   Excel Settings

Location	Make these settings:
View, Toolbars	Deselect all toolbars except the Standard and Formatting.
View	Use the Normal view and display the Formula Bar and the Status Bar.

Creating a New Workbook

When you launch Excel 97, a new blank workbook named Book1 automatically opens for you, and you can begin to enter data.

TASK 1: TO CREATE A NEW WORKBOOK:

1   Click the Start [Start] button and point to Programs.

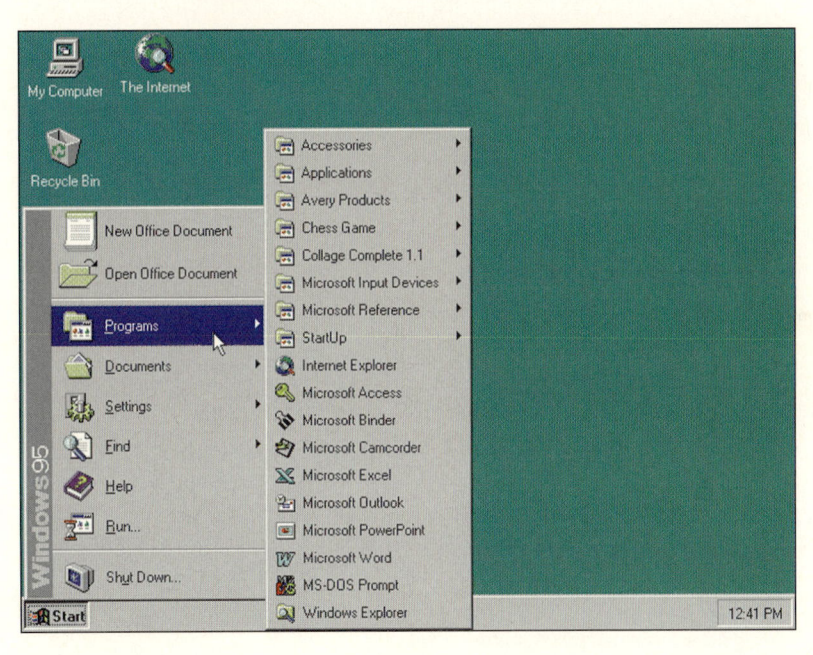

2   Choose Microsoft Excel.
The program launches and creates a workbook called Book1.

> **Note** If Excel is already started and you don't see a workbook on the screen, click the New [ ] button, and Excel will create one for you.

Moving Around in a Worksheet and a Workbook

To enter data in a worksheet like the one shown in Figure 1.2, you must move to the desired cell. The *active cell* is outlined with a black border. You make a cell the active cell by clicking in the cell or by moving to the cell with keystrokes. Table 1.2 lists the navigational keystrokes used to move to the desired cell.

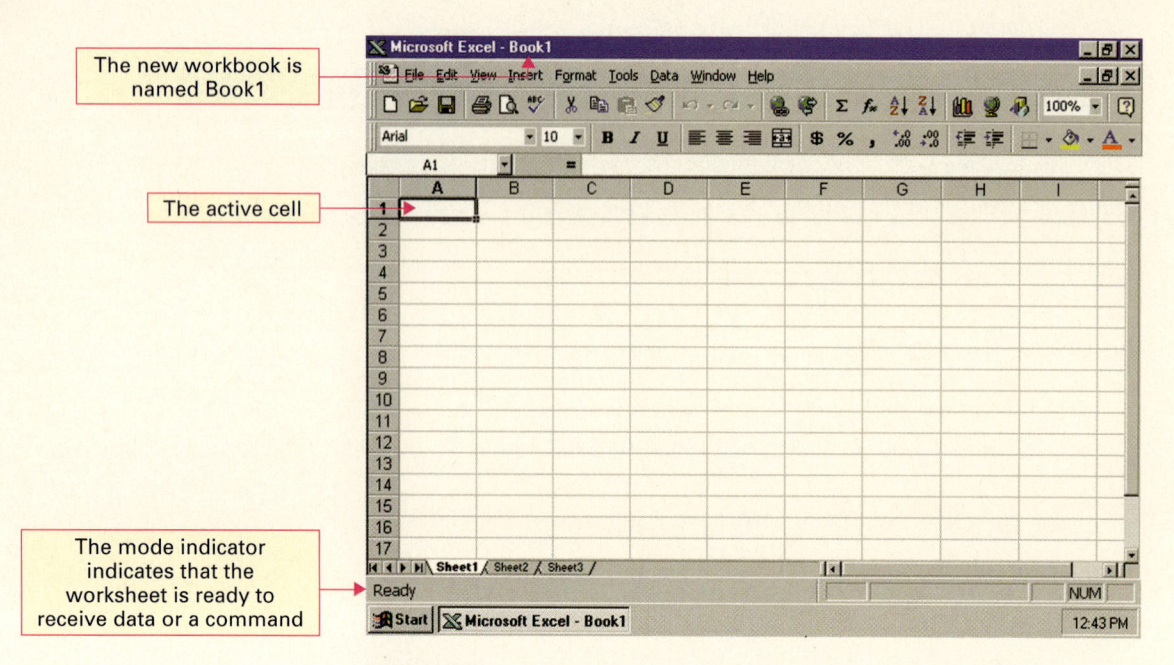

The new workbook is named Book1

The active cell

The mode indicator indicates that the worksheet is ready to receive data or a command

Figure 1.2

Note If you want to click in a cell you can't see on the screen, use the vertical or horizontal scroll bar to scroll the worksheet until you see the cell.

Table 1.2   Navigational Keystrokes

Target Location	Keystroke
Cell to the right of the active cell	→ or TAB
Cell to the left of the active cell	← or SHIFT+TAB
Cell below the active cell	↓ or ENTER
Cell above the active cell	↑ or SHIFT+ENTER
Upper-left corner of the worksheet	CTRL+HOME
Lower-right corner of the active area of the worksheet	CTRL+END
Down one screen	PGDN
Up one screen	PGUP
Right one screen	ALT+PGDN
Left one screen	ALT+PGUP

To display a different worksheet, click the worksheet tab. If you can't see the tab for the worksheet that you want to display, click the appropriate scroll button (the arrows just to the left of the worksheet tabs) to display the tab.

TASK 2: TO MOVE AROUND IN A WORKSHEET AND A WORKBOOK:

1 Press (PGDN).

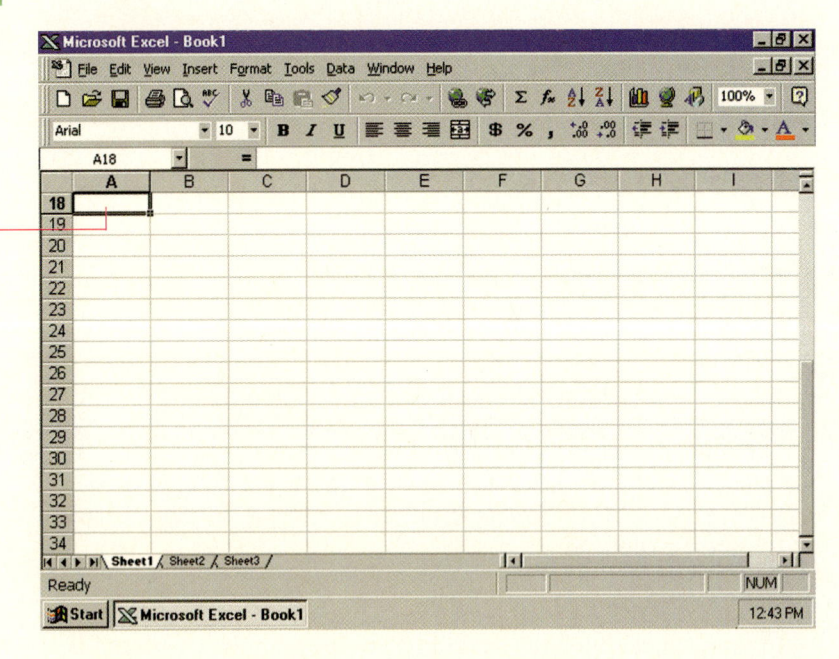

Cell A18 becomes the active cell

> **Note** The monitor's size and resolution determine the number of columns and rows displayed on a screen. When you press PgDn, PgUp, Alt+PgDn, or Alt+PgUp, the active cell may be different from those shown in the illustrations.

2 Press ⊙ five times.

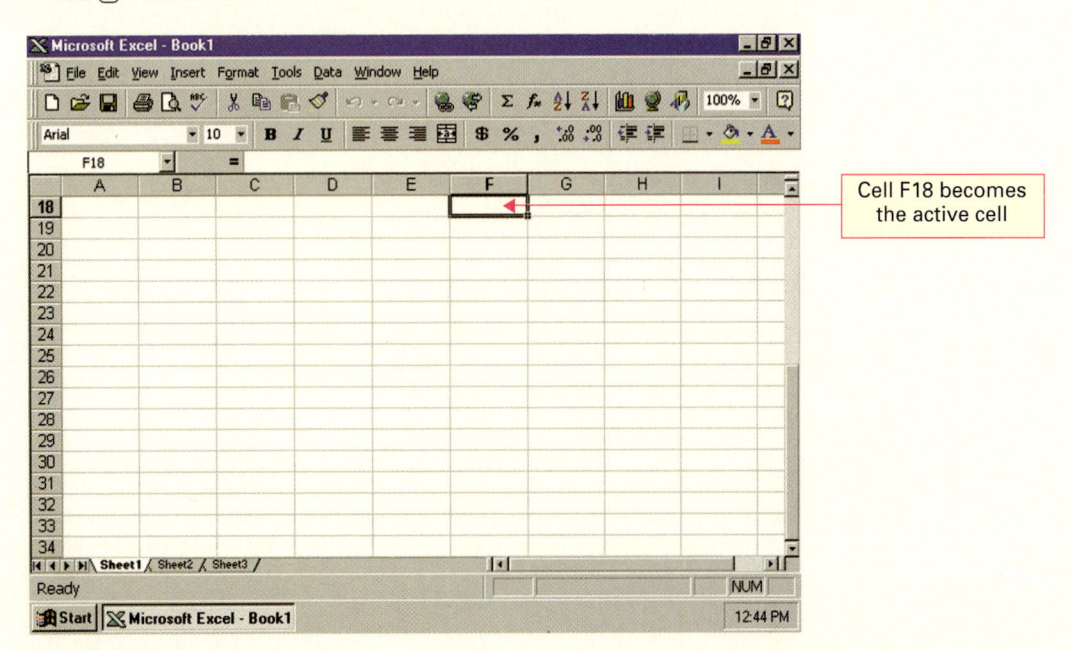

Cell F18 becomes the active cell

3 Type **88** and press ENTER.

The number displays in cell F18, and cell F19 becomes the active cell.

> **Note** Instead of pressing the Enter key to enter data in a cell, you can press any one of the arrow keys (Up, Down, Left, or Right) or any key that moves the cell pointer, such as the PgUp key or the PgDn key. When you enter data across a row, it's more efficient to use the Right arrow key than to use the Enter key.

4 Press CTRL+HOME.

Cell A1 becomes the active cell.

5 Drag the box in the vertical scroll bar until you see Row 4 in the ScrollTip box.

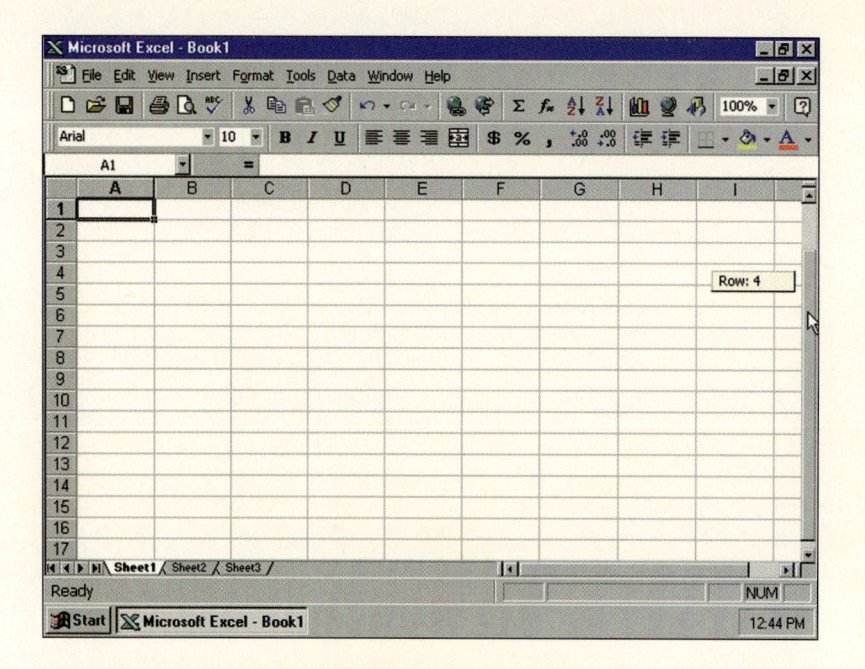

6 Click in cell D5.

Cell D5 becomes the active cell.

7 Press CTRL + END.

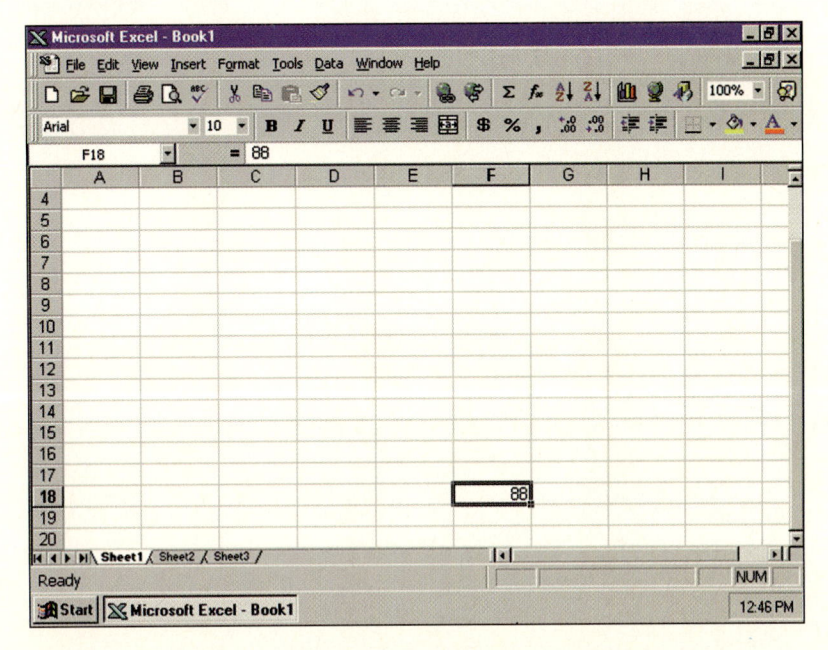

Note The lower right corner of the active worksheet is always the cell at the intersection of the last row and the last column used, and it doesn't necessarily contain data.

8 Press DEL.
The number is deleted.

9 Click the Sheet2 tab.
Sheet2 displays.

Naming Worksheets

The three worksheets created by default in a new workbook are named Sheet1, Sheet2, and Sheet3. Not very imaginative or meaningful names, are they? You can give the worksheets better names to help you identify the content of the worksheet.

TASK 3: TO NAME A WORKSHEET:

1 Point to the Sheet1 tab and right-click.

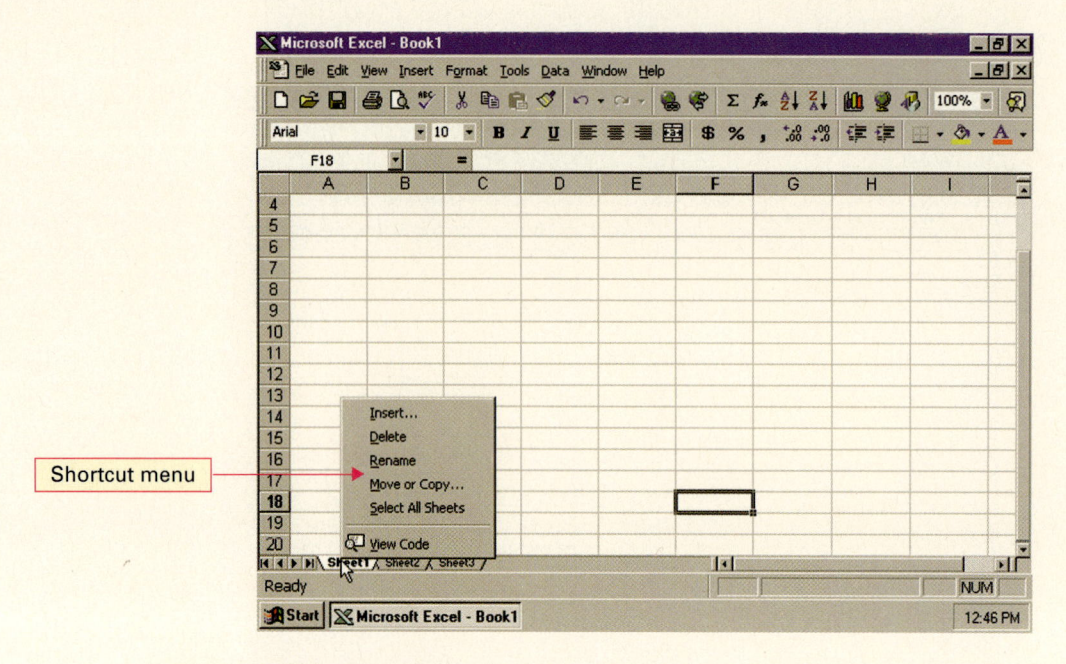

Shortcut menu

2 Choose Rename.
The current name on the tab is highlighted.

3 Type **Atrium Cafe** and press (ENTER).

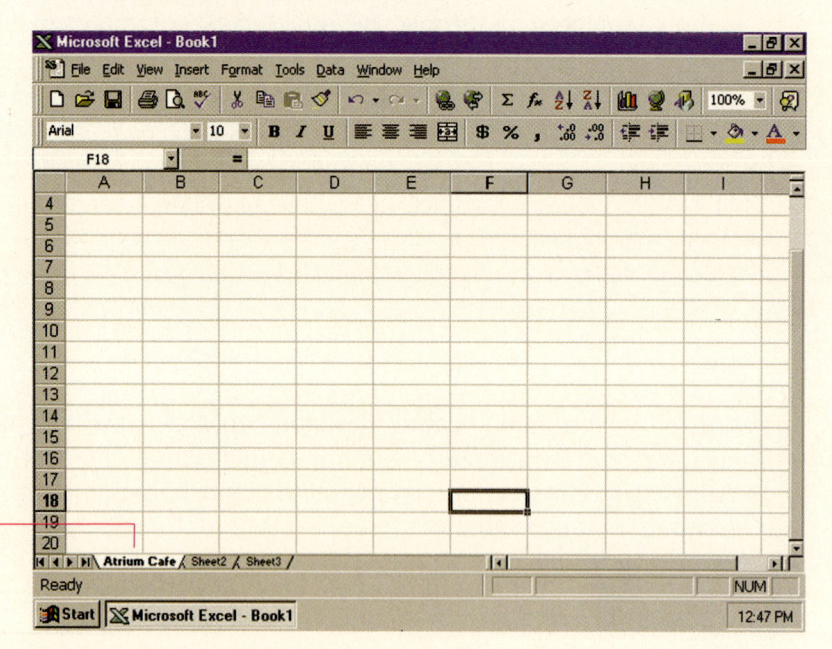

The new worksheet name appears on the tab

4 Point to the Sheet2 tab and right-click.
The shortcut menu displays.

5 Choose Rename.
The current name on the tab is highlighted.

6 Type **Willow Top** and press (ENTER).
The name displays on the tab.

Entering Data

Excel 97 recognizes several different types of data—text, dates, numbers, and formulas. Text can include any characters on the keyboard as well as special characters such as the symbols for the British pound or the Japanese Yen. Dates can be entered with numbers separated with a slash or a dash. Numbers can include only these characters:

1 2 3 4 5 6 7 8 9 0 + − ( ) , / $ % . E.

> **Tip** To enter a fraction instead of a date, precede the fraction with a zero. For example, to enter the fraction one-half, type 0 1/2 instead of 1/2 which Excel interprets as a date.

Entering Text

When you enter text in a cell, if the cell isn't wide enough to hold the text, the text will spill over into the next cell (if it's empty).

> **Tip** Any time you enter data that doesn't fit in a cell, you can widen the column and the data will display.

TASK 4: TO ENTER DATA IN THE WORKSHEET:

1 Click the Atrium Cafe tab.
The Atrium Cafe worksheet displays.

2 Click in cell A1.
Cell A1 becomes the active cell.

3 Type **Sales for the Atrium Cafe**.
Notice that the mode changes to **Enter** because you are entering data. Also notice that Excel adds an accent to the "e" in "cafe."

4 Press ⌨ENTER.

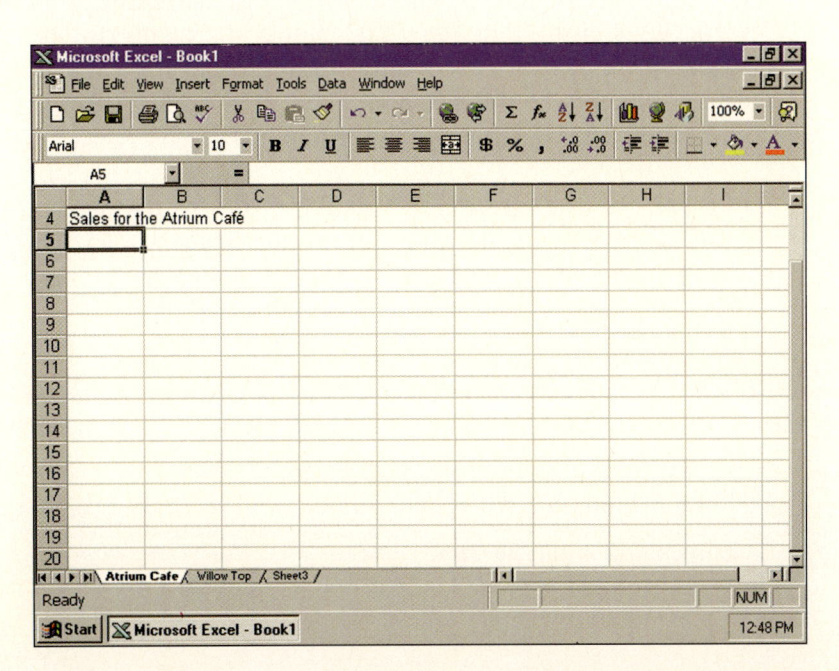

> **Tip** If you make a mistake while typing, simply press the Backspace key and retype the text before you press Enter. If you change your mind about entering the data in the current cell, press (ESC) before Excel enters the data.

5 Click the Willow Top tab.
The Willow Top worksheet displays.

6 Click in cell A1 if necessary.
Cell A1 becomes the active cell.

7 Type **Sales for the Willow Top Restaurant** and press (ENTER).

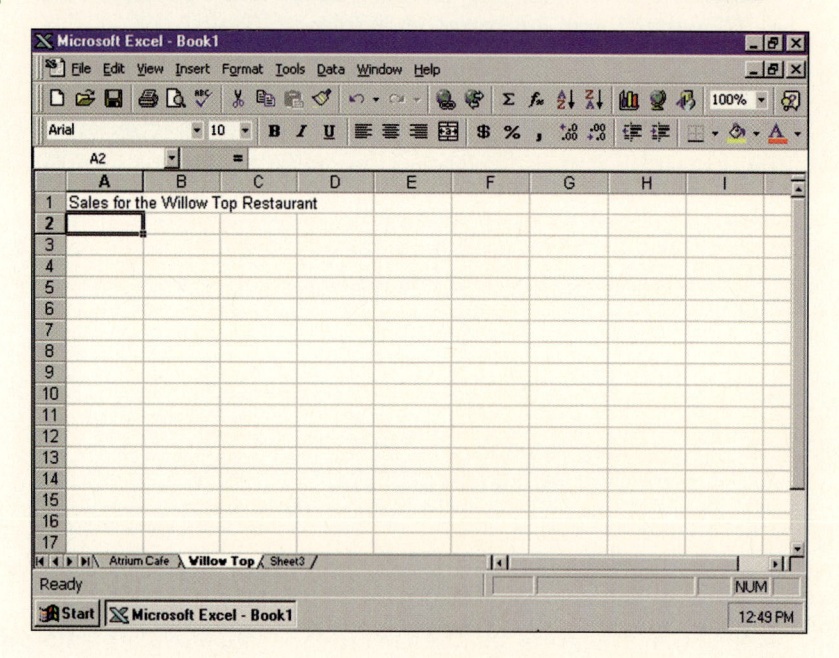

Entering Data on Multiple Worksheets

Sometimes the worksheets that you create have the same data entered several times. If the repetitive data that you are entering is text, the *Auto-Complete* feature of Excel 97 may complete the entry for you if the repetitive text appears in the same column. If the automatic completion isn't appropriate, just continue typing the text that you want.

If you are creating multiple worksheets in a workbook, you may want to use the same data for the column and row headings. To save time, you can enter the data that is the same on all worksheets at the same time.

TASK 5: TO ENTER THE SAME DATA ON MULTIPLE WORKSHEETS AT THE SAME TIME:

1 Press (CTRL) and click the Atrium Cafe tab.
Both the Atrium Cafe worksheet and the Willow Top worksheet are selected.

2 Click in cell B2 and type **Jan**.

Note The Group indicator displays in the title bar when multiple worksheets are selected.

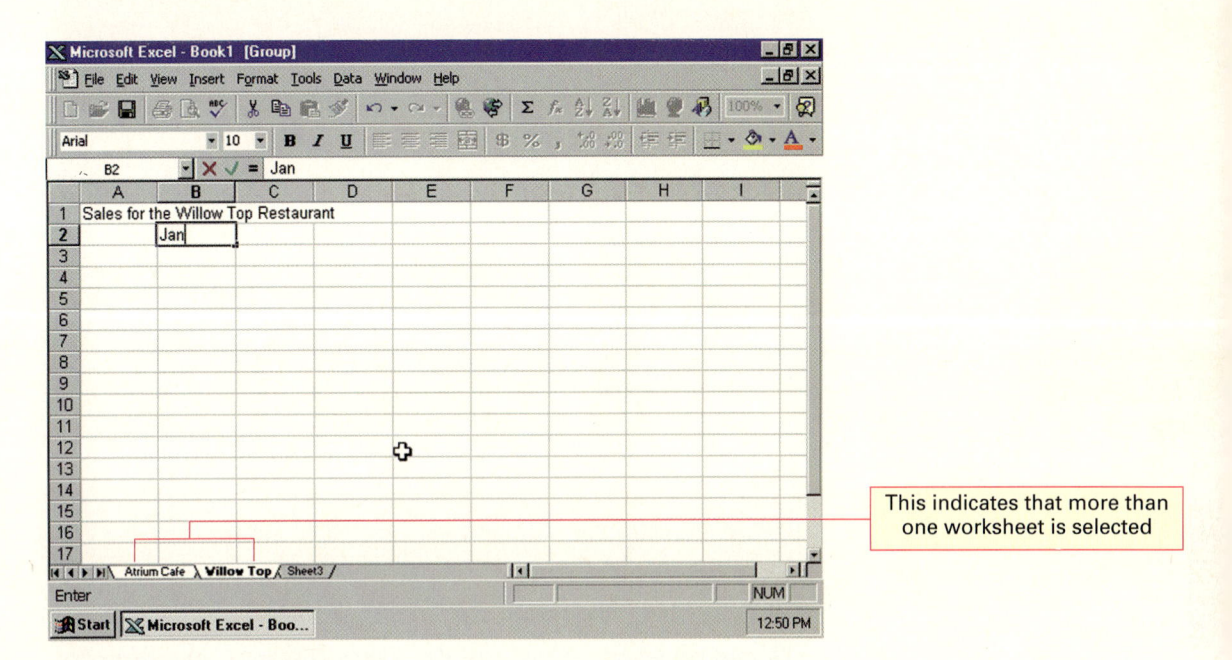

This indicates that more than one worksheet is selected

3 Press → and type **Feb**.

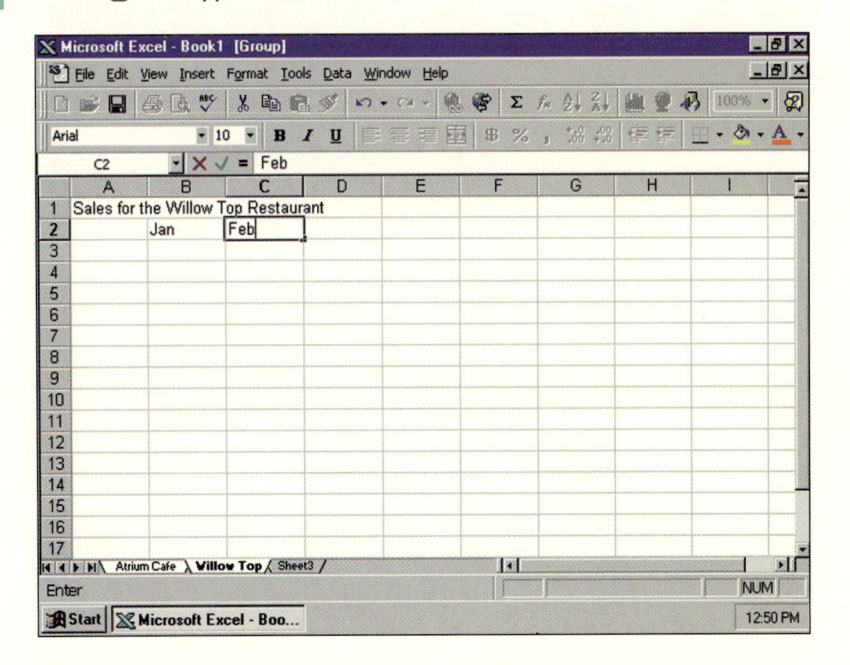

4 Press → and type **Difference**.

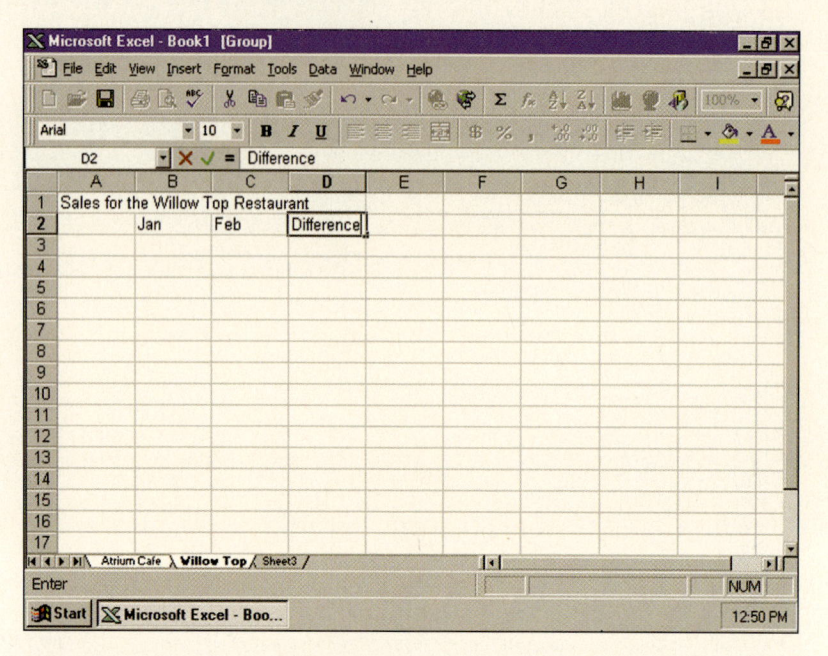

5 Click in cell A3 and type **Week 1**.

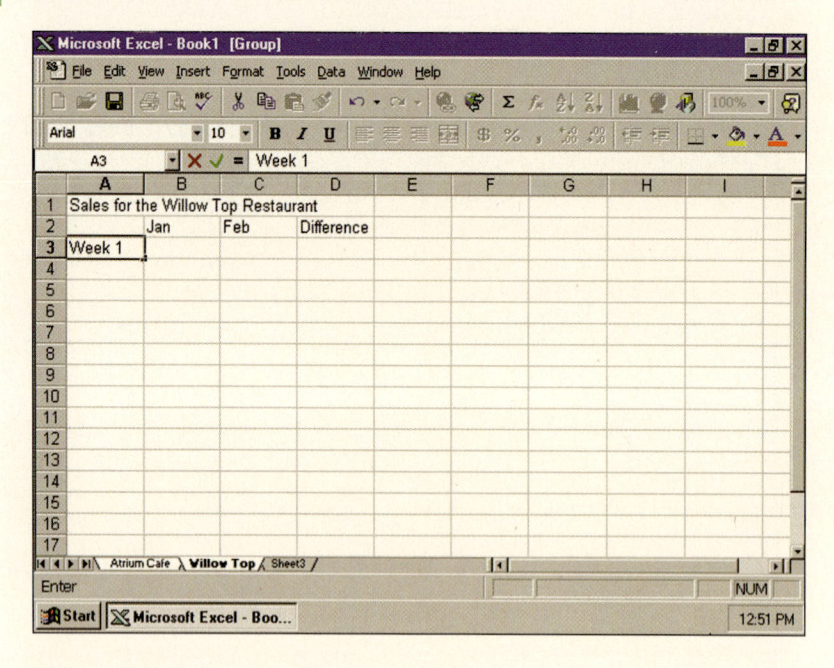

6 Press (ENTER) and type **Week**.
The AutoComplete feature completes the entry as Week 1.

7 Continue typing so that the entry is "Week 2" and then press (ENTER).

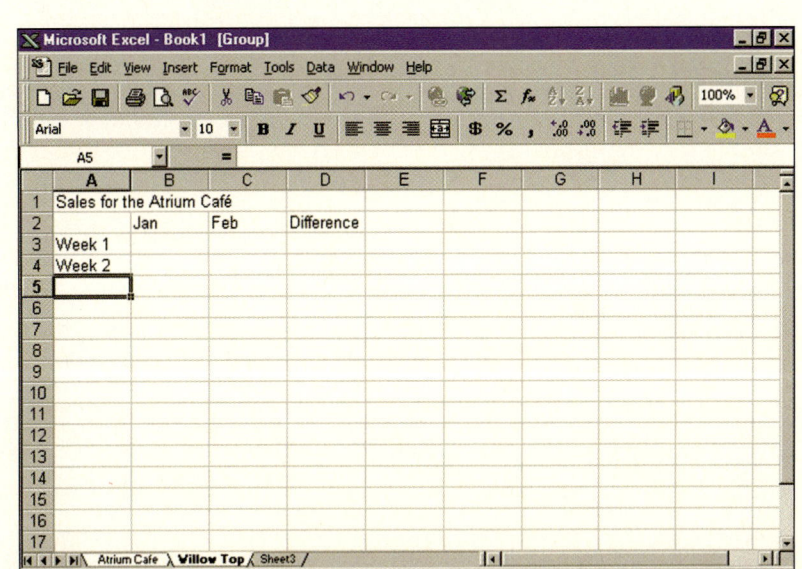

8 Click in cell A4.
Cell A4 becomes the active cell.

9 Point to the handle in the lower right corner of the cell.

Note The pointer appears as a plus when you point to the handle.

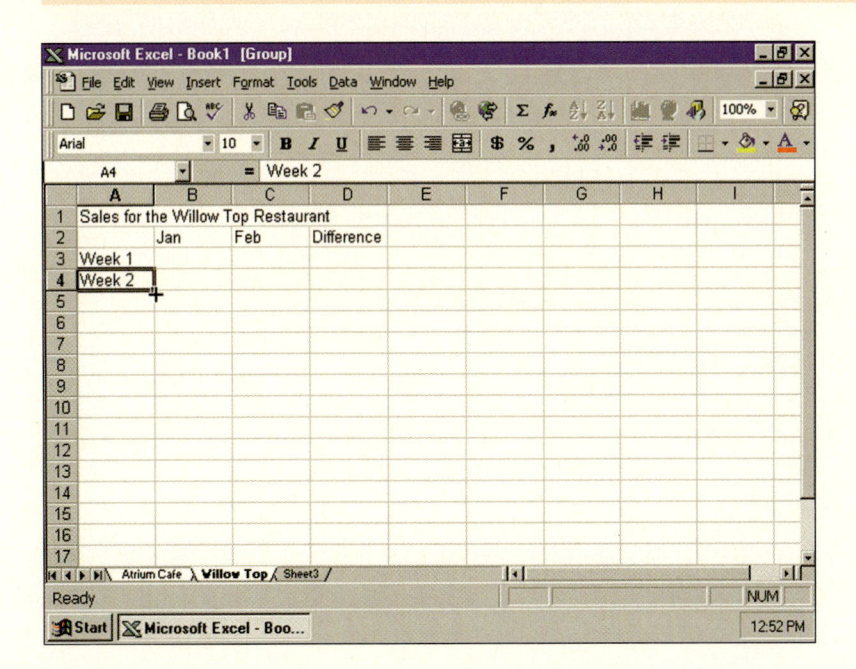

10 Drag the handle to cell A7.

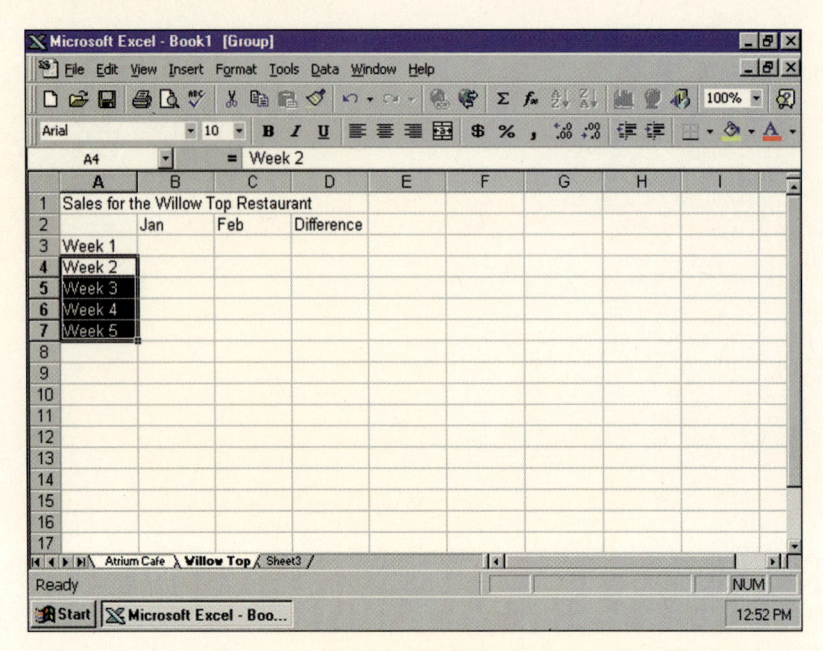

Tip You can use the dragging technique to enter almost any type of series (except the World Series, of course).

11 Click in cell A8, type **Total** and press (ENTER).

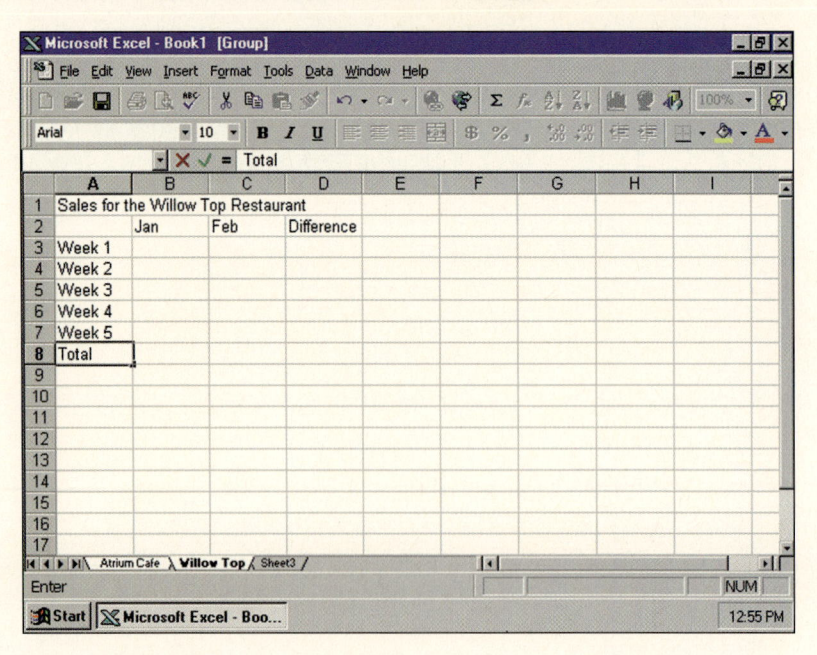

12 Click the Atrium Cafe tab.

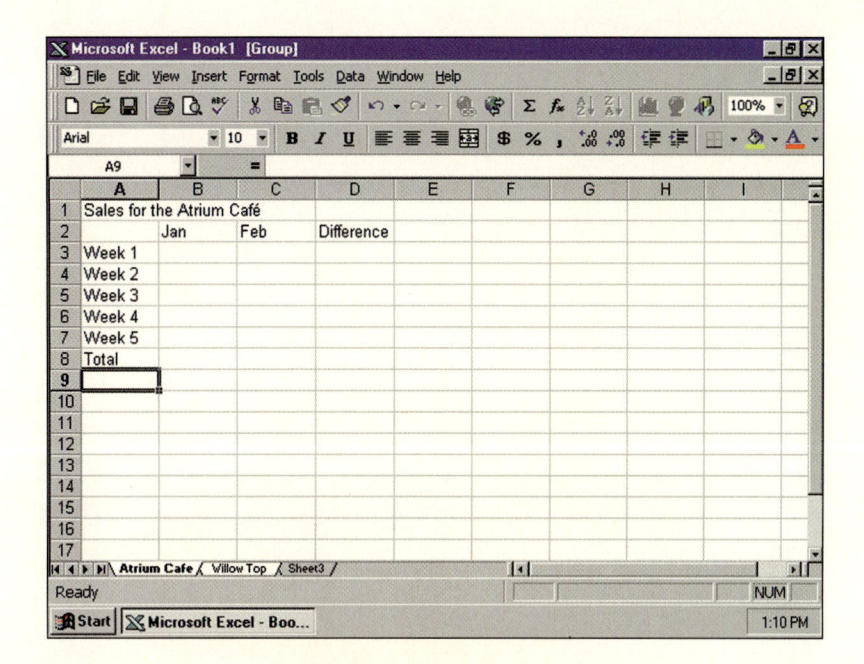

Now you will enter some numbers. The technique is the same.

Entering Numbers

If you enter a number that doesn't fit in a cell, Excel 97 either converts the number to *scientific notation* or displays pound signs (#) in the cell. If you enter a date that doesn't fit in a cell, Excel 97 displays pound signs.

> **Note** Scientific notation is a number format used for very large numbers and very small decimal numbers. For example, the scientific notation for 1,000,000,000 is 1E+09 which means 1 times 10 to the ninth power. Perhaps our government should consider using scientific notation to express the national debt; maybe it wouldn't look so bad.

TASK 6: TO ENTER NUMBERS IN THE WORKSHEETS:

1 Press (CTRL) and click the Willow Top tab.
The Willow Top worksheet is deselected and the Group indicator no longer displays in the title bar.

2 Enter the following numbers in columns B and C on the Atrium Cafe worksheet:

COLUMN B	COLUMN C
6570	2200
8345	7890
8650	9180
8990	8750
2130	4560

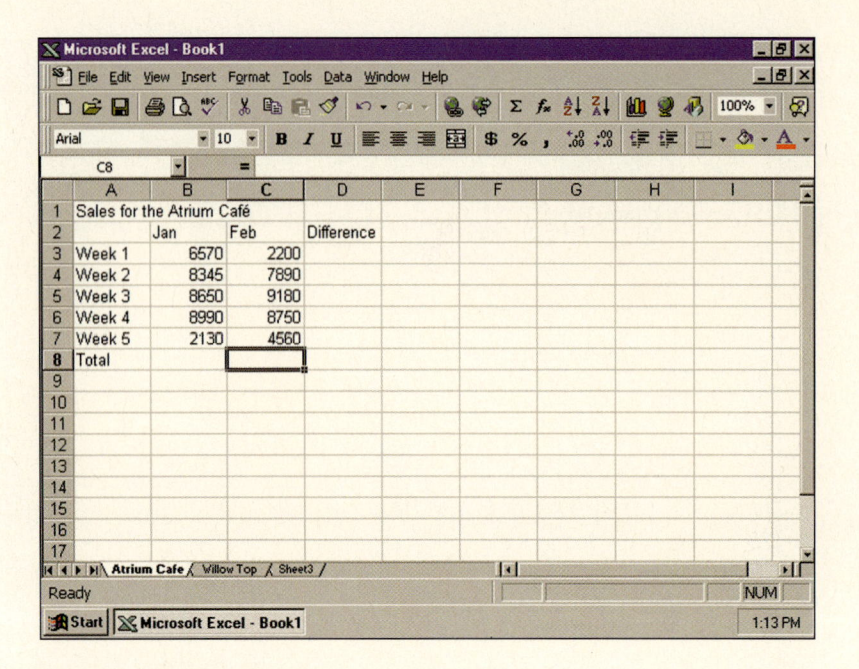

3 Click the Willow Top tab.
The Willow Top worksheet displays.

4 Enter the following numbers in columns B and C on the Willow Top worksheet:

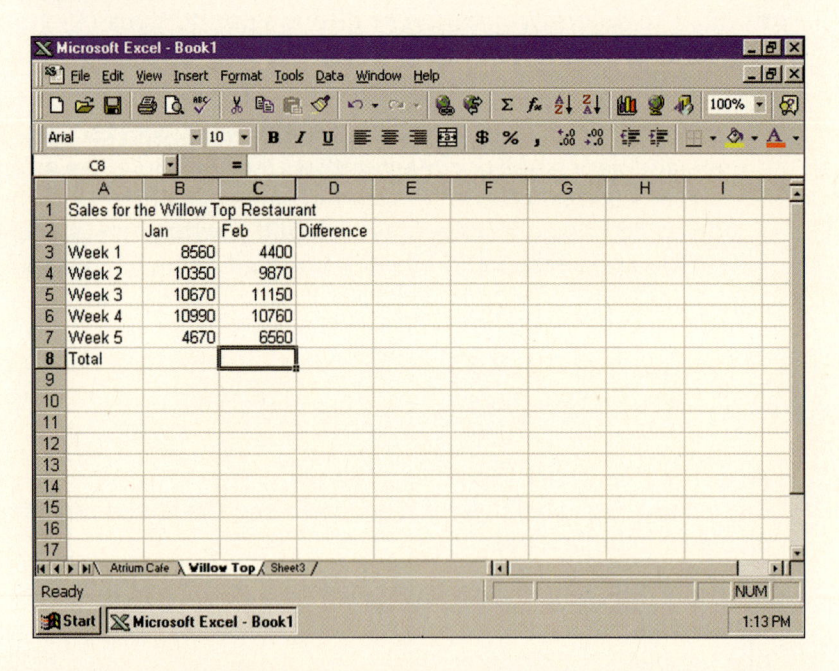

Entering Simple Formulas and Functions

Formulas and *functions* are mathematical statements that perform calculations. Formulas are made up and entered by the user to perform the specific calculation needed. Formulas and functions must start with the equal sign (=), and they can contain cell addresses, numbers, and *arithmetic op-*

erators. Table 1.3 describes the arithmetic operators and gives examples. Table 1.4 lists some of the commonly used functions.

Functions are formulas that are included in Excel 97. They perform calculations that are commonly used such as calculating a sum or an average. Functions require specific information, called *arguments,* to perform the calculations.

> **Tip** Some formulas and functions refer to a block of cells, called a *range.* The address of a range includes the first and last cells in the range separated by a colon. For example, the address of the range from cell A1 through cell B10 is A1:B10.

Table 1.3   Arithmetic Operators

Operator	Meaning	Example	Result (if A1 = 20 and A2 = 2)
+	Addition	=A1+A2	22
−	Subtraction	=A1−A2	18
*	Multiplication	=A1*10	200
/	Division	=A1/A2	10
%	Percent	=A1%	.2
^	Exponentiation	=A1^A2	400

Table 1.4   Commonly Used Functions

Function	Meaning	Example	Result (if A1 = 1, A2 = 2 and A3 = 3)
=SUM(*argument*)	Calculates the sum of the cells in the argument	=SUM(A1:A3)	6
=AVERAGE(*argument*)	Calculates the average of the cells in the argument	=AVERAGE(A1:A3)	2
=MAX(argument)	Finds the largest value in the cells in the argument	=MAX(A1:A3)	3
=MIN(*argument*)	Finds the smallest value of the cells in the argument	=MIN(A1:A3)	1
=COUNT(*argument*)	Counts the number of cells in the argument that have a numeric value	=COUNT(A1:A3)	3

TASK 7: TO ENTER FORMULAS AND FUNCTIONS:

1 Press (CTRL) and click the Atrium Cafe tab.
Both worksheets are selected, and the data you enter will display on both worksheets. Notice that the Group indicator displays in the title bar.

2 Click in cell D3 and click the equal sign in the formula bar. (If the Office Assistant opens, choose No, don't provide help now.)

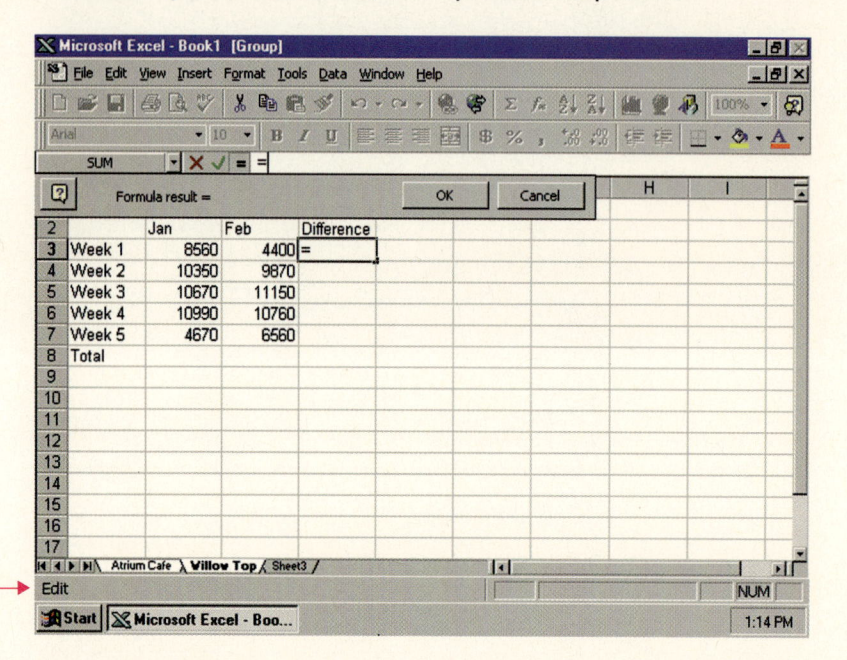

The mode changes to Edit because the data is being entered in the formula bar

3 Click in cell B3.
The mode changes to **Point** because you are pointing to cells to build the formula.

4 Type a minus sign (−).

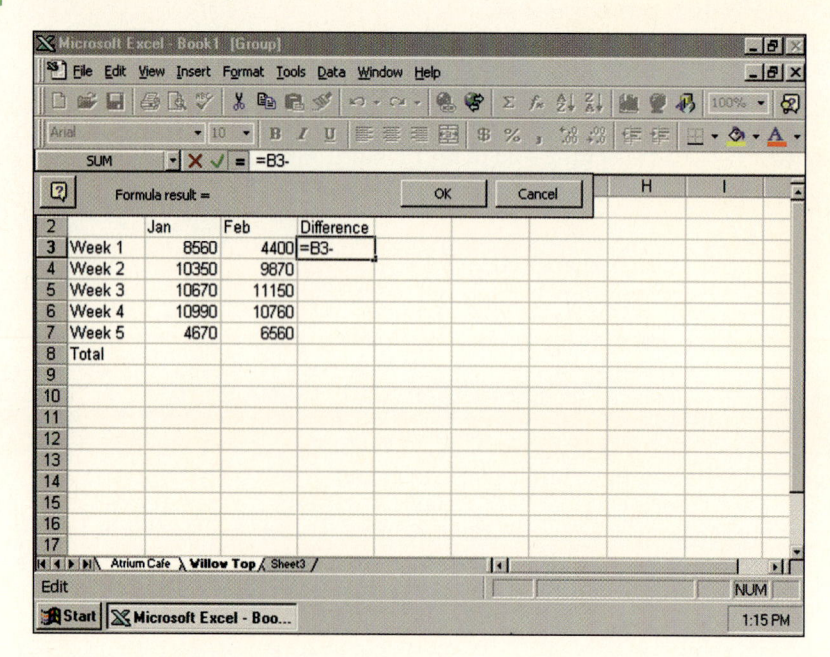

5   Click in cell C3 and the click the Enter ✓ button in the formula bar.

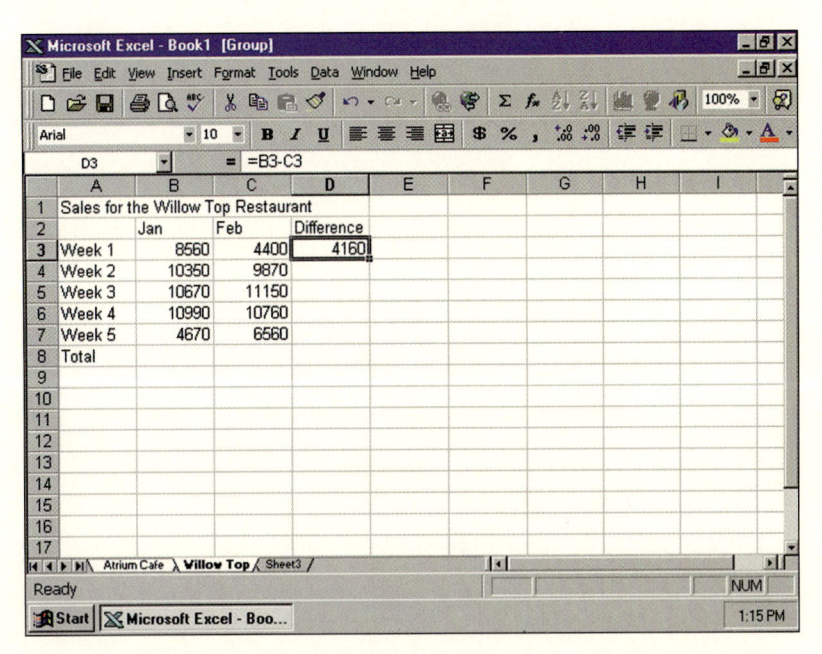

6   Click in cell B8 and type **=sum(**.

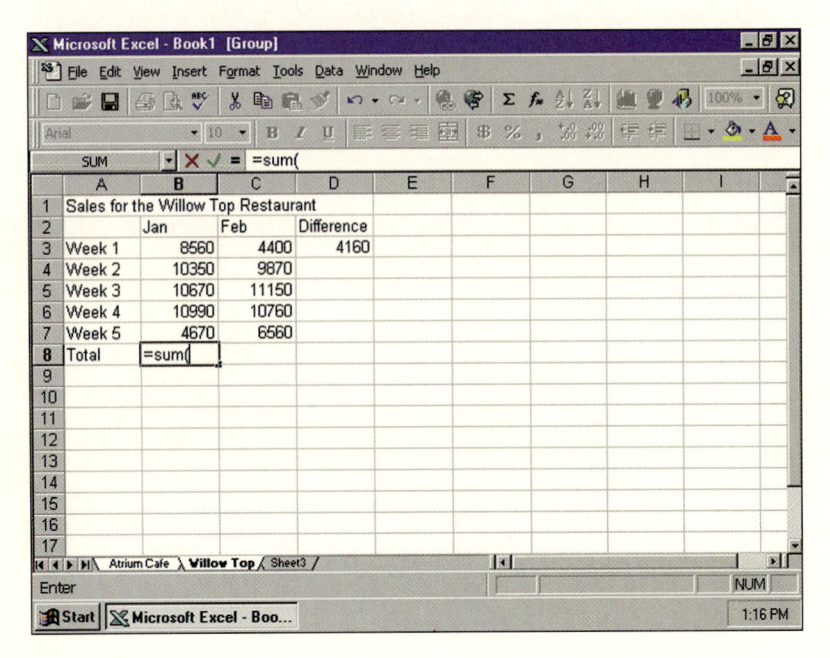

7 Drag the cursor from cell B3 through cell B7.

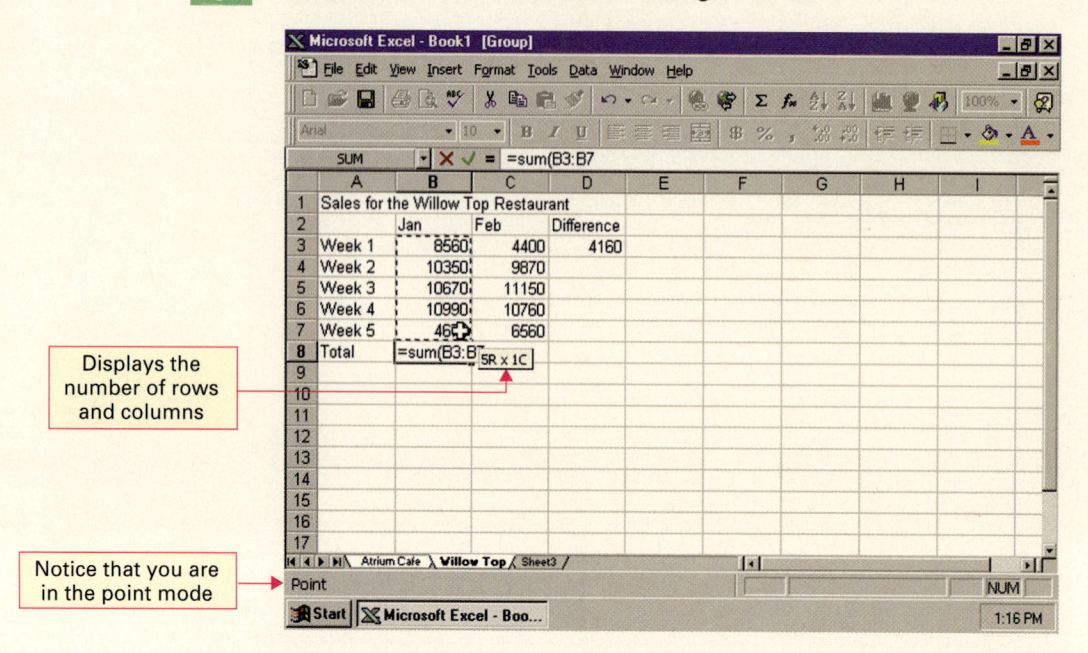

Displays the number of rows and columns →

Notice that you are in the point mode →

8 Press ENTER.

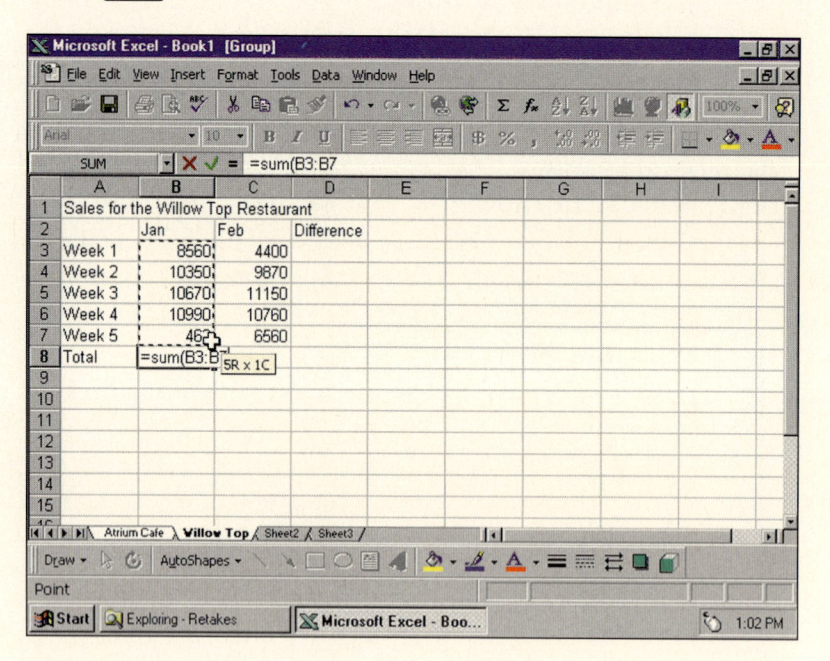

9 Click in cell C8 and click the AutoSum Σ button.

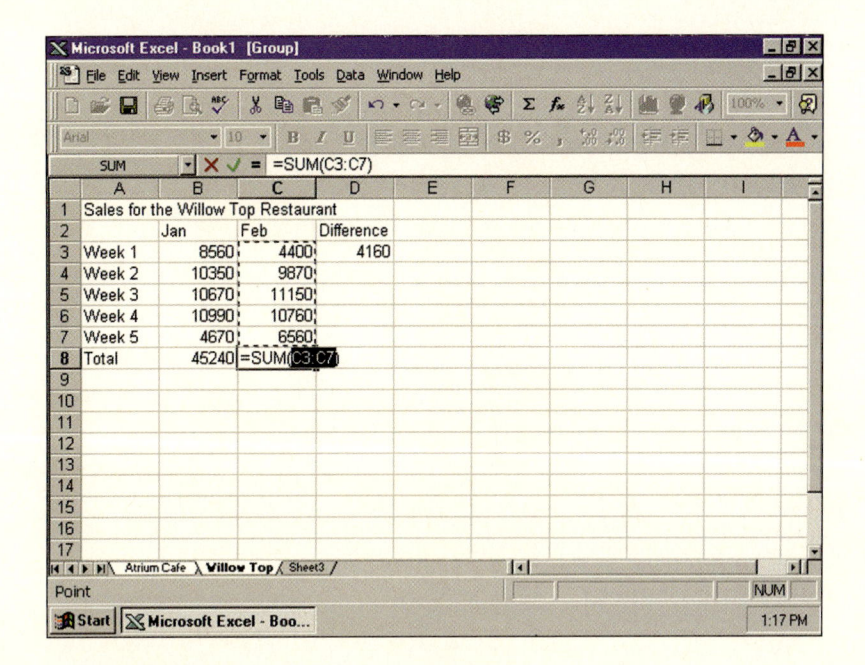

10   Press (ENTER).
The numbers in column C are totaled.

> **Note** If you change a number in a cell, Excel 97 automatically recalculates all formulas or functions that might be affected.

> **Key Concept** When a formula has more than one operation, Excel 97 follows an order of precedence to determine the sequence in which each operation should be performed. The order is as follows: exponentiation first, then multiplication or division (from left to right), and finally addition or subtraction (from left to right). If the formula has parentheses, the operation(s) in the parentheses are performed first. You can use the phrase "Please excuse my dear Aunt Sally" to remember "p" for parentheses, "e" for exponent, "m" for multiplication, "d" for division, "a" for addition, and "s" for subtraction.

Saving a Workbook

If you want to keep the data that you have entered in a workbook, you must save the file. When saving the file, you specify a name for the document and a location where it will be stored.

> **Tip** Because Excel 97 is written for Windows 95, the name of a workbook can be a *long filename.* Long filenames (including the full path of the file) can use up to 255 characters. Although you can use as many spaces and periods in the filename as you want, you can't use ? or : or *. Older versions of Excel prior to Excel 7.0 do NOT use long filenames and will convert a long filename to eight characters (plus the extension).

TASK 8: TO SAVE A WORKBOOK:

1 Click the Atrium Cafe tab if it isn't the displayed worksheet.
The Atrium Cafe worksheet displays.

2 Press (CTRL) and click the Willow Top tab.
The Willow Top worksheet is deselected.

> **Tip** When you are ready to save and close a workbook and you have more than one worksheet selected, you might want to deselect all but one worksheet by pressing (CTRL) and clicking the tabs you want to deselect. If you don't deselect worksheets, the next time you open the workbook, the worksheets will still be selected and any changes you make will be made on all worksheets.

3 Click the Save 🖫 button.

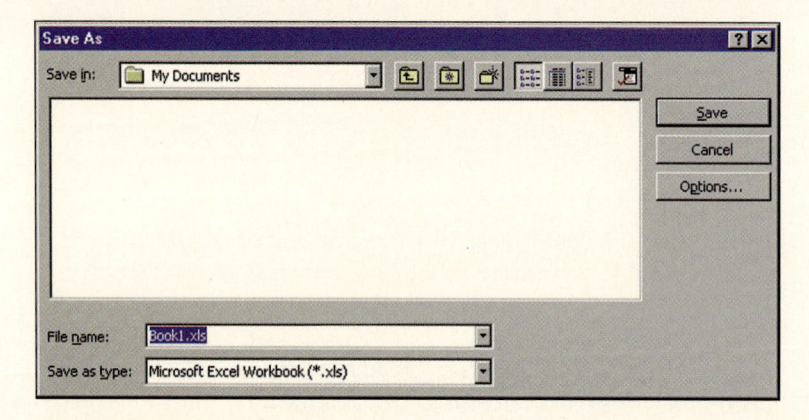

4 Type **Restaurant Sales** in the File Name text box.
Excel 97 adds the default extension xls to the filename when the file is saved.

5 Click the down arrow in the Save In text box and choose drive A: (or the drive and folder designated by your professor or lab assistant).

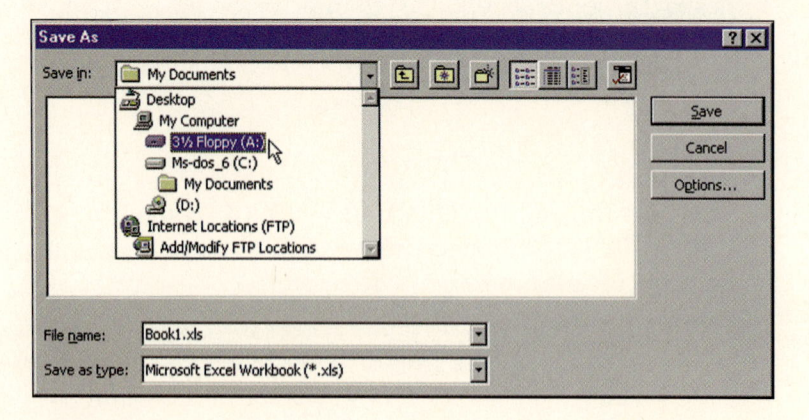

6 Click Save.
The dialog box closes, the file is saved on the disk, and the title bar displays the name of the file.

Previewing and Printing a Worksheet

Before you print a file, you should preview it to see if it looks like what you expect. (You don't want any surprises.) The *Print Preview* shows the full page of the current worksheet and allows you to zoom in on the worksheet so you can actually read the data, if necessary.

You can print a worksheet in the Print Preview mode or in Normal view. Clicking the Print button prints one copy of the complete workbook. If you want to print only part of the workbook or more than one copy, you should use the Print command from the File menu.

TASK 9: TO PREVIEW AND PRINT A WORKSHEET:

1 Click the Print Preview [📖] button.

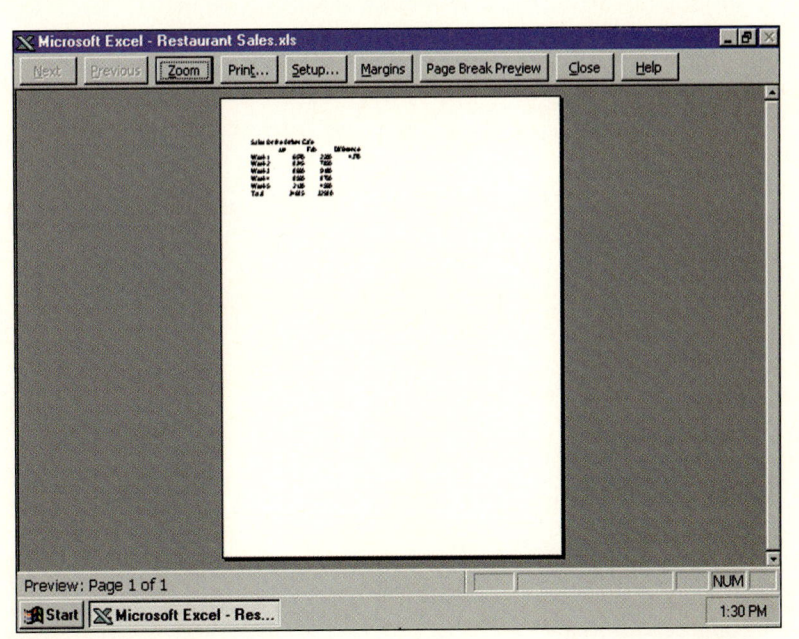

2 Click the pointer, shaped like a magnifying glass, at the top of the worksheet.

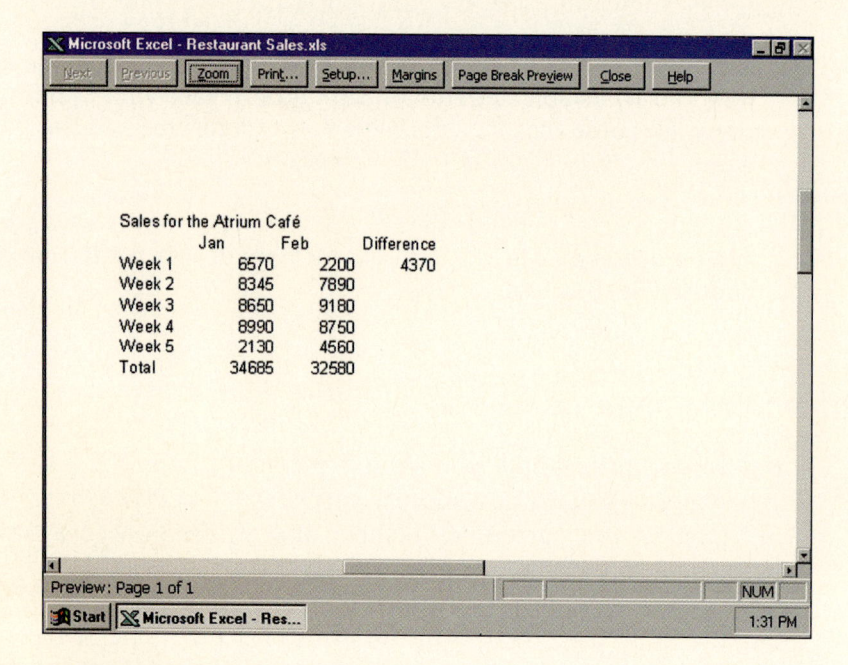

3 Click again.
The full page displays again.

4 Click Close in the Print Preview toolbar.
The Print Preview mode closes and the worksheet screen displays.

5 Ensure that the computer you are using is attached to a printer and that the printer is online.

6 Choose File from the menu bar.

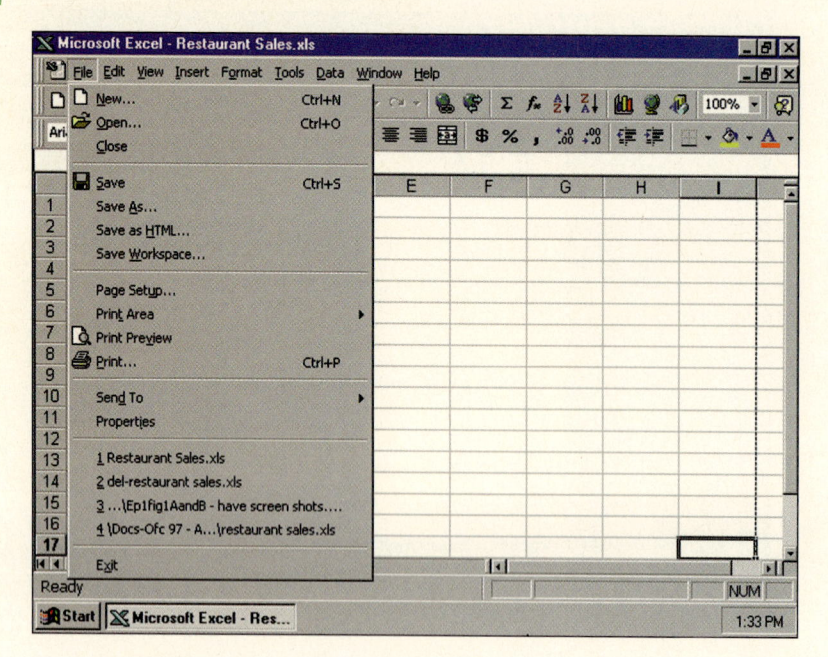

7 Choose Print.

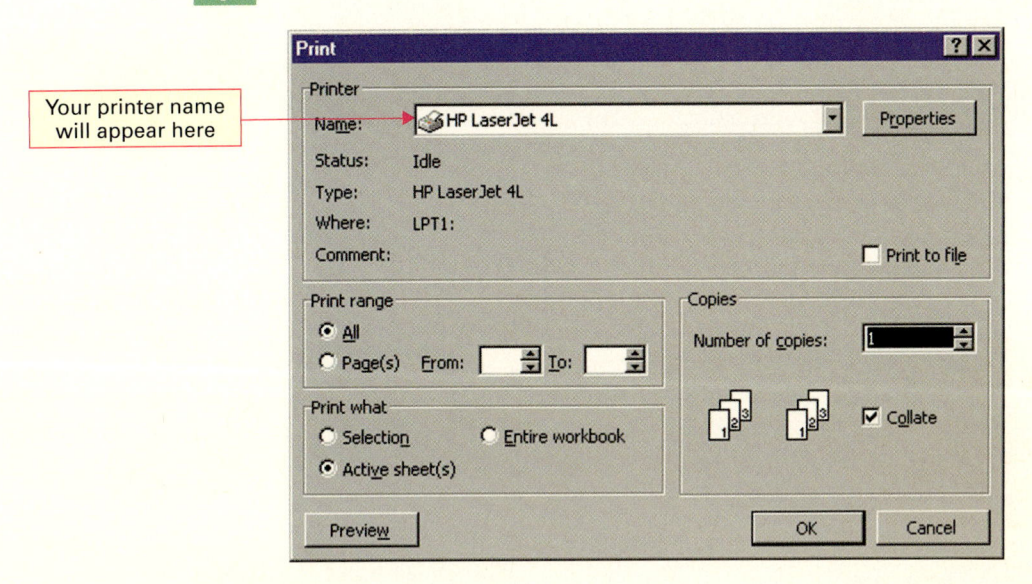

Your printer name will appear here

8 Click OK.
The workbook prints.

Closing a Workbook

When you are finished with a workbook, you can close it. If you have made changes that you want to keep, you should save the workbook before closing it. If you forget to save a workbook before closing, Excel 97 asks if you want to save changes.

TASK 11: TO CLOSE A FILE:

1 Click 💾.
The worksheet is saved.
The File menu displays.

2 Click ☒.
The file closes.

The Conclusion

You can exit Excel 97 now by clicking ☒, or you can work on the Review Exercises and Assignments.

Summary and Exercises

Summary

- When you launch Excel 97 a workbook named Book1 is created automatically.
- To enter data in a worksheet, the cell pointer must be positioned in the desired cell.
- By default, a new workbook has three worksheets.
- Excel 97 recognizes several different types of data: text, dates, numbers, and formulas.
- Formulas and functions are mathematical statements that perform calculations.
- Files can be saved with long filenames.
- Before you print a worksheet, you can preview it to see if it looks acceptable.
- When you close a file, if you haven't saved changes to the file, Excel 97 asks if you want to save the changes.

Key Terms and Operations

Key Terms	Operations
active cell	close a workbook
arithmetic operators	create a workbook
AutoComplete	enter data
Edit mode	enter formulas and functions
Enter mode	move in a workbook
formula	name a workbook
function	preview a worksheet
order of precedence	print a worksheet
Point mode	save a workbook
Print Preview mode	
range	
scientific notation	

Study Questions

Multiple Choice

1. Using the order of precedence, solve the formula 5–2*(8+2). What is the answer?
   a. 26
   b. −15
   c. −9
   d. 30

2. To move to the cell below the active cell, press
   a. Enter.
   b. PageDown.
   c. Tab.
   d. Ctrl + the down arrow.

3. Which of the following is a range address?
   a. D1;D10
   b. D1,D10
   c. D1 D10
   d. D1:D10

4. Which of the following can not be included in numeric data?
   a. 1
   b. 2
   c. E
   d. $

5. Which of the following is an example of scientific notation?
   a. 1.5E+11
   b. 1^10
   c. 7.8!
   d. A2

6. If A1 is 10, A2 is 15, and A3 is 20, what is the result of =SUM(A1:A2)?
   a. 10
   b. 15
   c. 25
   d. 45

7. If A1 is 10, A2 is 15, and A3 is 20, what is the result of =AVERAGE(A1:A3)?
   a. 10
   b. 15
   c. 25
   d. 45

8. If A1 is 10, A2 is 15, A3 is 20, and A4 says "Total," what is the result
   of =COUNT(A1:A4)?
   a. 3
   b. 15
   c. 45
   d. 4

9. The Preview mode shows
   a. all pages of a workbook.
   b. the current page of the workbook.
   c. the formulas.
   d. the formulas and functions.

10. When you press Ctrl + End, what cell becomes the active cell?
    a. IV65536
    b. The last cell in the current column.
    c. The cell in the lower right corner.
    d. The cell in the lower right corner of the active area of the worksheet.

Short Answer

1. What happens when you change a number in a cell that is included in a
   formula?

2. What should you do before you close a workbook?

3. How do you rename a worksheet?

4. What is the order of precedence?

5. What displays in a cell if you enter 1/10?

6. How can you make 1/10 display as a fraction in a cell?

7. Write the formula to add the numbers in from cell A1 through cell A5.

8. Write the function to add the numbers in from cell A1 through cell A5.

9. How do you enter the same data on more than one worksheet?

10. What function finds the smallest value?

For Discussion

1. Describe a situation in which you would use several worksheets in the same workbook.

2. The cell displays #######. What caused the problem and how can you solve it?

3. Discuss the reasons you might rename worksheets in a workbook.

4. What is a range and how is it addressed?

Review Exercises

1. Creating an Expense Account

Your good friend Karl Klaus, the head chef at the 4-star restaurant in *The Grande Hotel,* has asked you to create an expense report for him because he can't type. In this exercise, you will create a worksheet that lists the expenses Karl had on a recent trip for the hotel.

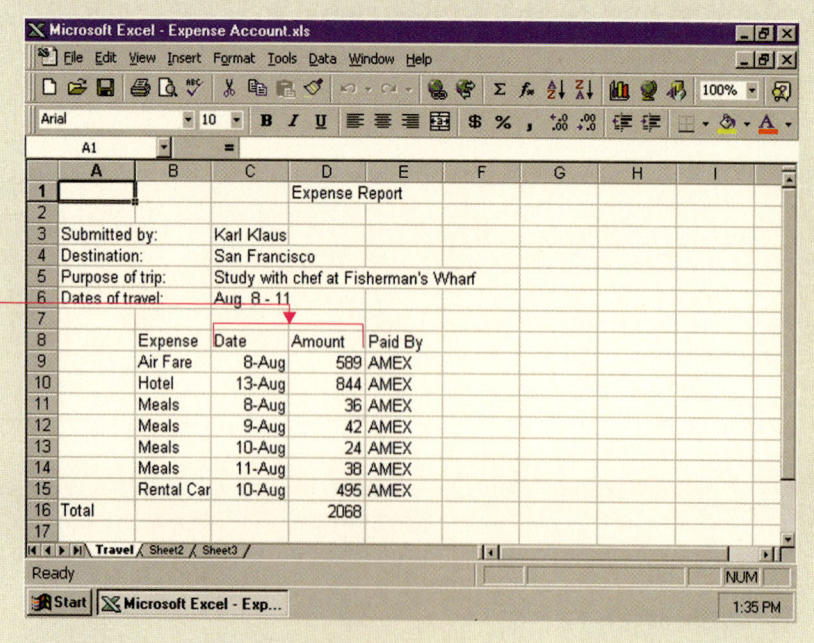

Figure 1.3

1. Create a new workbook.

2. Rename Sheet1 to Travel.

3. Enter the data shown in Figure 1.3.

Note The format for dates might be different on your computer.

4. Use the AutoSum button to calculate the total expenses.

5. Save the workbook as *Expense Account.xls*.

2. Calculating Savings

In this exercise, you will use a worksheet to calculate the amount of money you will have in twenty years, based on different variables such as the amount you can save each year and the rate of interest you earn.

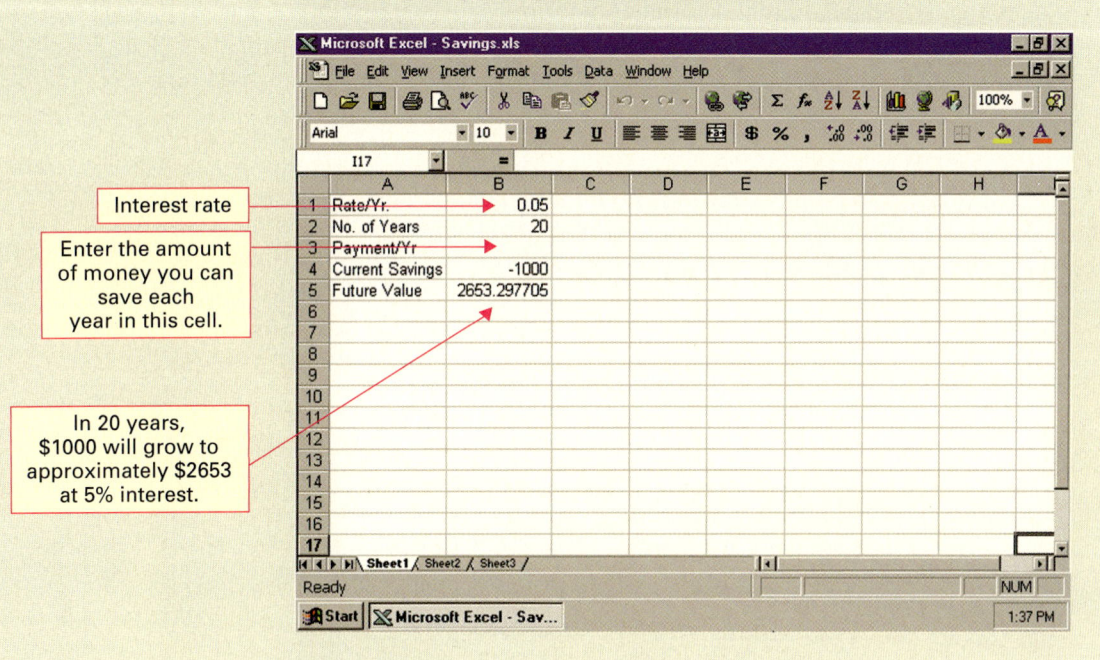

Figure 1.4

1. Go to this address on the Web:
http://www.finaid.org/finaid/calculators/finaid_calc.html.

2. Select the Savings Plan Designer.

3. If you currently have $1000 in savings and you can get 5 percent interest, how much will you have to save each month to have $200,000 in 20 years?

4. Create a new worksheet and enter the data shown in Figure 1.4. Be sure to enter the data in the same cells shown in the figure.

Note The values for current savings is a negative number due to the use of debits and credits in standard accounting procedures.

5. In cell B5, type this function: =FV(B1,B2,B3,B4,1).

6. In cell B3, enter the number that is 12 times the answer you got in step 3. Precede the number with a minus sign. The answer in cell B5 should be approximately 200,000.

7. Change the Payment/Yr amount to −2000 and change the Rate/Yr to .15.

8. Save the worksheet as *Savings.xls*.

Assignments

1. Creating a Timesheet

Create a workbook with a worksheet for each of your classes. List the dates and the number of hours that you spend for each class (including class time, lab time, and homework) in a week. Total the number of hours. Save the worksheets and workbook, using an appropriate filename.

2. Creating a Worksheet that Compares Menu Prices

Go to http://www.metrodine.com and follow links to find restaurant menus that list entrees and prices, or go to http://www.pvo.com/pvo/search.html and search for "menu." Create a worksheet that lists the entrees and prices for at least two restaurants. Use the MIN and MAX functions to show the lowest and highest priced entree for each restaurant. Save the worksheets and workbook, using an appropriate filename.

Editing a Workbook

Moving a title to a different location, deleting last week's totals, copying this month's totals to the summary worksheet, adding comments to a cell, checking the spelling — an Excel user's work is never done! In this project, you will edit a workbook and modify the data using some basic editing tasks.

Objectives

After completing this project, you will be able to:

- ➤ **Open a workbook**
- ➤ **Find data**
- ➤ **Edit data**
- ➤ **Work with data**
- ➤ **Add comments**
- ➤ **Check spelling**

The Challenge

Mr. Gilmore was impressed at how quickly you created his "down-and-dirty" worksheet, but he wants a few changes made to it. Specifically, he wants you to add some comments and create a new worksheet that includes the January sales figures from both restaurants.

The Solution

To make the changes Mr. Gilmore wants, you will open the Restaurant Sales workbook, revise some of the data, move and copy some of the cells, add comments, and check the spelling. The finished workbook will look like Figure 2.1.

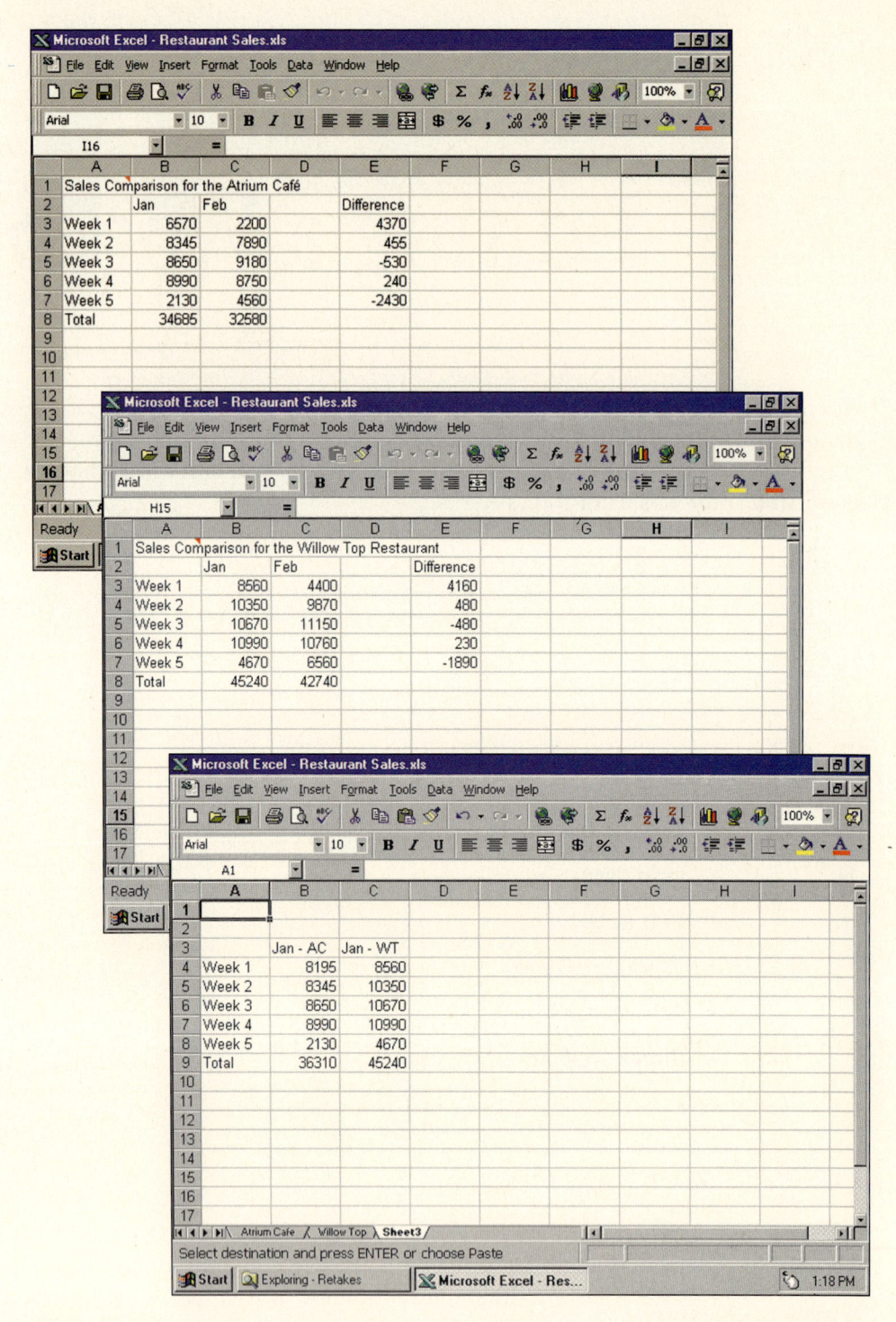

Figure 2.1

The Setup

So that your screen will match the illustrations in this chapter and to ensure that all the tasks in this project will function as described, you should set up Excel as described in Table 2.1. Because these are the default settings for the toolbars and view, you may not need to make any changes to your setup.

Table 2.1   Excel Settings

Location	Make these settings:
View, Toolbars	Deselect all toolbars except Standard and Formatting
View	Use Normal and display the Formula Bar and the Status Bar.

Opening a Workbook

When you want to view or revise a workbook that you have saved, you must open the workbook first. The worksheet and cell that were active when you last saved and closed the workbook are active when you open the workbook.

> **Tip** If the workbook is one that you have opened recently, you may see it listed at the bottom of the File menu. To open the file, simply select it from the menu.

TASK 1: TO OPEN A WORKBOOK:

1 Click the Open 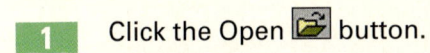 button.

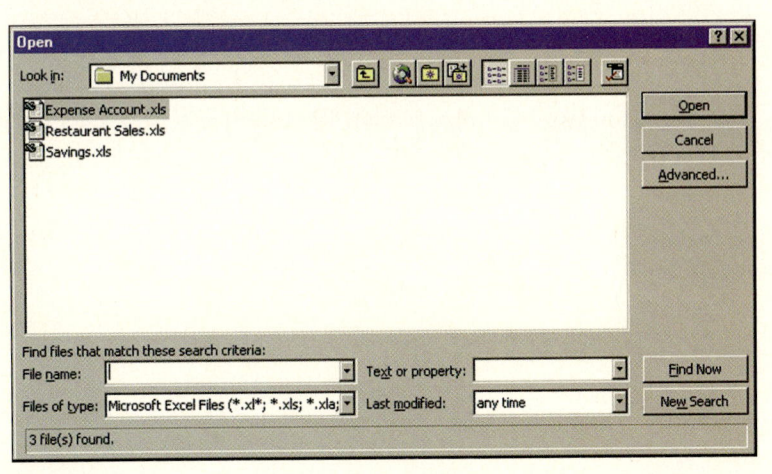

Click on the arrow in the Look in text box to display the drop down list.

2 Select the correct path and folder.
The folder name appears in the Look in text box.

3 Double-click *Restaurant Sales.xls*.

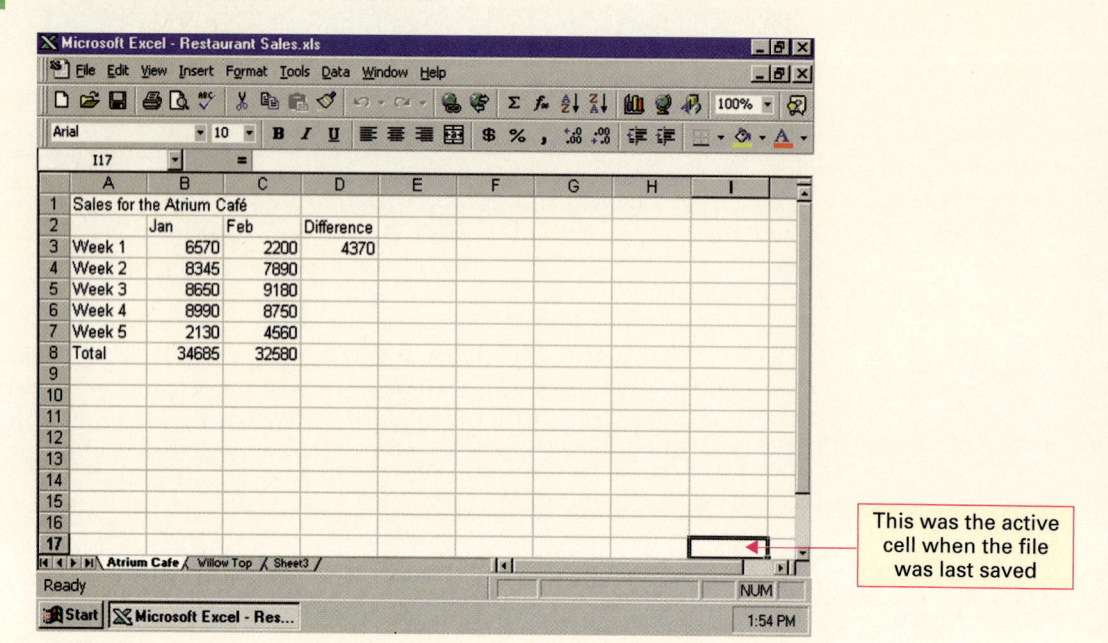

This was the active cell when the file was last saved

When you open a workbook, it opens to the location where you were when you last saved and closed it.

4 Click the Atrium Cafe tab if necessary.
The Atrium Cafe worksheet displays.

Finding Data

The Find command helps you find specific text or values in a worksheet. The command is very useful if the worksheet is large, but it also can be useful in small worksheets to find text and values that aren't shown on the screen. For example, you can use the Find command to find a word, number, or cell address that is in a formula.

TASK 2: TO FIND DATA:

1   Choose Edit.

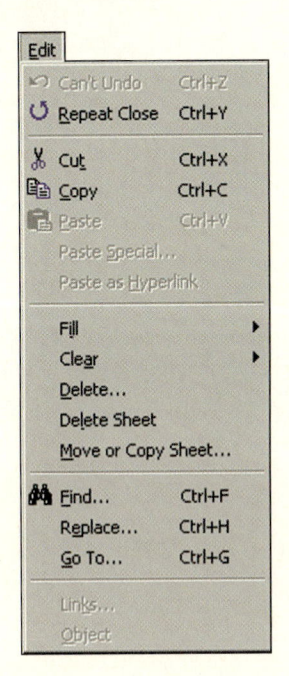

2   Choose Find.

3   Type **Sum** in the Find what text box and ensure that Formulas is selected in the Look in text box.

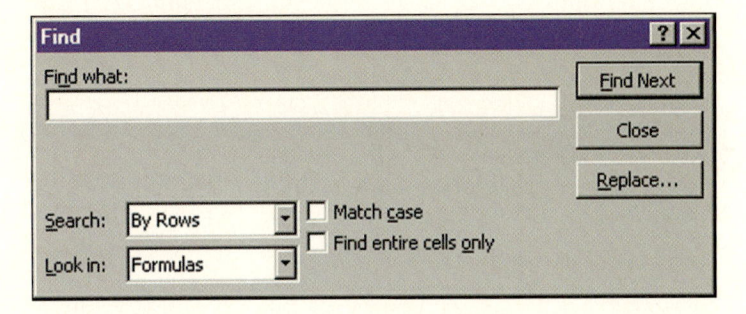

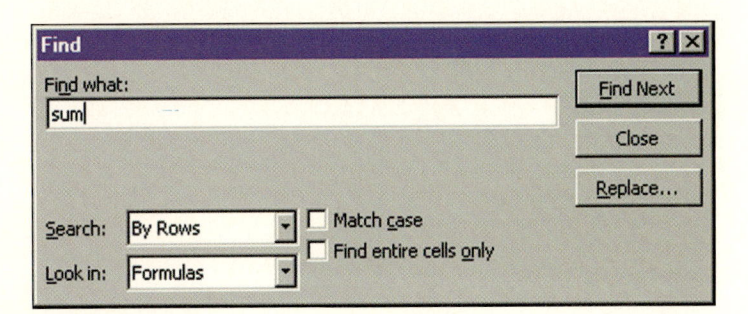

4   Click Find Next.
Cell B8 becomes the active cell.

5   Click Find Next.
Cell C8 becomes the active cell.

6 Click Find Next.
Cell B8 becomes the active cell again even though the next worksheet has a SUM function.

> **Tip** The Find command searches only the current worksheet.

7 Click Close.
The Find dialog box closes.

Editing Data

If you want to change the data that is entered in a cell, just click in the cell and type the new data. If the data is lengthy, it is more efficient to edit the existing data unless the new data is completely different. If the cell that you edit is used in a formula or function, Excel 97 recalculates automatically to update the worksheet.

TASK 3: TO EDIT DATA IN A CELL:

1 Click in cell A1 in the Atrium Cafe worksheet.
Cell A1 becomes the active cell.

2 Click in the formula bar before the "f" in "for."

The insertion point should be here

	A	B	C	D	E	F	G	H	I
1	Sales for t								
2		Jan	Feb	Difference					
3	Week 1	6570	2200	4370					
4	Week 2	8345	7890						
5	Week 3	8650	9180						
6	Week 4	8990	8750						
7	Week 5	2130	4560						
8	Total	34685	32580						
9									
10									

Microsoft Excel - Restaurant Sales.xls
File Edit View Insert Format Tools Data Window Help
Arial 10 B *I* U
Sales for the Atrium Café

3   Type **Comparison** and then press (SPACE BAR).

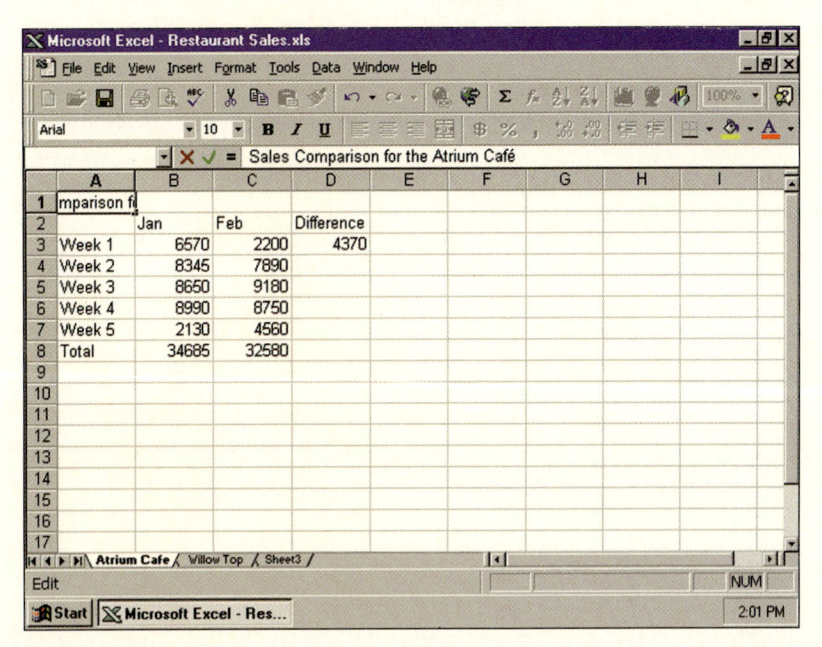

4   Press (ENTER).

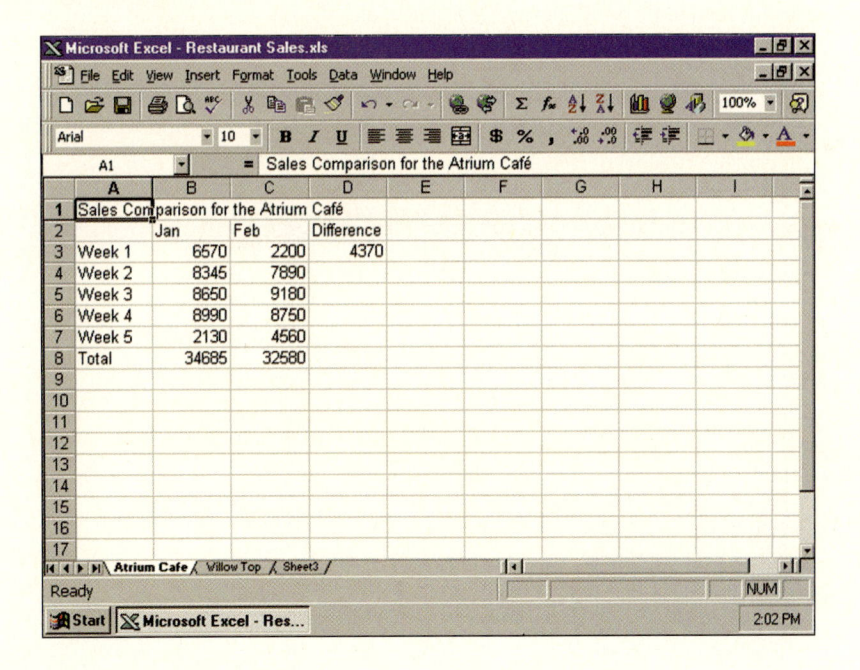

5   Click the Willow Top tab.
The Willow Top worksheet displays.

6   Click in cell A1.
Cell A1 becomes the active cell.

7 Click in the formula bar before the "f" in "for."

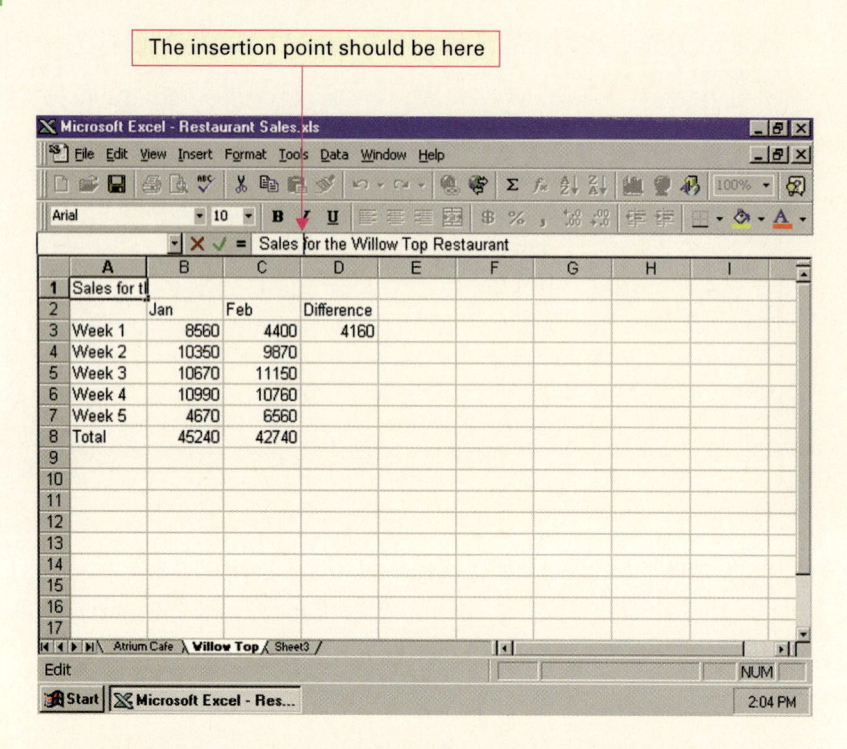

8 Type **Comparison**, press (SPACE BAR), and press (ENTER).

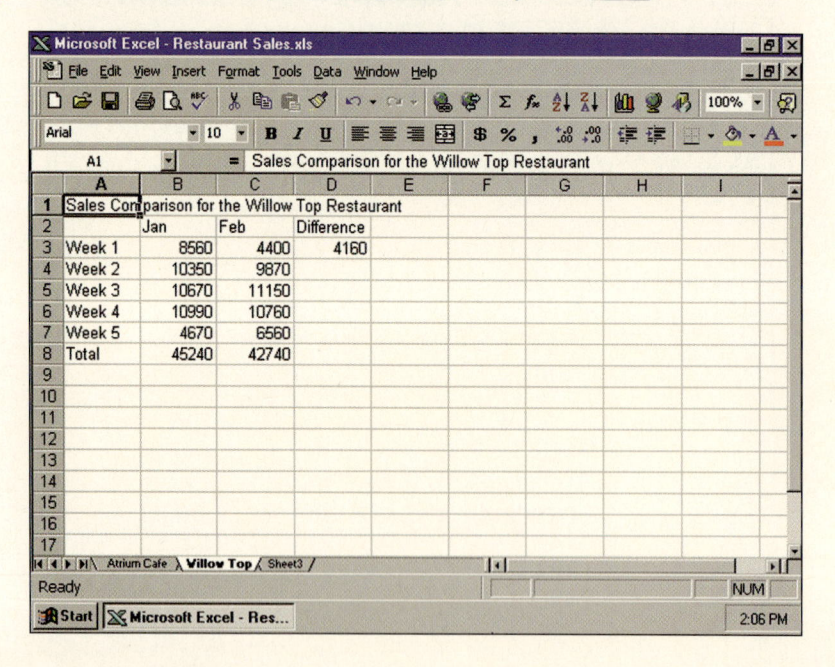

9 Click in cell B3.
Cell B3 becomes the active cell.

10 Type **8195** and press (ENTER).

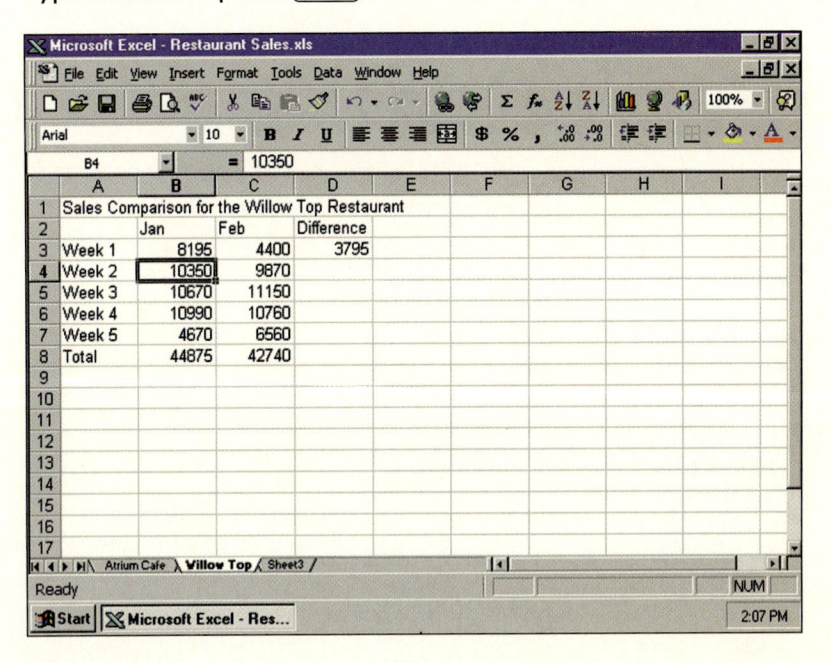

Working with Data

After you have entered data in a worksheet, you may find that you need to make some changes. You may have to copy, delete, or move the data. All of these types of revisions require selecting cells.

Selecting Cells

When you select cells, they are highlighted. In most cases, the easiest way to select cells is to drag the mouse pointer over the cells, but Table 2.2 describes other ways of selecting cells that are appropriate in many situations.

Table 2.2   Selection Methods

Selection	Method
Entire column	Click the column letter at the top of the column.
Entire row	Click the row number at the left of the row.
Entire worksheet	Click the blank button above the row numbers and to the left of the column letters.
Adjacent columns	Drag the pointer through the column letters.
Adjacent rows	Drag the pointer through the row numbers.
Non-adjacent ranges	Select the first range (the range can be an entire column or row) and then press (CTRL) while you select additional ranges.

TASK 4: TO SELECT RANGES:

1 Click the column letter above column A.

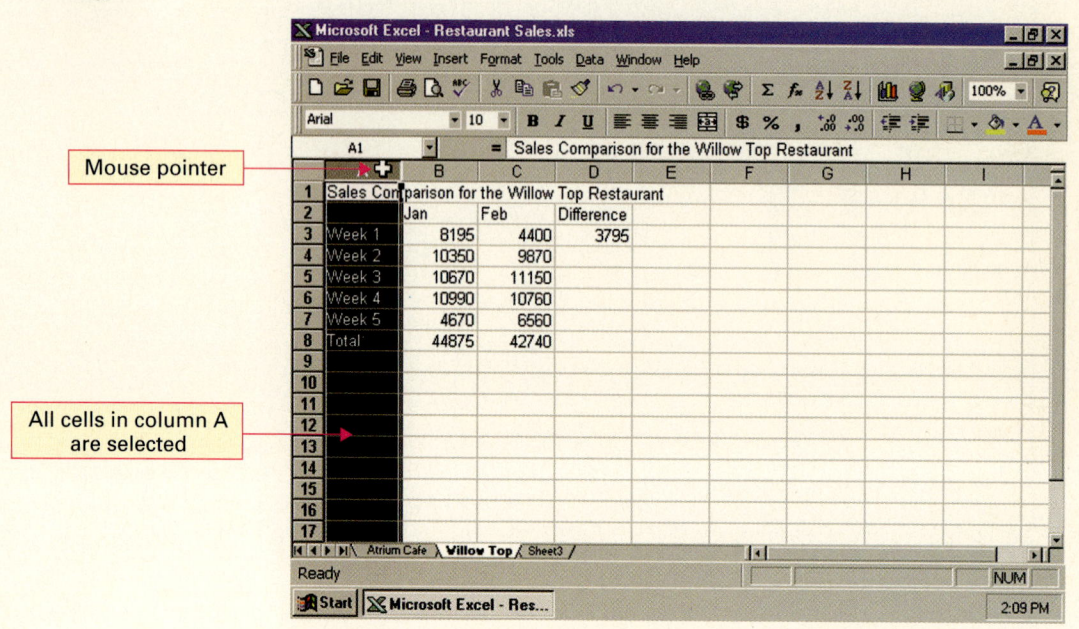

Mouse pointer

All cells in column A are selected

2 Drag the pointer through row numbers 3 and 4.

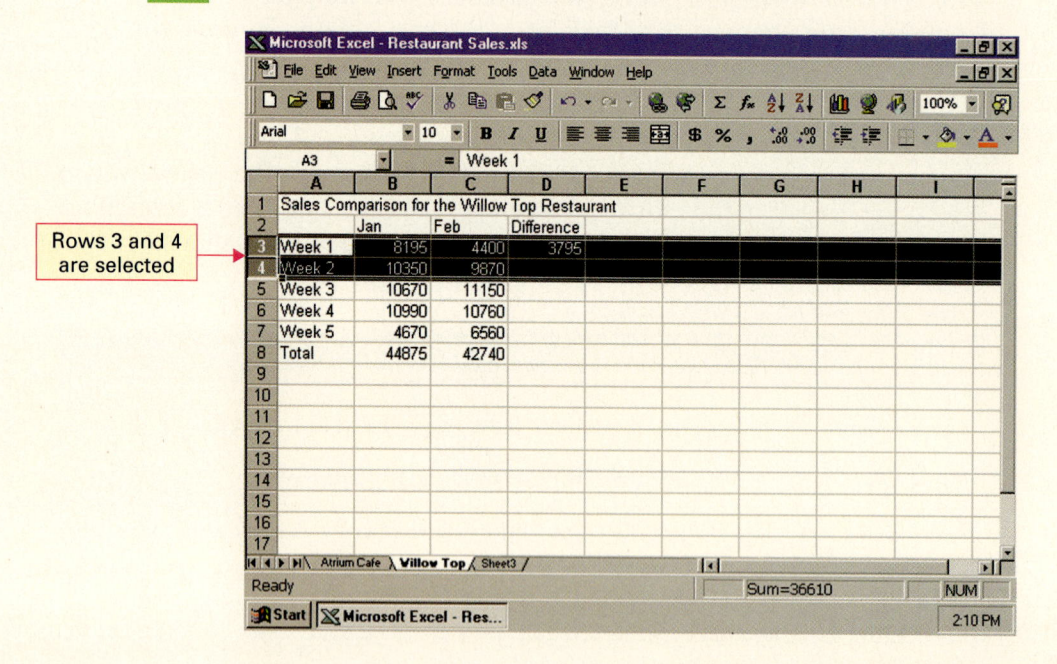

Rows 3 and 4 are selected

3 Select column C and then press (CTRL) while you select column F, row 8, and the range from cell H6 through cell I9.

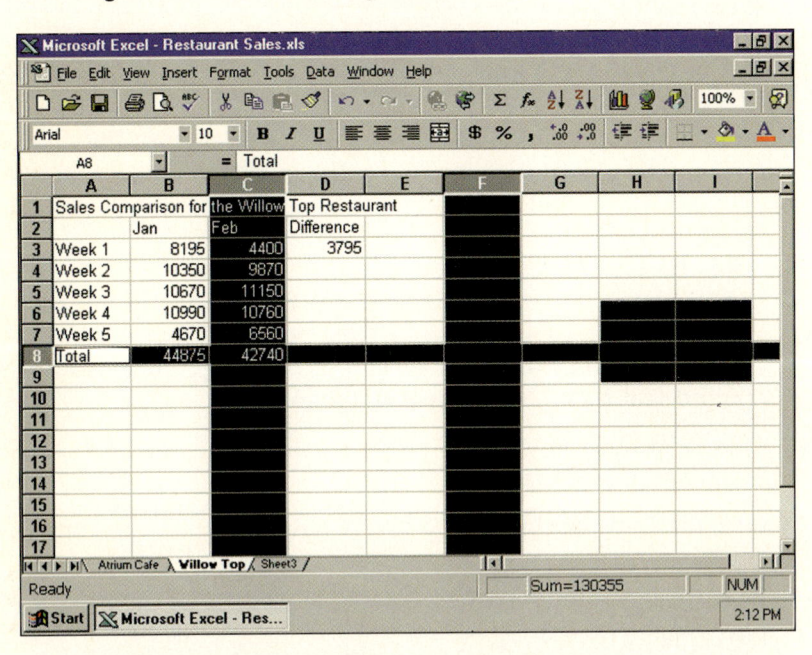

4 Select cell B3 through cell B7.

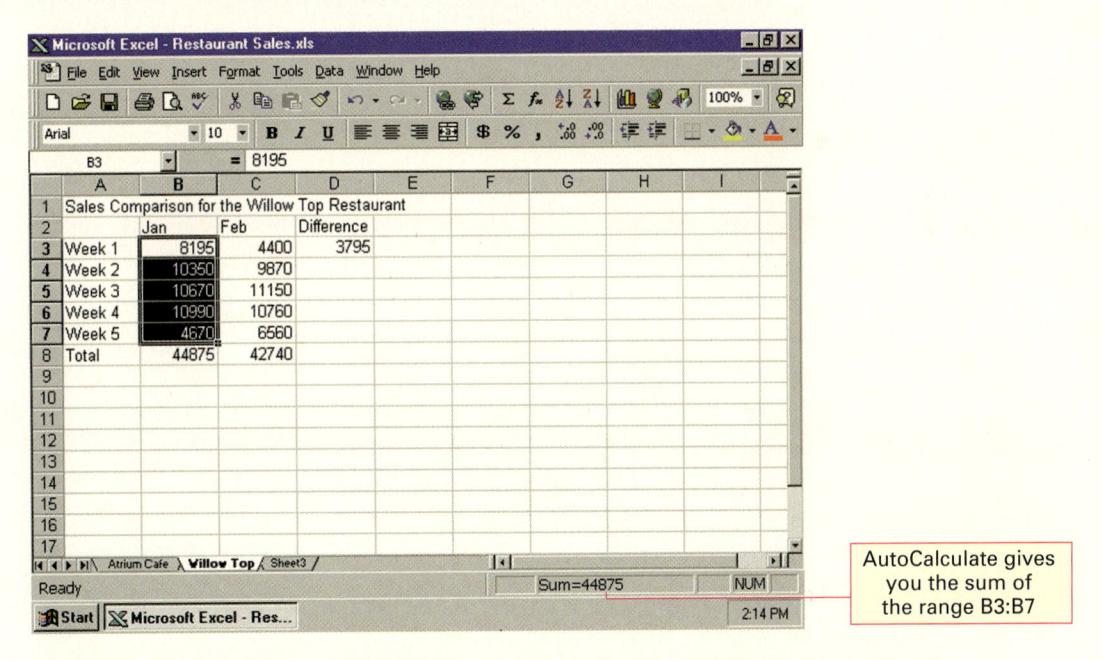

AutoCalculate gives you the sum of the range B3:B7

Tip When you select a range with values, the *AutoCalculate* feature displays a calculation in the status bar. To change the type of calculation, right-click the calculation and choose a different one.

Copying Data

When you copy data, Excel 97 stores the data in a memory area called the *Clipboard.* Data in the Clipboard can be pasted in any cell, or range of cells in any worksheet or any workbook. If you copy or cut additional data, the new data replaces the existing data in the Clipboard. The Clipboard is erased when you exit Excel 97. Pasting data from the Clipboard does not remove data from the Clipboard; therefore, you can paste it repeatedly.

TASK 5: TO COPY DATA:

1 Press CTRL and click the Atrium Cafe tab.
The Atrium Cafe worksheet and the Willow Top worksheet are both selected, and the Willow Top worksheet still displays.

2 Click in cell D3.
Cell D3 becomes the active cell.

3 Click the Copy 🖺 button.

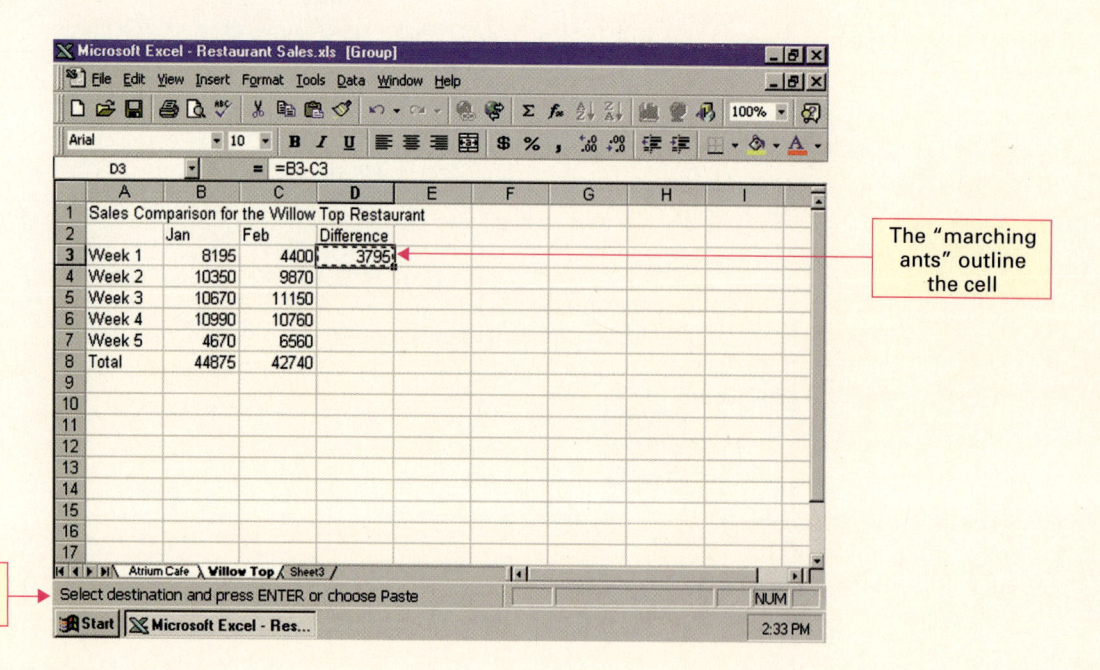

The "marching ants" outline the cell

The status bar tells you what to do next

4   Select the range from cell D4 through cell D7.

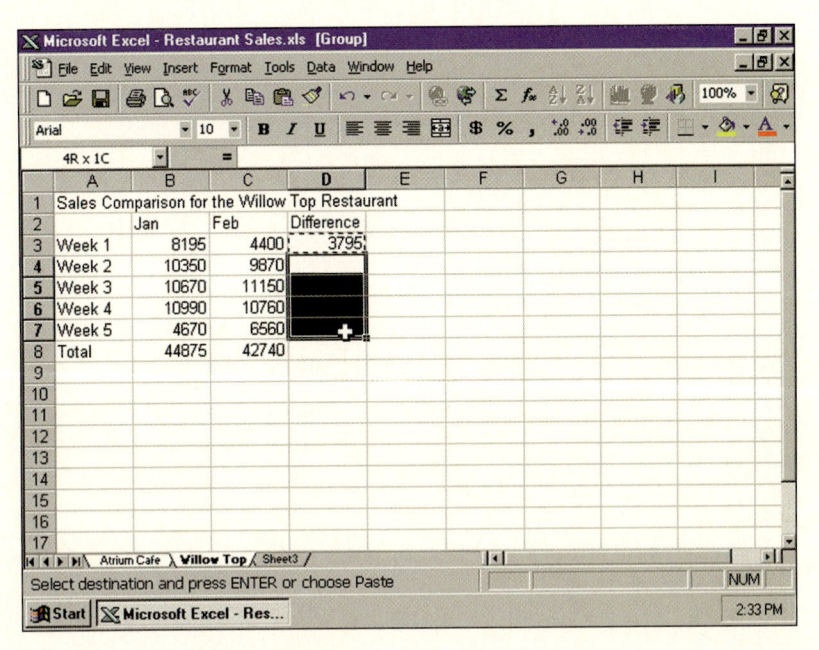

5   Click the Paste 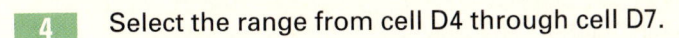 button.

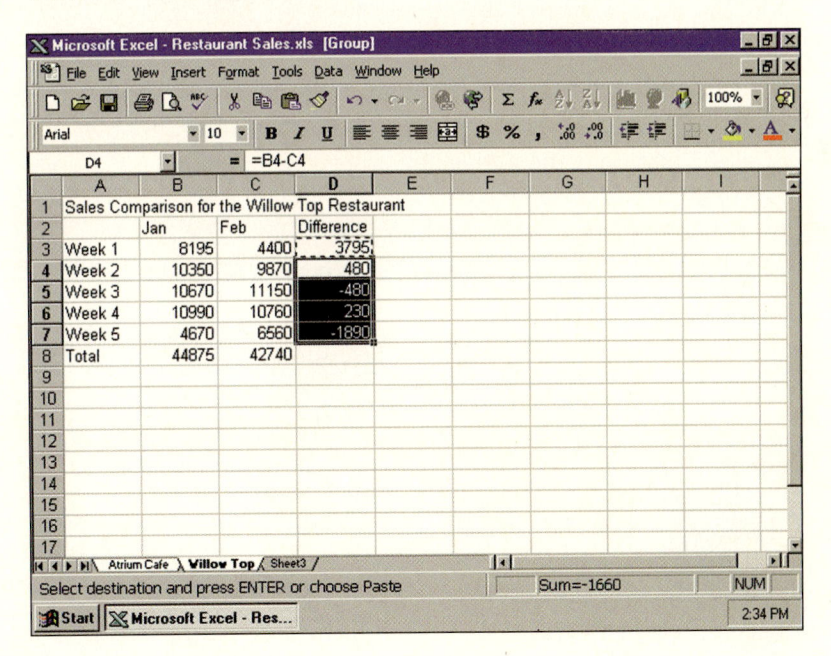

6   Click the Atrium Cafe tab.
The Copy command has been executed on this worksheet, too.

7   Press (CTRL) and click the Willow Top tab.
The Willow Top worksheet is deselected.

8 Select the range from cell B2 through cell B8.

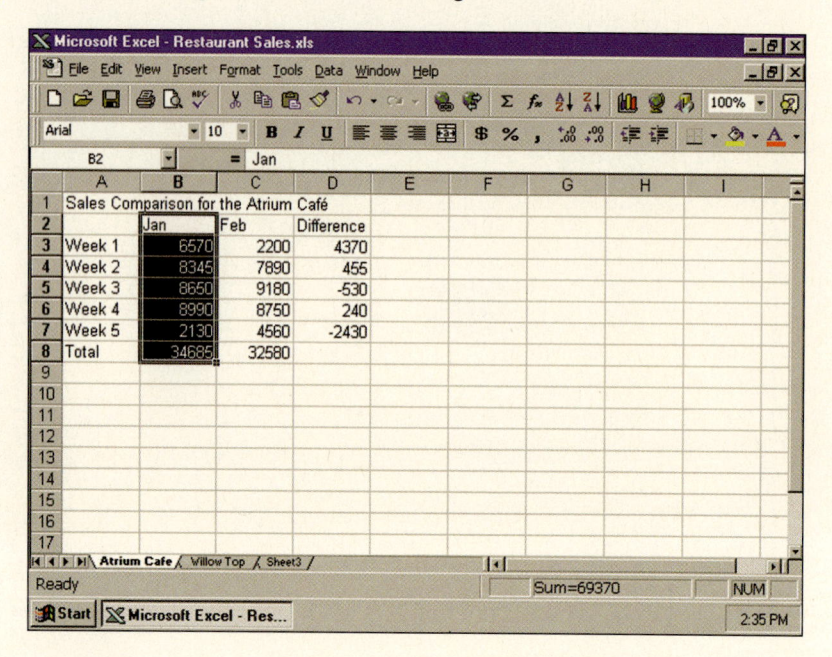

9 Click 📋.
The cells are copied to the Clipboard.

10 Click the Sheet3 tab.
The Sheet3 worksheet displays.

11 Click in cell A3.
Cell A3 becomes the active cell.

12 Click 📋.

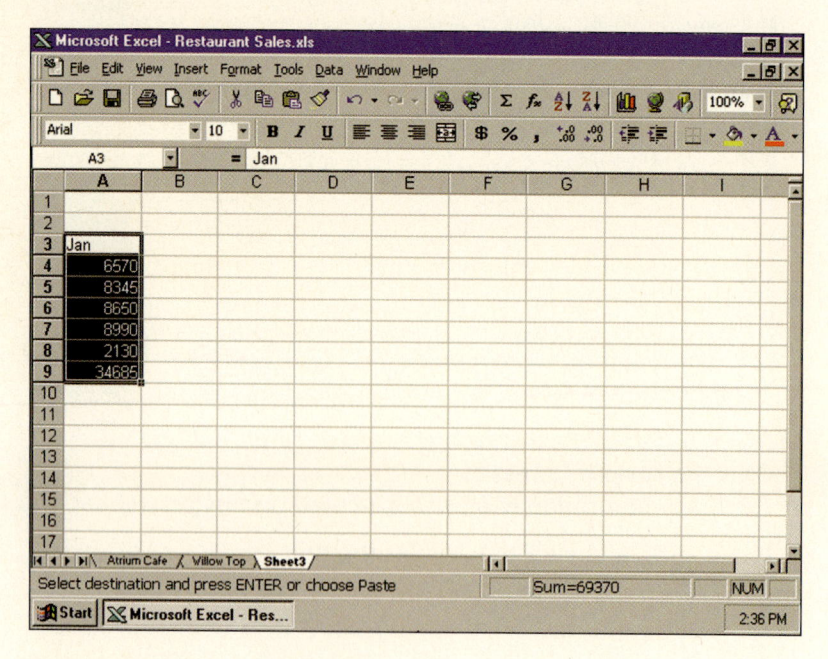

Caution Pasting data into cells automatically replaces data already contained in the cells — without notice. Use the Undo feature to restore data, if necessary.

13 Copy and paste the same range from the Willow Top worksheet to cell B3 in Sheet3.

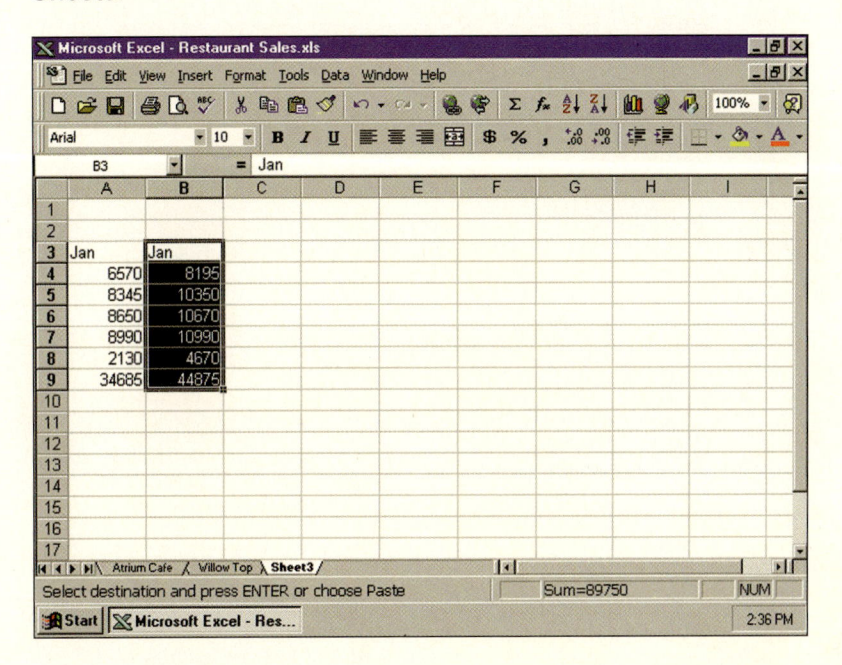

14 Rename Sheet3 to "January."
The name January appears on the tab.

Deleting Data

To erase the data in a cell or a range of cells, simply select the cells and press the Delete key. If you change your mind, click the Undo button.

Warning Some users try to erase cells by passing the space bar. Although the cell looks blank, it really isn't; it contains the character for a space. You should never use this method to erase a cell; you could get arrested by the SSP (Special Spreadsheet Police).

Note The Edit, Clear command accomplishes the same as pressing the Delete key.

TASK 6: TO DELETE DATA:

1 Select cell A8 through cell B8 on the January worksheet.

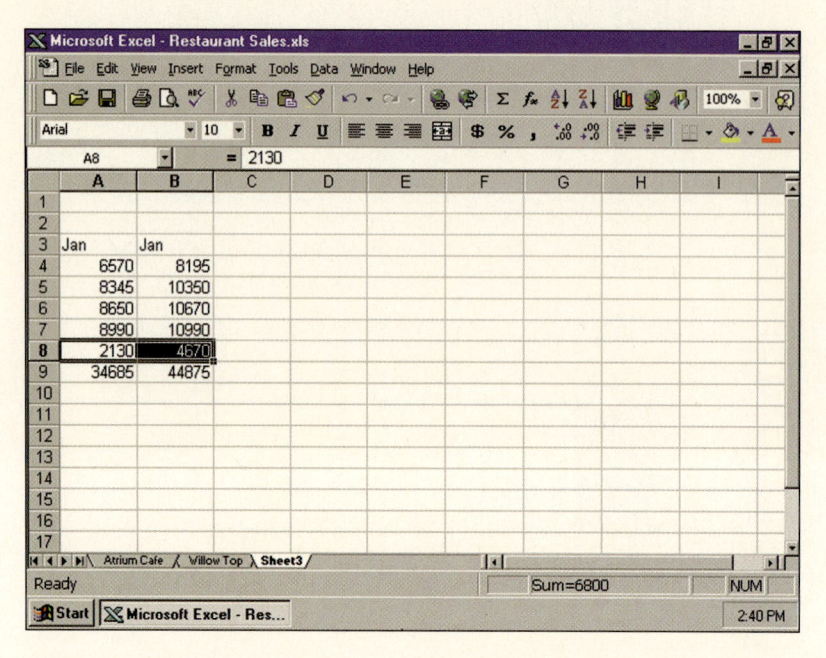

2 Press `DEL`.

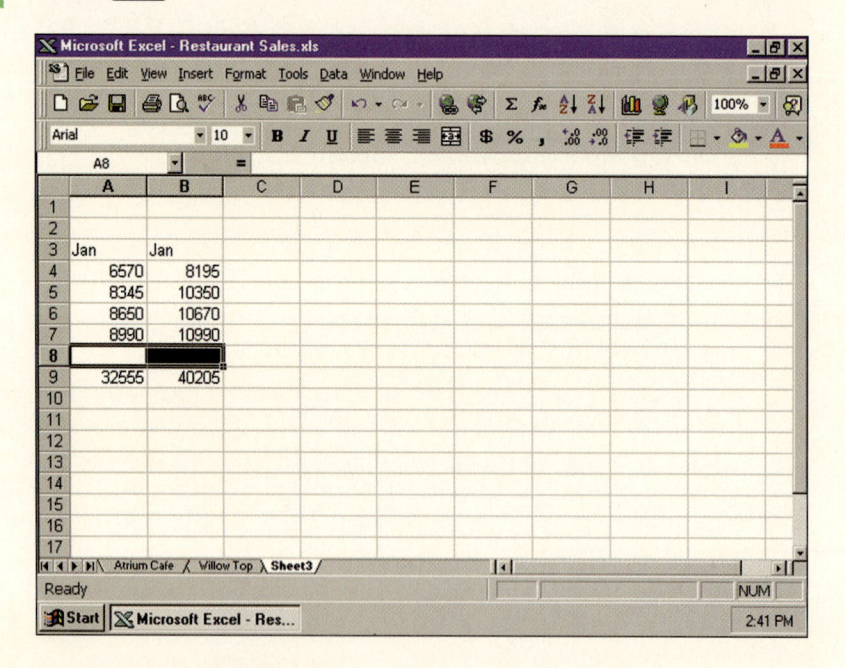

3 Click the Undo button.
The data appears again.

> **Tip** When you delete text with the Delete key, the text isn't stored in the Clipboard and therefore it can't be pasted in another location. You can press Shift+Delete or choose Edit, Delete if you want deleted text placed in the Clipboard.

Moving Data

You can move data to a different location in the same worksheet or to a location in a different worksheet.

TASK 7: TO MOVE DATA:

1 Click on the Atrium Cafe tab.
The Atrium Cafe worksheet displays.

2 Select cell D2 through cell D7.

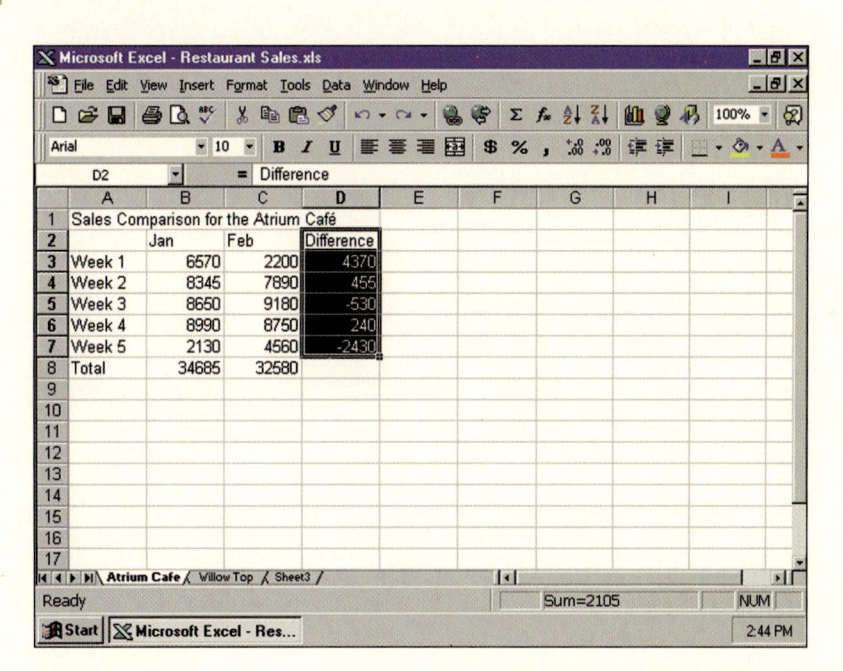

3 Click the Cut button.

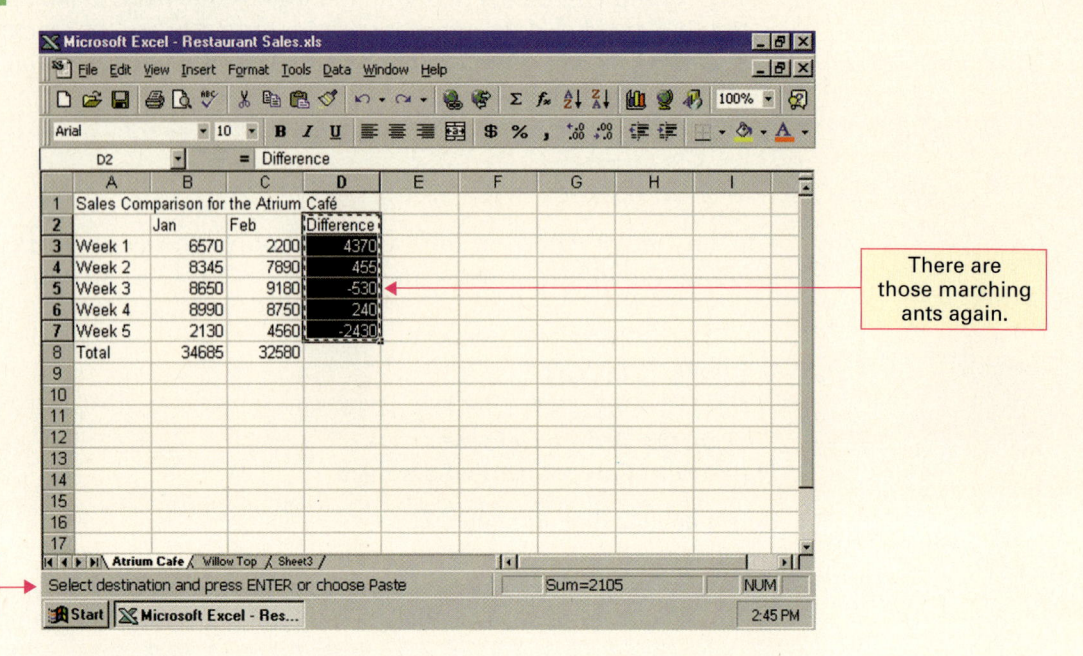

There are those marching ants again.

The status bar tells you what to do next

4 Click in cell E2.
Cell E2 becomes the active cell.

5 Click.

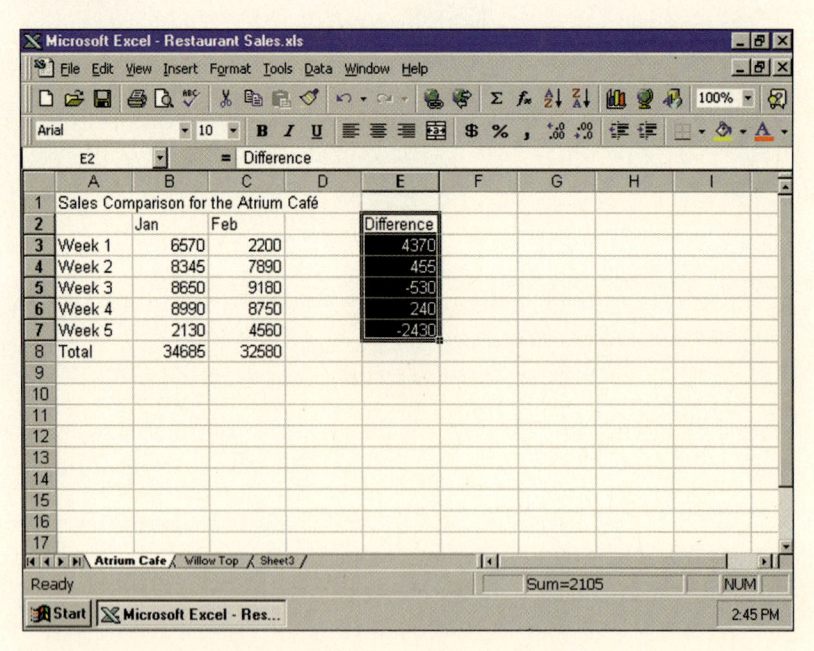

Warning Pasting anything that has been cut (or copied) to a new location that contains data overwrites the data.

6 Display the Willow Top worksheet and move the range D2 through D7 to cell E2.

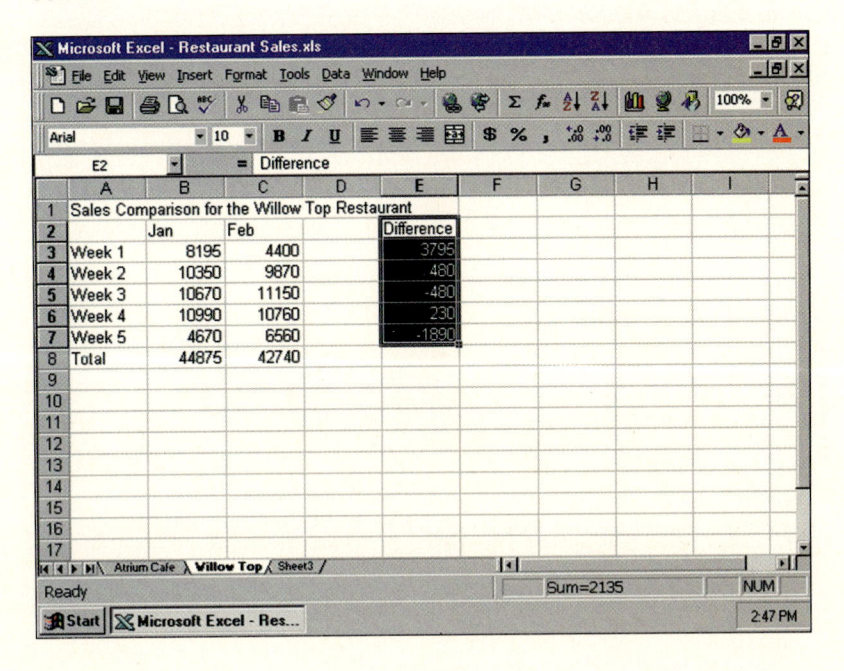

Adding Comments

You can attach **comments** to cells in a worksheet to provide additional information. The comment will contain the user name that is specified on the User Information page of the Options dialog box. The text in a comment displays on the screen and it can be made to print as well.

TASK 8: TO ADD COMMENTS:

1 Click in cell A1 on the Willow Top worksheet.
Cell A1 becomes the active cell.

2 Choose Insert.

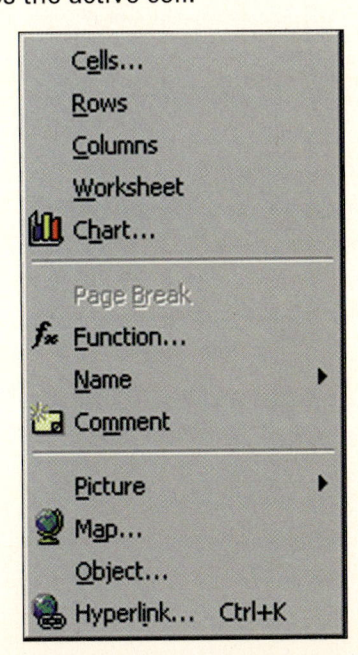

3 Choose Comment.

The user name precedes the comment

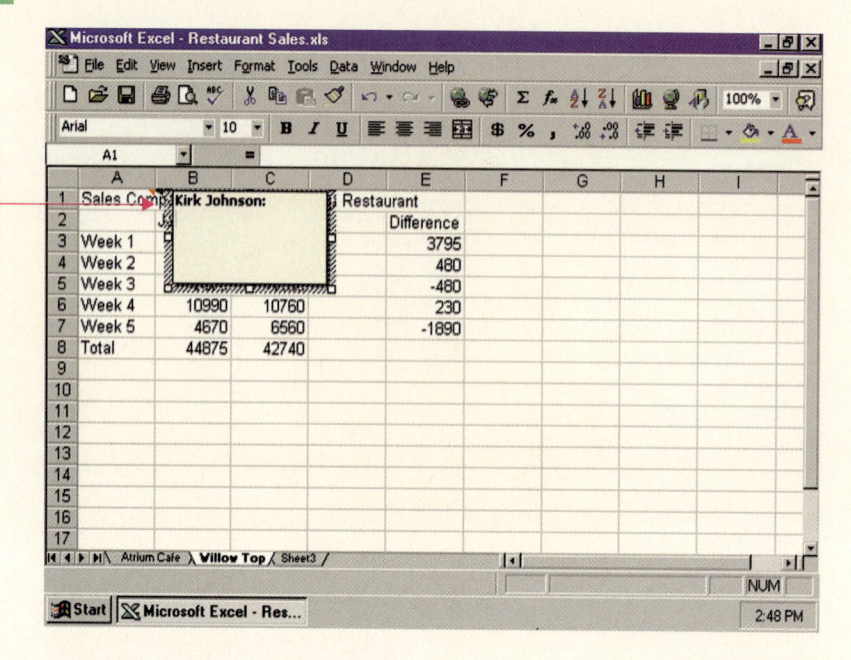

4 Type **Open for dinner only.**

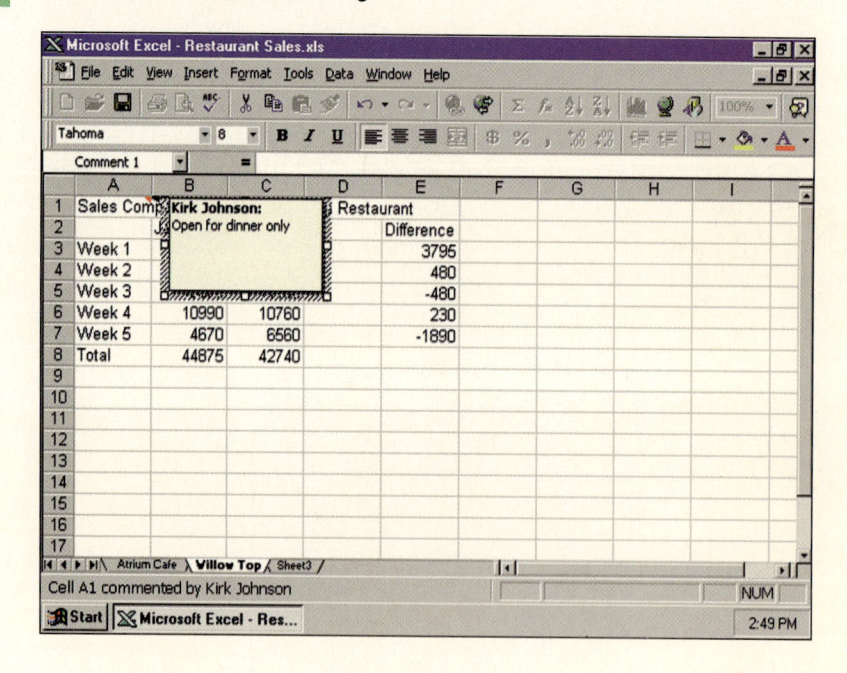

5   Click anywhere outside the comment box.

The red mark denotes a comment

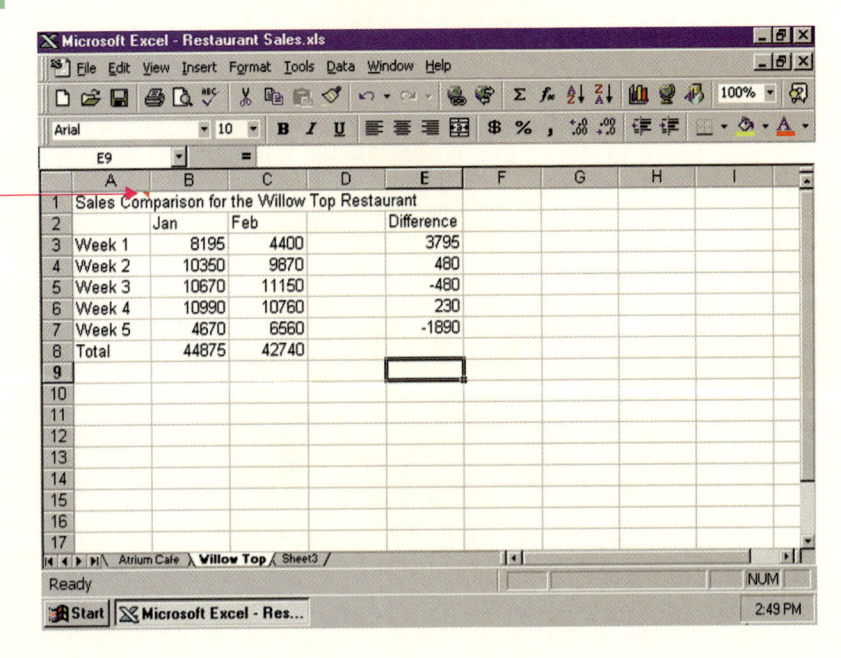

6   Click the Atrium Cafe tab.
The Atrium Cafe worksheet displays.

7   Click in cell A1.
Cell A1 becomes the active cell.

8   Choose Insert, Comment, and type **Open for breakfest, lunch, and dinner.**
Do not correct the spelling of "breakfast."

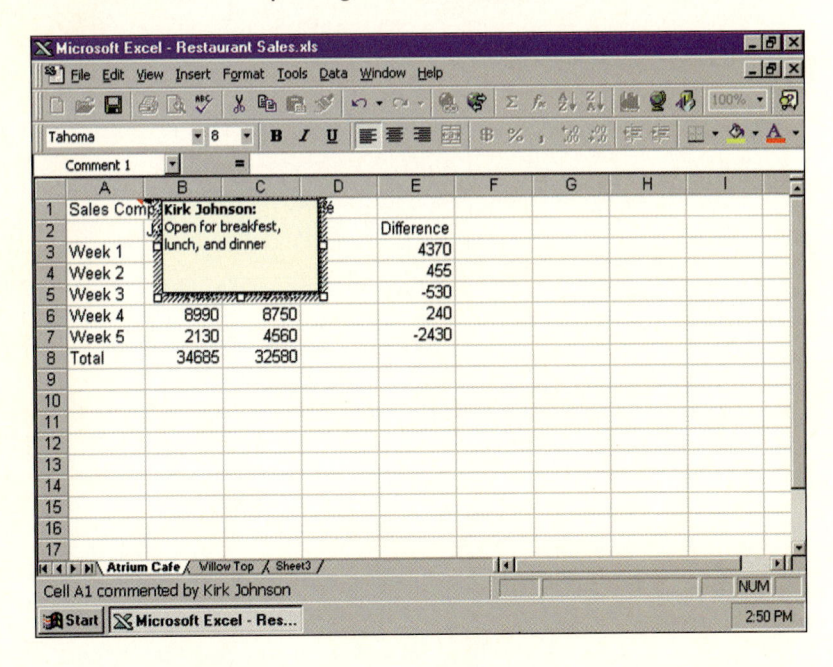

9   Click anywhere outside the comment box.
A red mark appears in cell A1.

If you want to see the comments on a worksheet, you can point to the cell that has a red mark and the comment box will pop up, or you can turn on the Comment view and all the comments will be visible.

TASK 9: TO TURN ON THE COMMENT VIEW AND TURN IT OFF AGAIN:

1 Choose View.

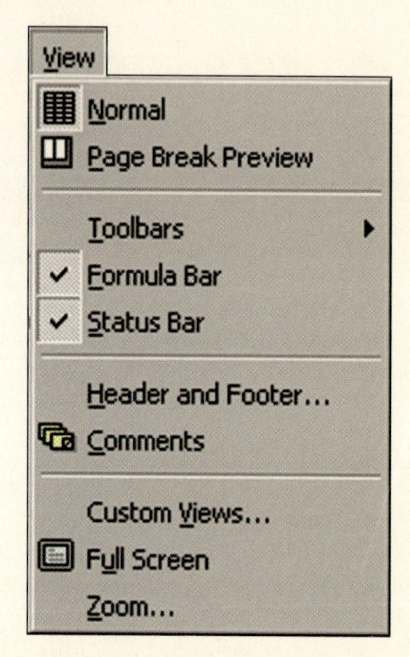

View

- Normal
- Page Break Preview
- Toolbars ▶
- ✓ Formula Bar
- ✓ Status Bar
- Header and Footer...
- Comments
- Custom Views...
- Full Screen
- Zoom...

2 Choose Comments.

The Reviewing toolbar displays when you turn on the Comments view

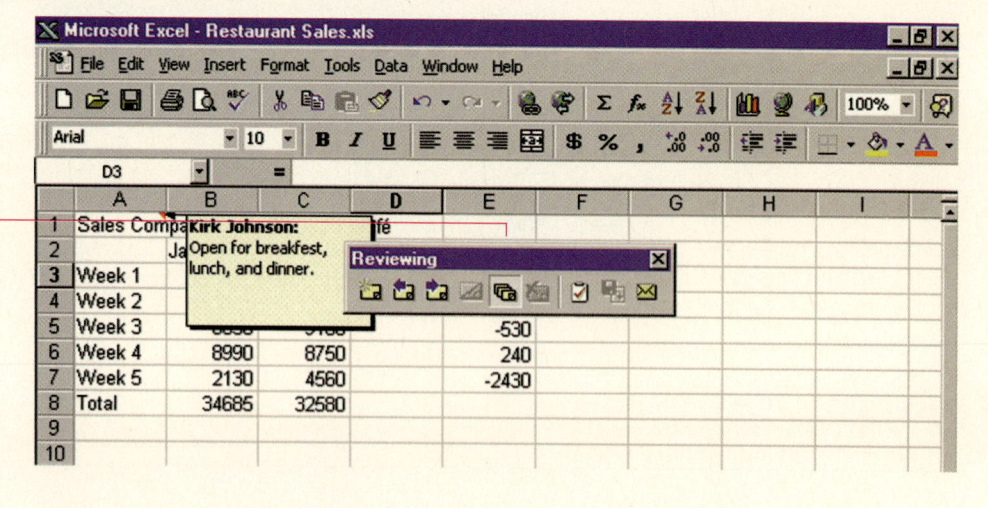

3 Click the Willow Top tab.

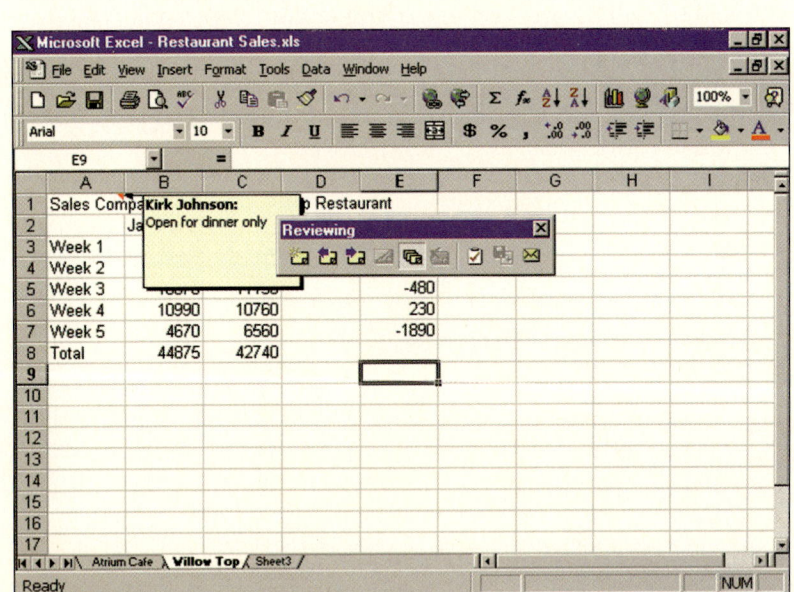

4 Click ☒ on the Reviewing toolbar.
The toolbar closes.

5 Choose View, Comments.
The comments are hidden.

> **Tip** Use the Find command to find text or values in comments.

Checking Spelling

When you have made all the revisions in a worksheet, it is a good idea to check the spelling, especially since Excel 97 doesn't underline spelling errors as you make them (as Word 97 does).

> **Note** Even though Excel 97 doesn't check your spelling as you go, it does make automatic corrections for many typing errors.

TASK 10: TO CHECK THE SPELLING:

1 Click the Atrium Cafe tab.
The Atrium Cafe worksheet displays.

2 Click in cell A1.
Excel 97 will begin its check of the spelling with cell A1.

3 Click the Spelling button.

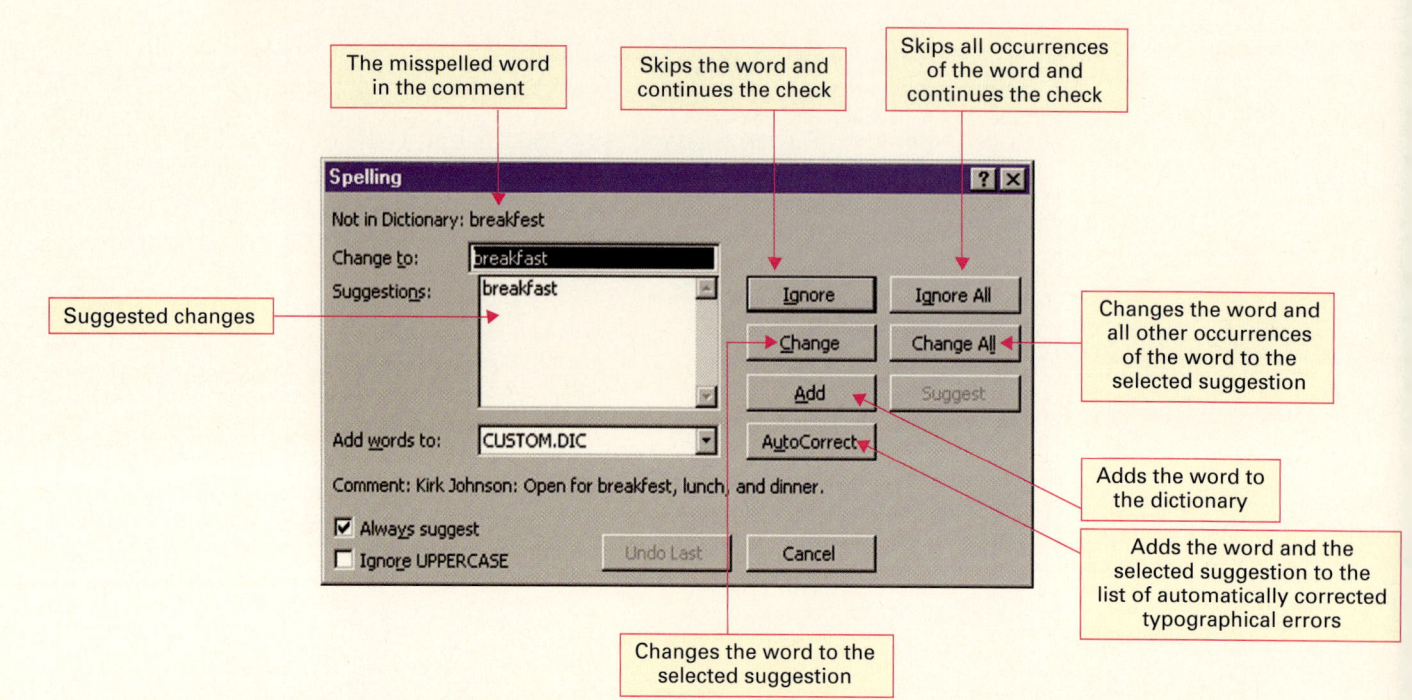

- The misspelled word in the comment
- Skips the word and continues the check
- Skips all occurrences of the word and continues the check
- Suggested changes
- Changes the word and all other occurrences of the word to the selected suggestion
- Adds the word to the dictionary
- Adds the word and the selected suggestion to the list of automatically corrected typographical errors
- Changes the word to the selected suggestion

4 Choose Change.
If there is another word not found in the dictionary, Excel 97 lists it, but if there are no more words, a message displays telling you that the spell check is complete.

5 Click OK.
The worksheet redisplays.

> **Note** If you have used multiple worksheets, you must spell check each sheet individually. Sorry!

Conclusion

If you have time, you may want to spell check the other worksheets. Then save the file and close it.

Summary and Exercises

Summary

- The Find command finds specific text or values in a worksheet.
- You can edit the data in a cell or simply reenter the data.
- Excel 97 automatically recalculates formulas if the numbers in the cells change.
- When you copy data it is stored in the Clipboard.
- Comments provide additional information in a workbook.
- You can check the spelling of worksheets in a workbook.

Key Terms and Operations

Key Terms
AutoCalculate
Clipboard
comment

Operations
add comments
copy data
delete data
edit data
find data
move data
open a workbook
paste data
select cells
spell check a worksheet

Study Questions

Multiple Choice

1. A workbook's name may appear at the bottom of the File menu,
   a. if it is in the current path.
   b. if the workbook has multiple worksheets.
   c. unless it is on a floppy disk.
   d. if it has been opened recently.

2. To edit a cell, first
   a. select the cell.
   b. click in the formula bar.
   c. activate the edit mode.
   d. press F4.

3. The easiest way to select the entire worksheet is to
   a. triple-click in any cell.
   b. click the button above the row numbers and to the left of the column letters.
   c. drag the pointer through all the cells in the worksheet.
   d. select all the rows in the worksheet.

4. The Find command can find
    a. only text.
    b. only numbers.
    c. only cell addresses.
    d. text in comments.

5. The Spell Checker will
    a. not check all worksheets at once.
    b. not check comments.
    c. only start in the first cell of a worksheet.
    d. not add words to the dictionary.

6. When you press Delete, the
    a. contents of the selected cells are erased.
    b. selected cells are removed from the worksheet.
    c. contents of the selected cells are stored in the Clipboard.
    d. same result is achieved as when you choose Edit, Delete.

7. The Find command
    a. searches only the current worksheet.
    b. searches all worksheets in the workbook.
    c. searches only formulas.
    d. is useful only in large worksheets.

8. Which of the following do not require pressing the (CTRL) key?
    a. non-adjacent columns
    b. non-adjacent rows
    c. adjacent columns
    d. a range of cells

9. To move data, use the
    a. Cut and Paste buttons.
    b. Copy and Paste buttons.
    c. Move and Paste buttons.
    d. Cut and Insert buttons.

10. A comment
    a. is attached to the worksheet.
    b. is attached to a cell.
    c. is only visible when you point to the cell.
    d. displays when you click a cell.

Short Answer

1. When you open a workbook, what is the location of the active cell?

2. How do you use the AutoCalculate feature?

3. What happens if you copy data to a range that already contains data?

4. What toolbar displays when you turn on the Comments view?

5. How would you select both Column C and the range A1 through A10?

6. How do you move data?

7. What happens to the data in the Clipboard when you copy new data?

8. What happens to the data in the Clipboard when you exit Excel 97?

9. How do you select several consecutive rows?

10. How do you insert a comment?

For Discussion

1. What do you do if you need to find all the formulas that reference cell B3?

2. Discuss the two methods of changing data in a cell and when you use each method.

3. Describe several scenarios in which comments are useful.

4. Describe several scenarios in which the AutoCalculate feature could be used.

Review Exercises

1. Revising the Restaurant Sales Worksheet

In this exercise, you will revise the Restaurant Sales worksheet, revising data and adding a comment.

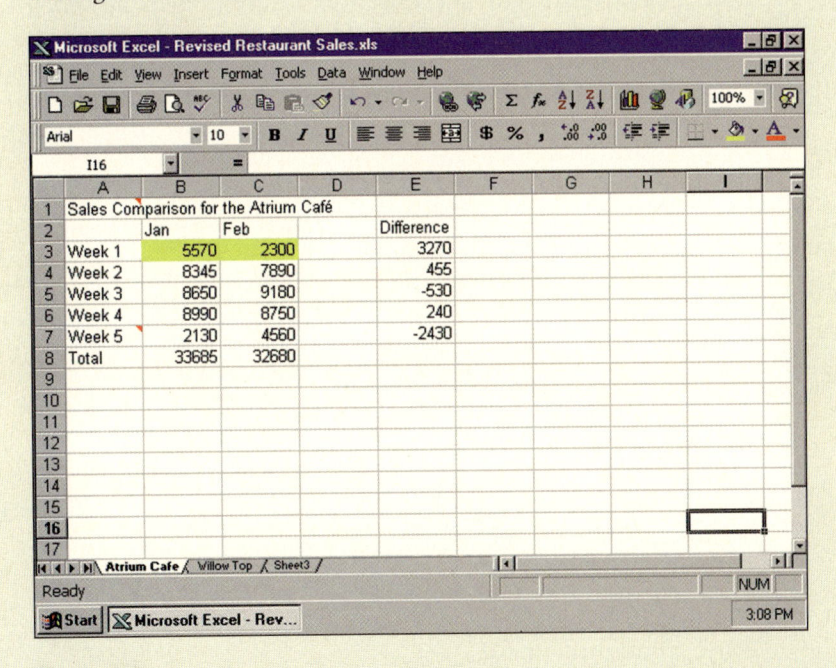

Figure 2.2

1. Open the workbook named *Restaurant Sales.xls,* unless it is already open.

2. Make the revisions (highlighted in yellow) shown in Figure 2.2.

3. Add a comment to cell A7 in the Atrium Cafe worksheet that says "This week had 4 days in January and 3 days in February."

4. Make sure the numbers on the January worksheet match the numbers on the Atrium Cafe and Willow Top worksheets.

5. Save the file as *Revised Restaurant Sales.xls* and close it.

2. Revising a Time Sheet

In this exercise, you will revise a time sheet workbook.

1. Ask your instructor how to obtain the file *Tmsheet.xls*. (If you have Internet access, you can download this file from the Addison Wesley Longman website at www.awl.com/is/select/).

2. Open the file and find the word "sum" in a formula in the Smith worksheet. Copy the formula to the next six cells on the right.

3. Delete the text in row 4.

4. Move the data in cell B1 to cell D1.

5. Copy A1:H9 to the Jones worksheet.

6. Save the file as *Times.xls* and close it.

Assignments

1. Creating and Revising a Budget

Create a worksheet that lists expenses for your personal budget. List expense items in column A starting in row 4. List the projected amounts for the next three months in columns B through D. Total each month at the bottom of the column. Save the worksheet as *My Budget.xls*. Revise the amounts so they are more conservative. Move the totals to row 3. Add comments for expenses that need further explanation. Save the revised worksheet as *Lower Budget.xls*.

2. Tracking the American Stock Exchange (Optional Exercise)

Go to the web site http://www.amex.com and click on the link Market Summary. Create a worksheet to contain the five columns of information shown in the summary. Save the worksheet as *Amex.xls*. Check the summary on several different days and add the information to the worksheet.

3

Enhancing the Appearance of a Workbook

Now that you can create and edit a worksheet, it's time for you to add a little pizzazz to the worksheet with various formatting techniques. In this project you will use borders and colors to give the worksheet a classy look.

Objectives

After completing this project, you will be able to:

- ➤ **Format text**
- ➤ **Change cell alignment**
- ➤ **Format numbers**
- ➤ **Format dates**
- ➤ **Format numbers as text**
- ➤ **Add borders and fill**
- ➤ **View and change a page break**
- ➤ **Use AutoFormat**

The Challenge

Mr. Williams, the manager of the golf and tennis property at The Willows, has created a worksheet named *Income.xls* that estimates the income for the upcoming Pro-Celebrity Tournament. He has entered all the data and formulas, but he wants you to format the worksheet so it looks better and is easier to read.

The Solution

You will open the workbook, format the numbers and dates, add a border to the important information and emphasize the totals with shading. Additionally, you will format and align the data in some of the cells and use AutoFormat to format a group of cells automatically. The formatted worksheet will look like Figure 3.1 when you are finished. (The Full Screen view is used in Figure 3.1.)

Before you can begin you must download *Income.xls* from the Addison Wesley Longman web site. The file is stored at this address: www.awl.com/is/select/. If you are unable to download, obtain the file from your instructor.

Figure 3.1

The Setup

So that your screen will match the illustrations in this chapter and to ensure that all the tasks in this project will function as described, you should set up Excel as described in Table 3.1. Because these are the default settings for the toolbars and view, you may not need to make any changes to your setup.

Table 3.1   Excel Settings

Location	Make these settings:
View, Toolbars	Deselect all toolbars except Standard and Formatting.
View	Use the Normal view and display the Formula Bar and Status Bar.

Formatting Text

You can format text in a number of ways. You can make it bold, italic, or underlined, or change the font, the font size, and the font color. The Formatting toolbar includes buttons for many of the text formatting options. Before you begin formatting the worksheet, you will save it as *Income2.xls* so you can use the original again later.

TASK 1: TO FORMAT TEXT:

1 Open *Income.xls* and choose File, Select the drive or folder, type *Income2.xls* in the filename text box and click Save.

2 Select cells D3, B4, and F4.

Click the first cell to select it and then press Ctrl when you click the other cells

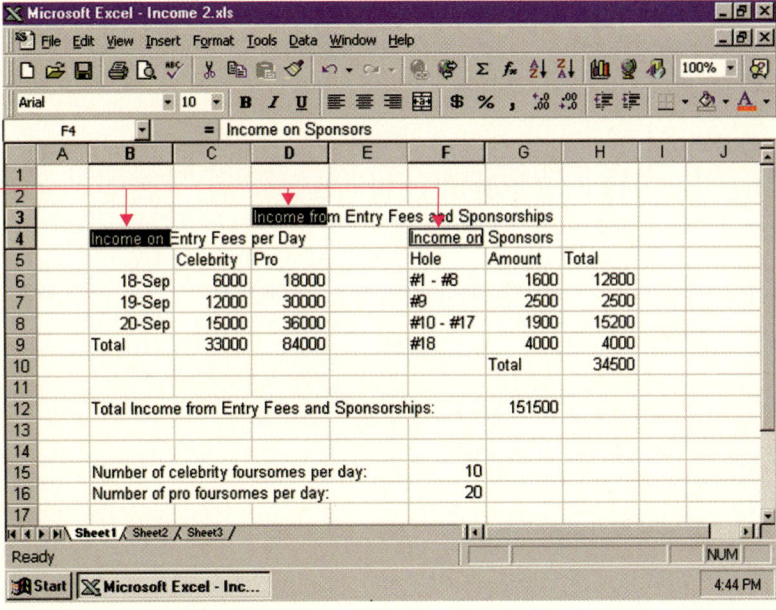

3 Click the Bold **B** button.
The text in all three cells changes to bold.

4 Select cell D3. Click the drop-down arrow for Font Size and choose 12.
The text in the cell changes from 10 point to 12 point.

5 Click the drop-down arrow bar Font and choose Arial Black.

The height of the row increases automatically to accommodate the size of the font

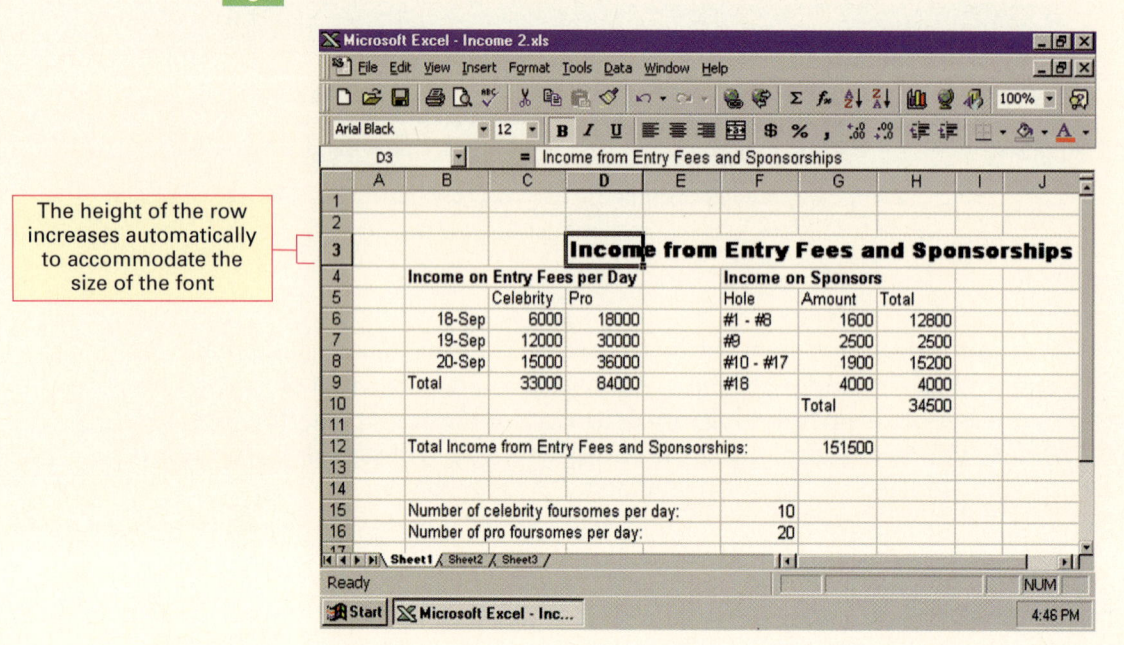

Changing Cell Alignment

Data in a cell can be aligned on the left, in the center, or on the right. Each type of data that you enter uses a default alignment — text is left aligned and numbers and dates are right aligned.

You can change the alignment of data in a selected cell by clicking on one of the alignment buttons in the Formatting toolbar. Sometimes you may want to align data across several cells; for example, you might want to center a title in the first row so that the title spans the columns used in the worksheet. In this case, you can merge the cells into one wide cell, and then center the data in the wide cell.

TASK 2: TO CHANGE THE CELL ALIGNMENT:

1 Select A3:I3.
The cells are highlighted.

2   Choose Format.

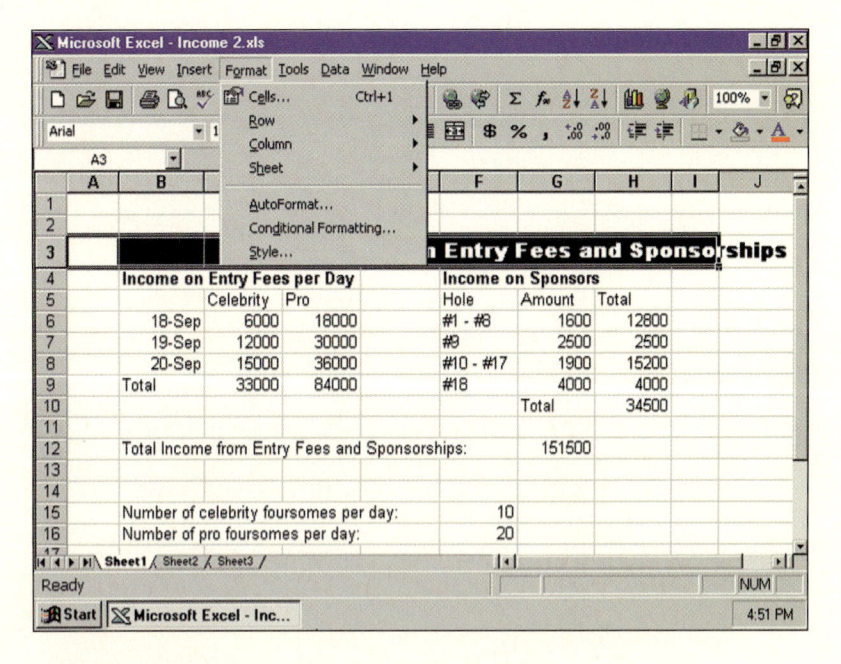

3   Choose Cells.

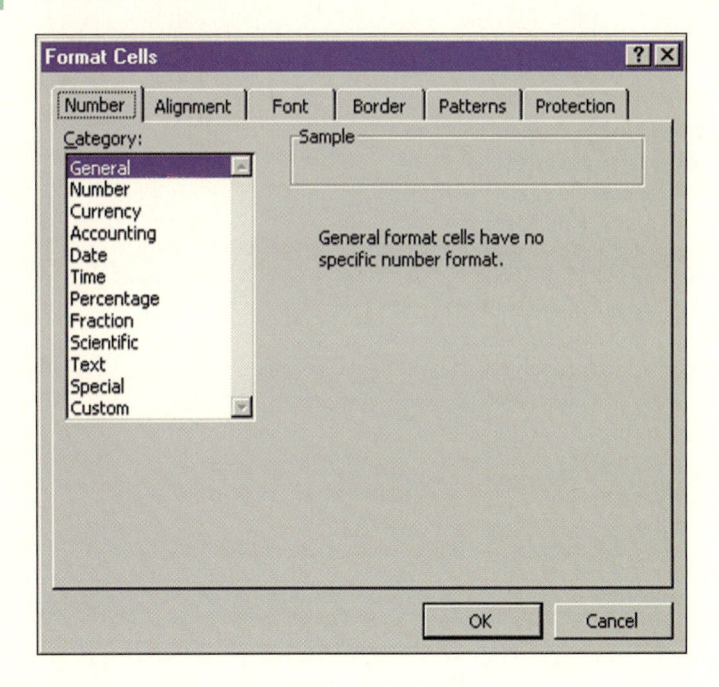

4 Click the Alignment tab.

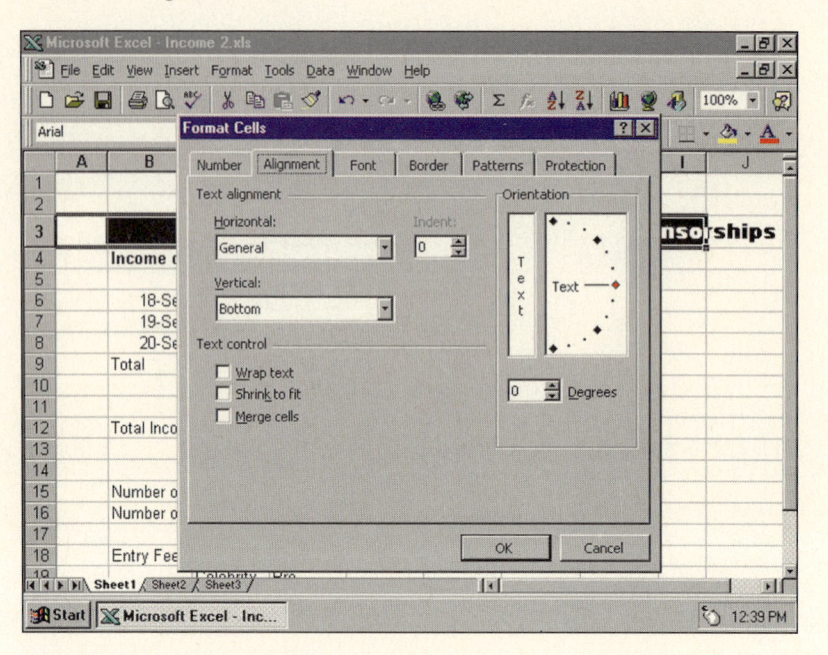

5 Choose Merge cells and click OK.
The cells become one cell.

6 Click the Center button.

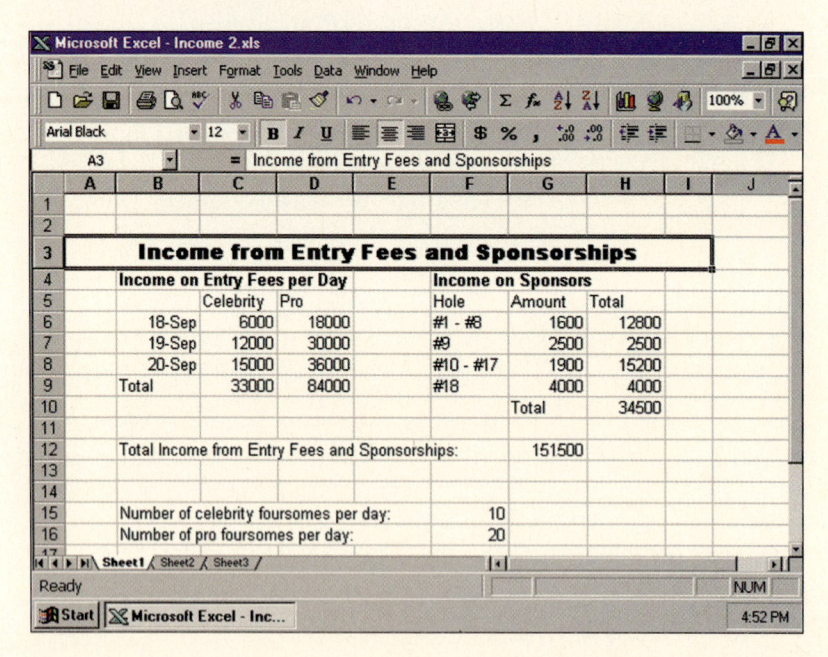

Tip To merge and center at the same time, select the cells and click the Merge and Center button.

7 Merge and align the remaining cells:
Merge the cells B4:D4 into one cell and center the text in the cell. Merge the cells F4:H4 into one cell and center the text in the cell. Center the text in cell F5. Select cells C5, D5, G5, and H5 and click the Align Right button.

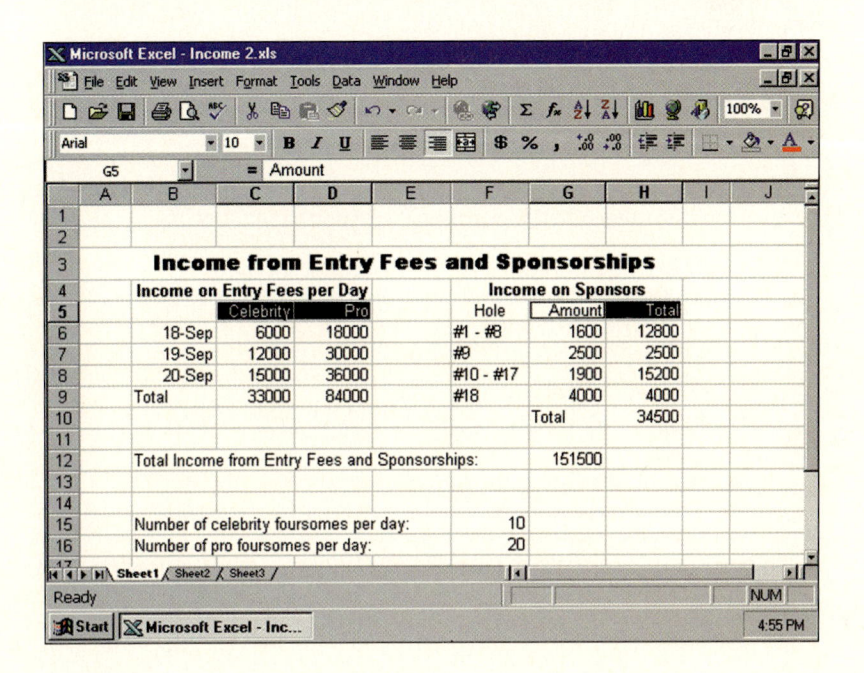

Formatting Numbers

The numbers you enter in a workbook can be "dressed up" with several different formats. As with text, you can make numbers bold, italic, change the font size, and font color. But there are other formatting options available for numbers. Table 3.2 describes the formats that are available in Excel and Figure 3.2 shows some examples.

Table 3.2 Number Formats

Format	Description
General	Numbers appear as entered except for fractions in the form of 1/2 which must be entered as **0 1/2**. Commas and decimal points can be entered with the numbers. If commas are not entered, they will not display automatically as in other formats. You can enter a minus or parentheses for negative numbers.
Number	Numbers have a fixed number of decimal places, comma separators can be displayed automatically, and negative numbers can be displayed with a minus, in red, with parentheses, or in red with parentheses.
Currency	Numbers have thousands separators and can have a fixed number of decimal places, a currency symbol, and negative numbers can be displayed with a minus, in red, with parentheses, or in red with parentheses.
Accounting	Numbers have thousands separators, a fixed number of decimal places, and can display a currency symbol. Currency symbols and decimal points line up in a column.
Date	Dates can display with numbers, such as 3/4/97 or 03/04/97, or with numbers and text, such as March 4, 1997 or March-97. Some date formats also display the time.
Time	Times can display as AM or PM or use the 24-hour clock, as in 13:15 for 1:15 PM.
Percentage	Numbers are multiplied by 100 and display a percent sign.
Fraction	Numbers display as one, two, or three digit fractions.
Scientific	Numbers display as a number times a power of 10 (represented by E).
Text	Numbers display exactly as entered but are treated as text; therefore, the number would not be used in a calculation.
Special	These formats are used for zip codes, phone numbers, and social security numbers.
Custom	Numbers display in a format created by the user.

	A	B	C	D	E
1	This column is formatted with the **General** Format which is the default.	This column is formatted with the **Number** format with two decimal places.	This column is formatted with the **Currency** format, two decimal places, a dollar sign, and negative numbers in red.	This column is formatted with the **Accounting** format and two decimal places.	This column is formatted with the **Scientific** format with two decimal places.
2					
3	1.37512349	1.38	$1.38	$ 1.38	1.38E+00
4	1000000000	1000000000.00	$1,000,000,000.00	$ 1,000,000,000.00	1.00E+09
5	-98	-98.00	$98.00	$ (98.00)	-9.80E+01
6	12345.6	12345.60	$12,345.60	$ 12,345.60	1.23E+04
7	10	10.00	$10.00	$ 10.00	1.00E+01
8					

Figure 3.2

TASK 3: TO FORMAT NUMBERS:

1   Select cells C6:D9, G6:H9, H10, and G12.
The cells are highlighted.

2   Choose Format, Cells, click the Number tab, and select Currency from the
Category list.

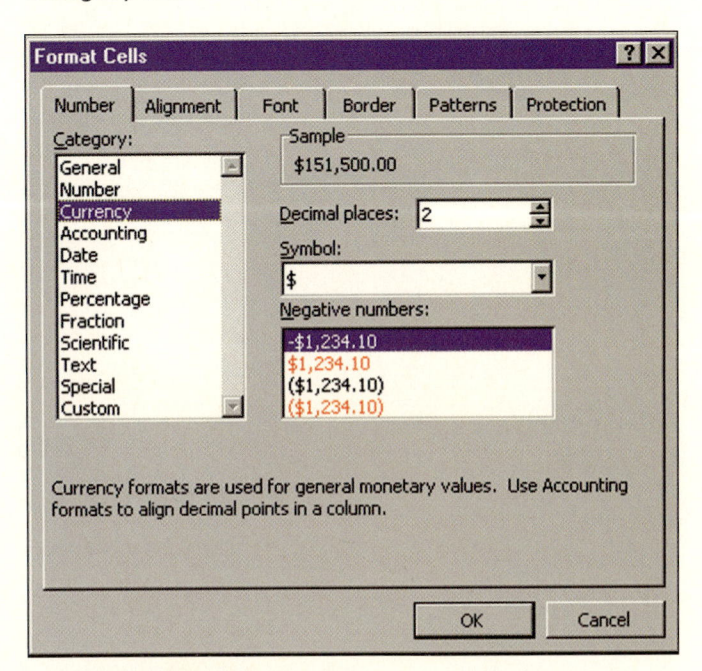

3   Select 0 for Decimal places and None for Symbol.

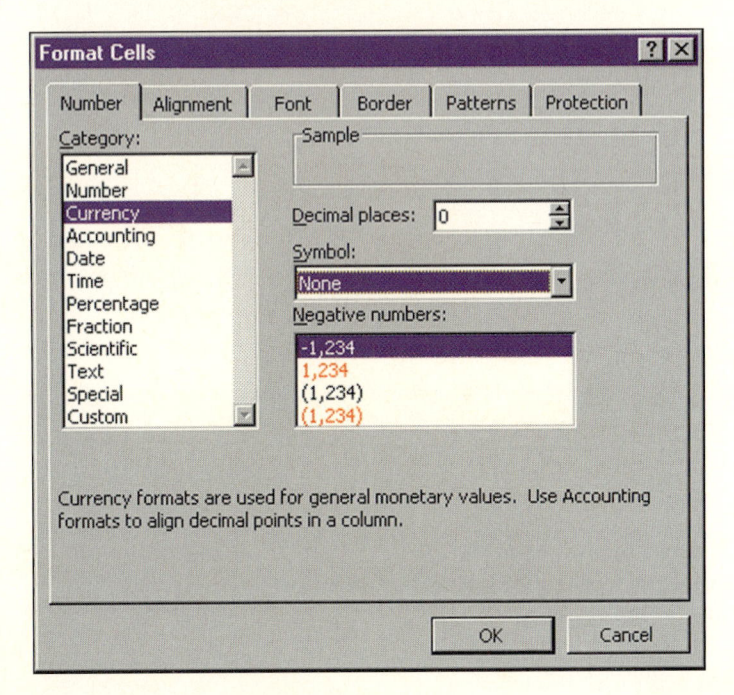

4   Click OK.
The format is applied.

Formatting Dates

The date format is included in the number formats because Excel stores dates as numbers. You can format dates in several ways. For example, if you enter the date 3/4/97, you can format it to look like any of the following:

3/4	Mar-97
3/4/97	March-97
03/04/97	March 4, 1997
4-Mar	M
4-Mar-97	M-97
04-Mar-97	

Some numbers that you enter are really text. For example, in Figure 3.1, shown on page 77 and again below, the range of 1–8 refers to holes 1 through 8 on the golf course. If you do not format "1–8" as text, Excel will interpret the entry as a date. You will learn how to format dates in Tasks 4 and 5.

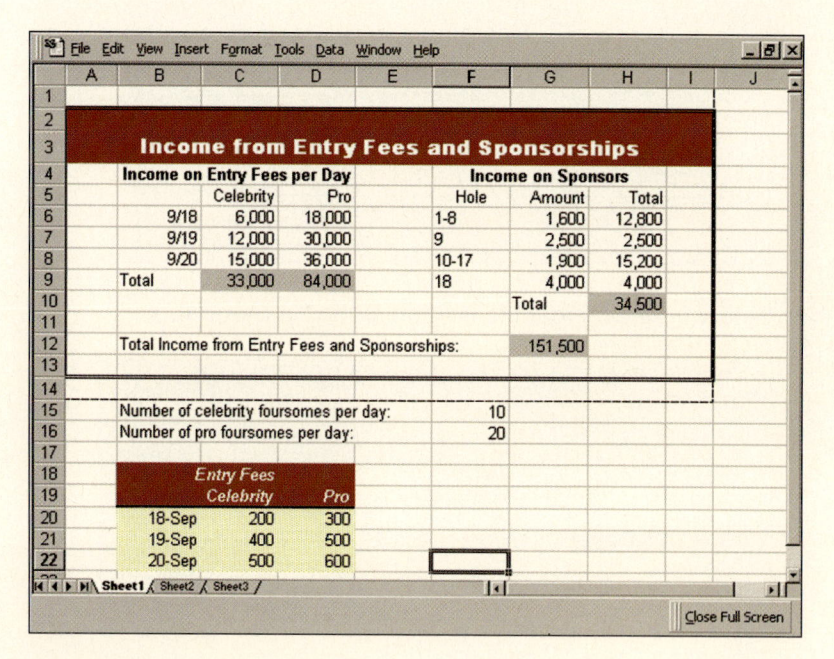

Figure 3.1

TASK 4: TO FORMAT DATES:

1 Select B6:B8.
The cells are highlighted.

2 Choose Format, Cells, and click on the Number tab (if necessary).
The default format is selected.

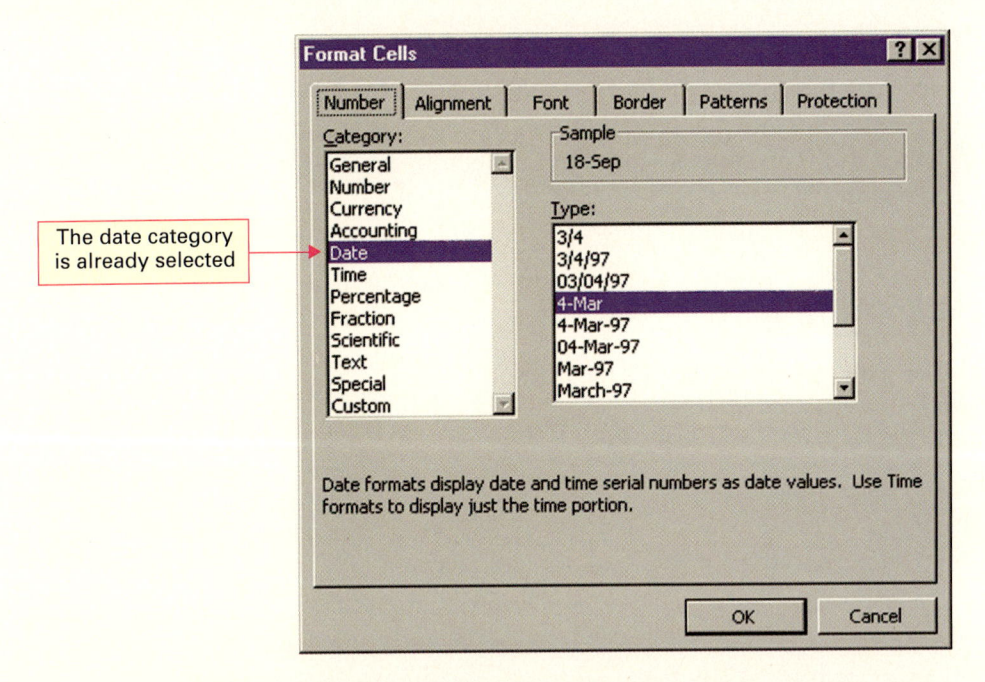

The date category is already selected

3 Select the first option from the Type list (3/4) and click OK.

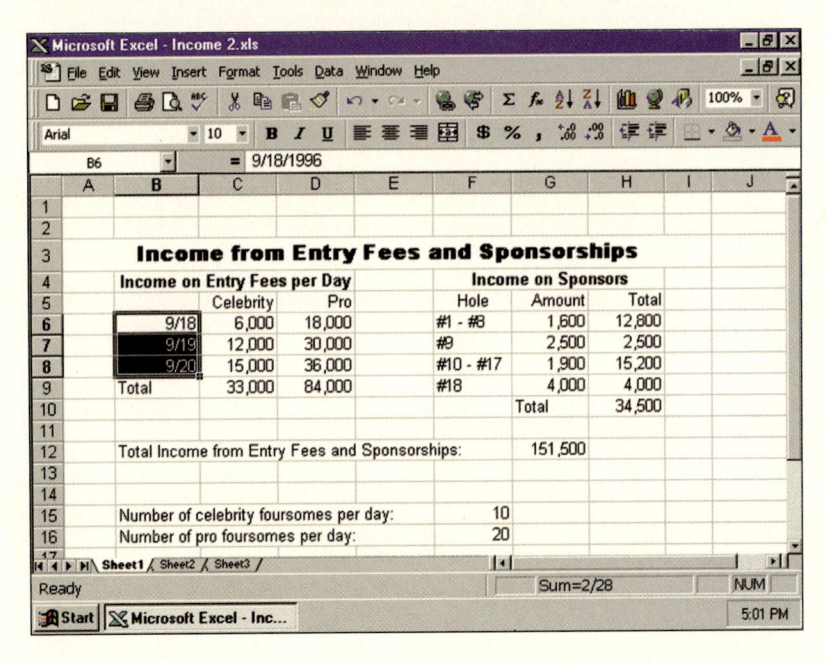

Formatting Numbers as Text

When you enter numbers with dashes or slashes in a worksheet, as we did in golf course holes 1–8 and 10–17 shown below, Excel interprets the entry as a date. To avoid this, you must format the numbers as text.

TASK 5: TO FORMAT NUMBERS AS TEXT:

1 Reenter the data in cells F6:F9 exactly as shown:
F6: **1 - 8**
F7: **9**
F8: **10 - 17**
F9: **18**

Excel has interpreted the text in these two cells as dates

			Microsoft Excel - Income 2.xls			

File Edit View Insert Format Tools Data Window Help

Arial   10   **B** *I* U

F10   =

	A	B	C	D	E	F	G	H	I	J
1										
2										
3		**Income from Entry Fees and Sponsorships**								
4		Income on Entry Fees per Day				Income on Sponsors				
5			Celebrity	Pro		Hole	Amount	Total		
6		9/18	6,000	18,000		8-Jan	1,600	12,800		
7		9/19	12,000	30,000		9	2,500	2,500		
8		9/20	15,000	36,000		17-Oct	1,900	15,200		
9		Total	33,000	84,000		18	4,000	4,000		
10							Total	34,500		
11										
12		Total Income from Entry Fees and Sponsorships:					151,500			
13										
14										
15		Number of celebrity foursomes per day:				10				
16		Number of pro foursomes per day:				20				

Sheet1 Sheet2 Sheet3

Ready   NUM

Start Microsoft Excel - Inc...   5:03 PM

2 Select cells F6:F9.
The cells are highlighted.

3 Choose Format, Cells, and click on the Number tab (if necessary). Select Text for the Category and click OK.

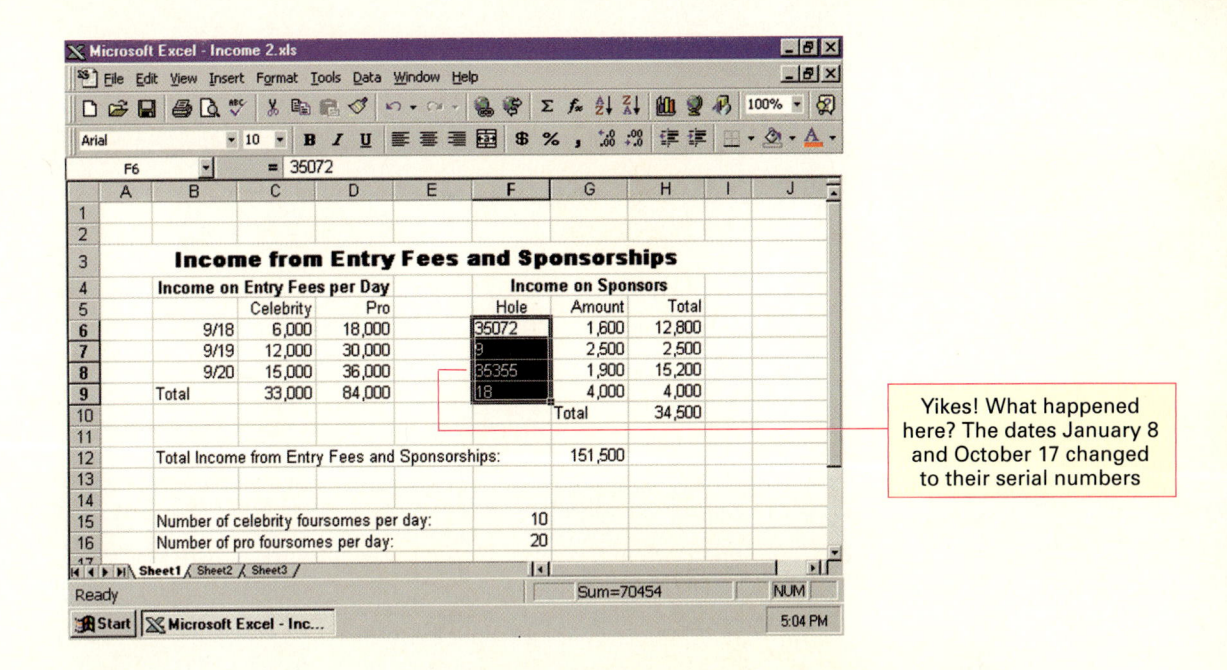

Yikes! What happened here? The dates January 8 and October 17 changed to their serial numbers

Note A serial number is a sequential number given to every day of every year since the turn of the century. So the number 35072 means that January 8, 1997 is the 35,072nd day of the 20th century.

4 Type **1 - 8** in cell F6. Type **10 - 17** in cell F8.

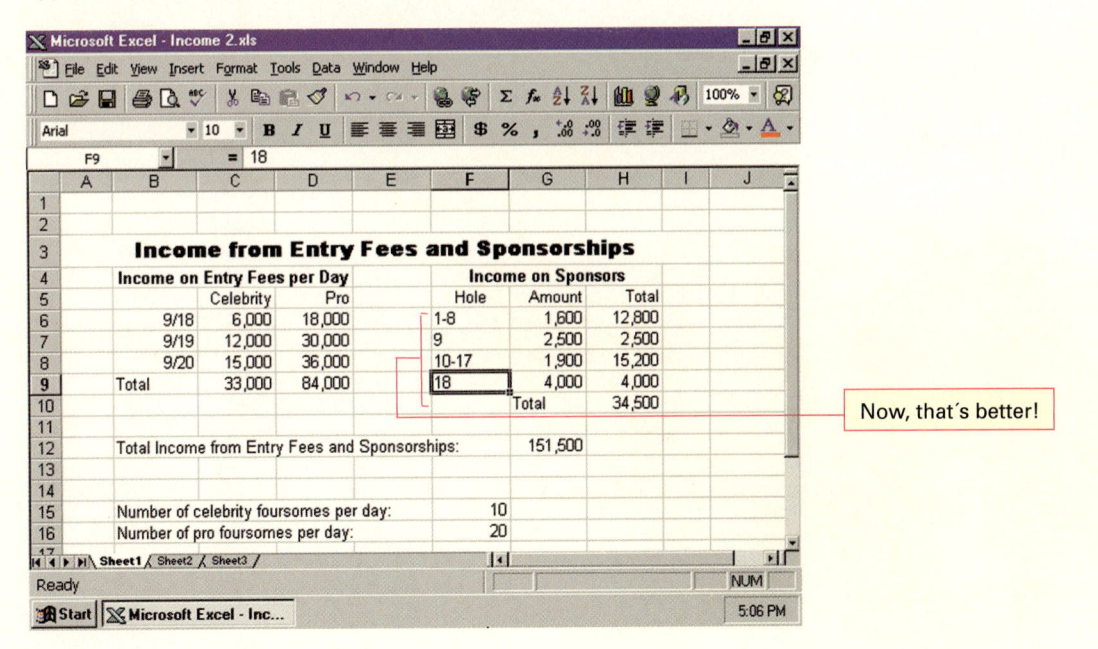

Now, that's better!

Adding Borders and Fill

A *border* is a line that displays on any side of a cell or group of cells. You can use borders in a variety of ways: to draw rectangles around cells, to create dividers between columns, to create a total line under a column of numbers, and so on.

Fill, also called *shading* or *patterns*, is a color or a shade of gray that you apply to the background of a cell. Use fill carefully if you do not have a color printer. Sometimes it doesn't look as good when it prints in black and white as it does on screen.

TASK 6: TO ADD A BORDER AND FILL:

1 Select cells A2:I13.
The cells are highlighted.

2 Choose Format, Cells, and click the Border tab.

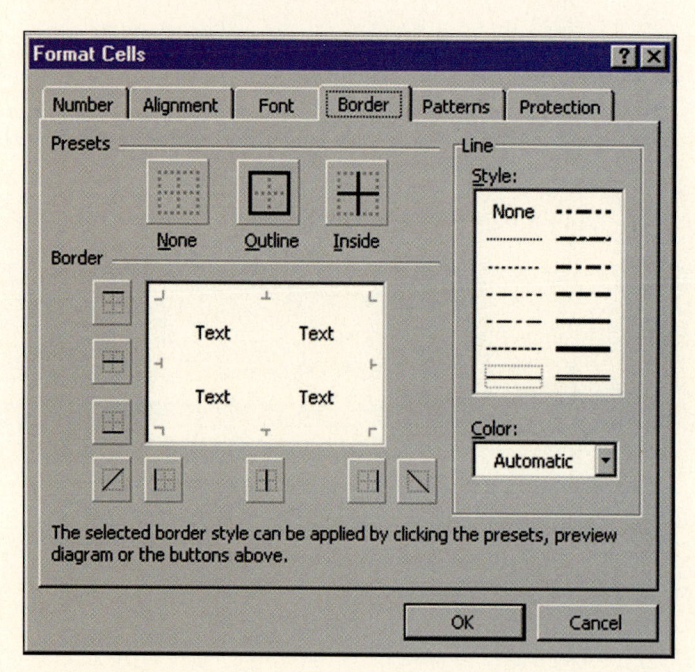

3 Select the double line in the Style box, click the Outline button, and click OK.

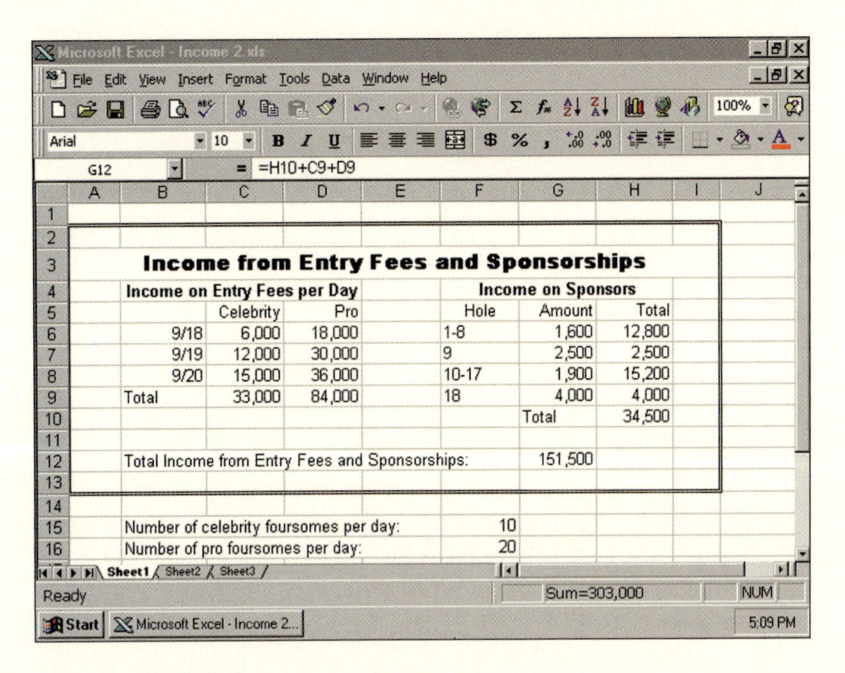

4 Select cells C9:D9, H10, and G12.
The cells are highlighted.

5 Choose Format, Cells, and click the Patterns tab.

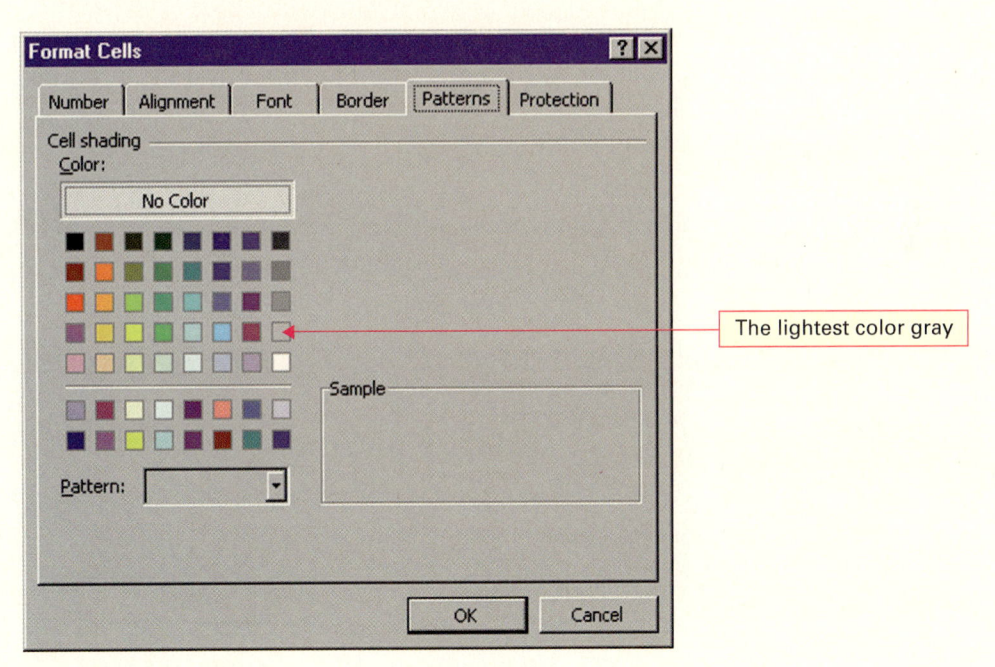

The lightest color gray

6 Select the lightest color gray and click OK.

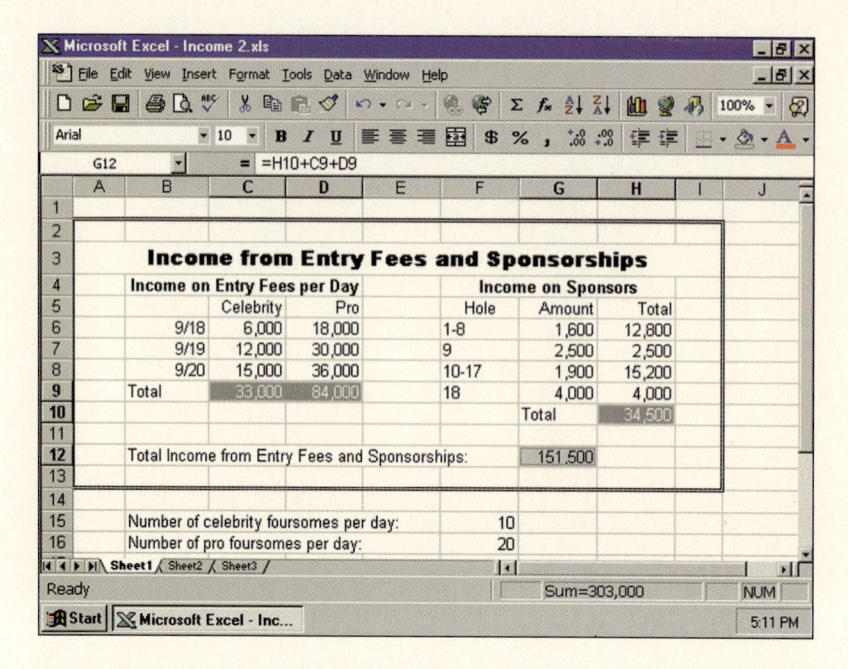

7 Select cells A2:I3 and format them with the first color on the second row of the color chart on the Patterns page.
The cells are shaded with the selected color.

> **Tip** You also can apply color by clicking the down arrow on the Fill Color button on the Formatting toolbar and selecting a color from a smaller palette.

8 Select cell A3.
The cell is highlighted.

9 To change the text color, click the down arrow in the Font Color **A** button and click the white rectangle in the color palette.

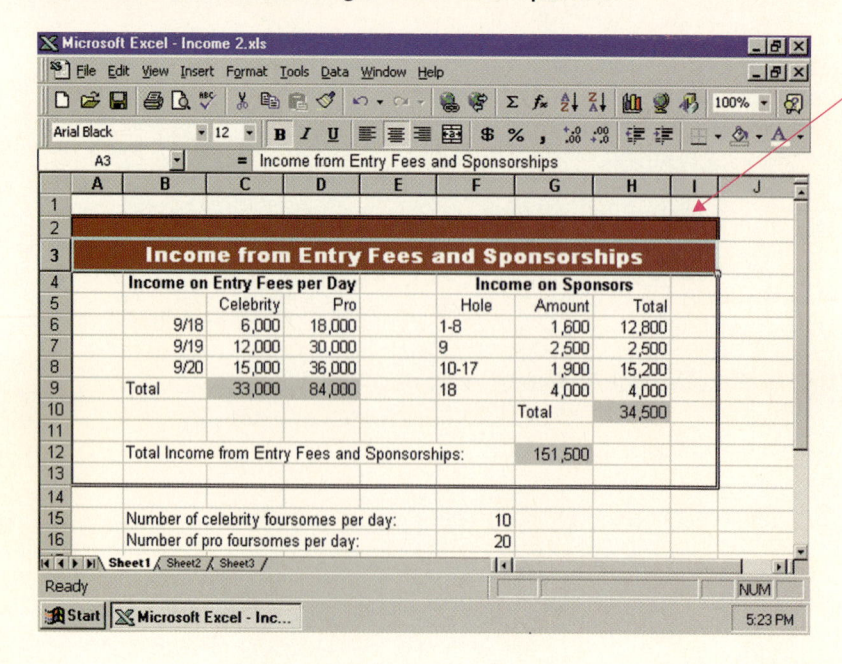

The border is in the same place, but it is hard to see because of the selected cells

Viewing and Changing a Page Break

Unlike word processing documents, worksheets are not represented on the screen by pages. The complete worksheet, all 16,777,216 cells of it, is one big page on the screen. So that you can see where the pages will break when the worksheet prints, Excel provides a *Page Break view*. You can adjust the location of the *page breaks* in this view.

TASK 7: TO VIEW THE PAGE BREAK IN THE INCOME WORKSHEET AND CHANGE IT:

1   Click the Print Preview button.

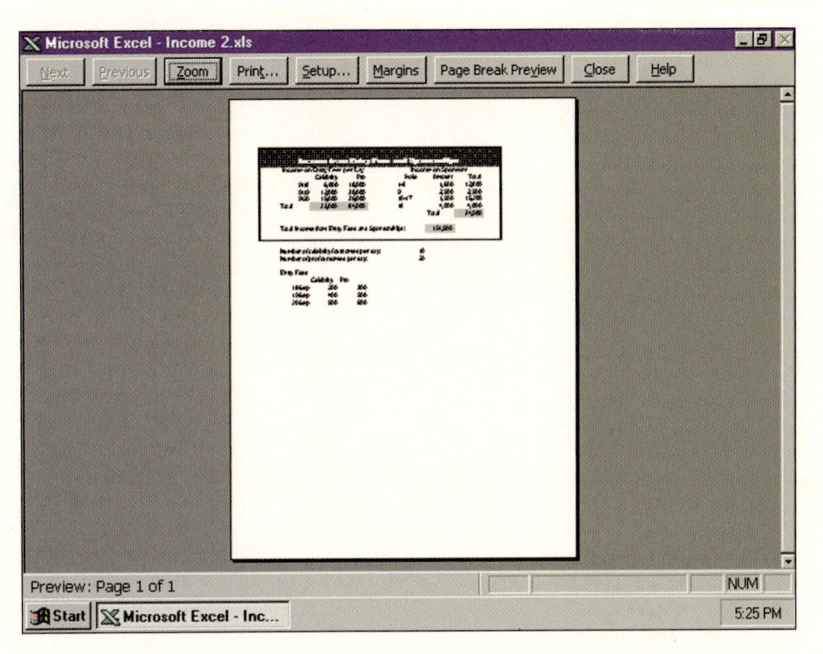

2   Click the Page Break Preview button. (Click OK if a message displays.)

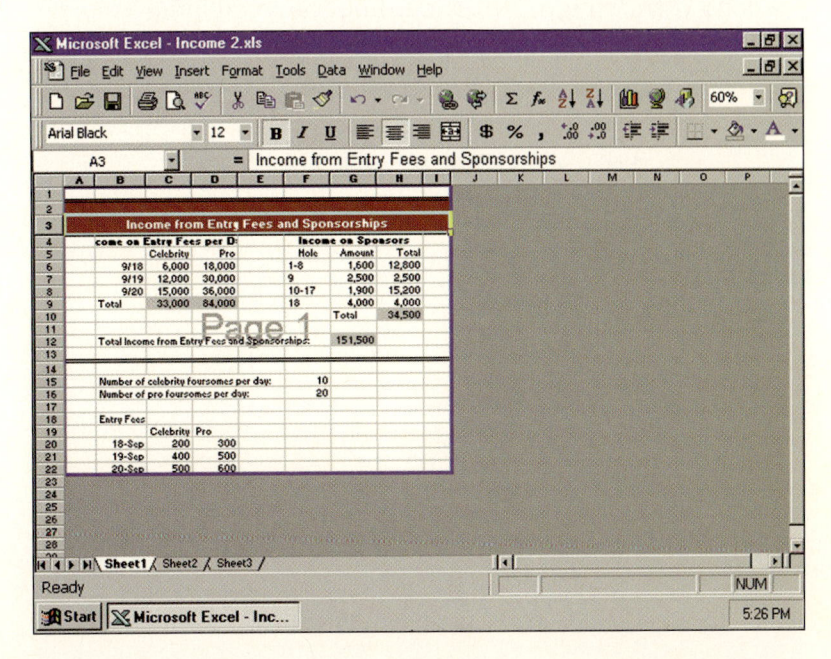

3 Drag the blue line at the bottom to just below row 14.

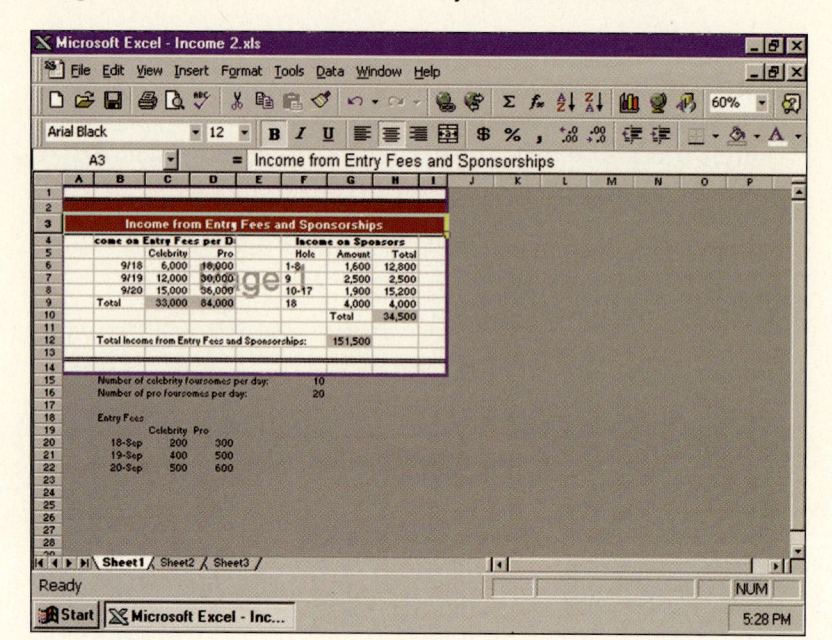

4 Click .
Now, only the bordered text displays in the print preview for page 1.

5 Click the Normal View button.
The worksheet displays in Normal view. Notice that the page break location is indicated with a dotted line.

Using AutoFormat

Excel provides several formats that you can apply to a complete worksheet or to a single range. The **AutoFormat** feature enables you to apply many formatting features automatically, creating very professional looking worksheets without much effort on your part. (Excel works hard so you don't have to.)

> **Note** AutoFormats are designed for worksheets or ranges that have row headings in the first column and column headings in the first row.

TASK 8: TO APPLY AN AUTOFORMAT:

1 Select B18:D22.
The cells are highlighted.

2   Choose Format, AutoFormat.

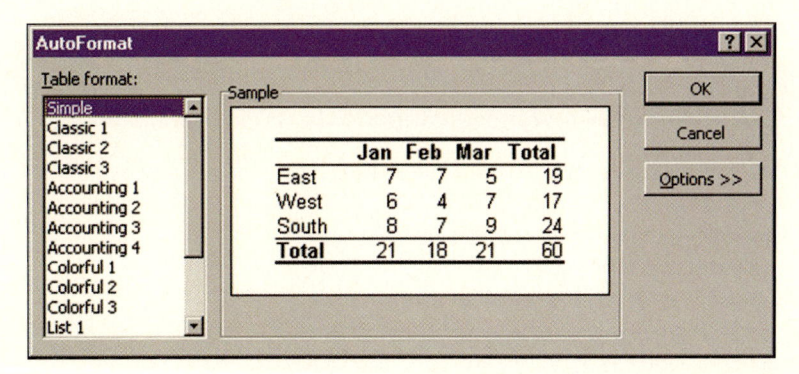

3   Select Colorful 2. Click Options, deselect Width/Height, and click OK. Click in a cell outside the selected range to see the true colors.

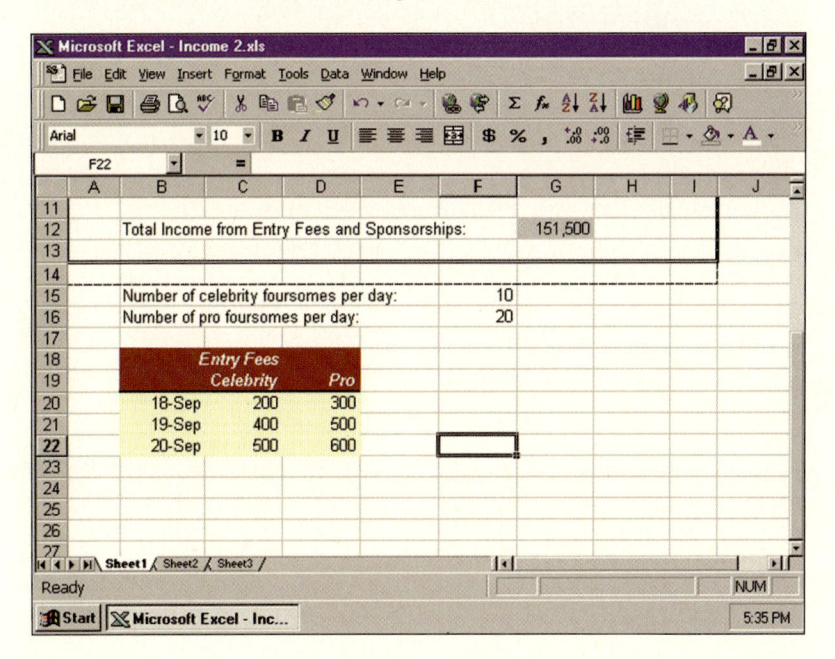

The Conclusion

If you have access to a printer, print page 1 of the worksheet. Save the workbook and close it.

Summary and Exercises

Summary

- You can format text with bold, italic, underline, different fonts and font sizes, and so on.
- Data in a cell can be left, right, or center aligned.
- Excel provides many formats for displaying numbers.
- You can apply a border to any side of a cell.
- You can apply a background color to a cell.
- The Page Break view shows where page breaks are located.
- An AutoFormat can be applied to a worksheet or a range.

Key Terms and Operations

Key Terms	Operations
border	add a border
fill	add fill
page break	align cells
Page Break view	AutoFormat
pattern	change a page break
shading	format dates
	format numbers
	format text
	view a page break

Study Questions

Multiple Choice

1. If you type text in cell A1 and you want to center the text across cells A1 through A5,
   a. merge the cells and click the Center button.
   b. select A1:A5 and click the Center button.
   c. select A1:A5 and choose Format, Cells, Alignment, Center, and click OK.
   d. merge the cells, and choose Format, Align, Center.

2. You can apply an AutoFormat
   a. to a cell.
   b. only to a complete worksheet.
   c. to a single range.
   d. to noncontiguous ranges.

3. To make text bold,
   a. click in the cell, type the text, click the Bold button, and press Enter.
   b. select the cell and click the Bold button.
   c. select the cell and choose Format, Bold.
   d. All of the above.

4. Borders can be applied to
   a. any side of a range.
   b. all sides of a range.
   c. the top and bottom sides of a range.
   d. All of the above.

5. To add shading to a cell, select the cell and
   a. click the drop-down arrow on the Shading button and choose the color.
   b. choose Format, Cells, Shading, select the color, and click OK.
   c. choose Format, Cells, Patterns, select the color, and click OK.
   d. choose Format, Shading, select the color, and click OK.

6. A page break is marked with
   a. a dotted line in the worksheet.
   b. a blue line in the Print Preview.
   c. a dotted line in the Page Break Preview.
   d. a blue line in the worksheet.

7. Which of the following format(s) (if any) would be used to achieve this format: $1,200.00?
   a. general format with a dollar sign symbol and two decimal places
   b. accounting format with a dollar sign symbol and two decimal places
   c. currency format with a dollar sign symbol and two decimal places
   d. number format with a dollar sign symbol and two decimal places

8. When you increase the point size of text,
   a. you must first increase the height of the row.
   b. the text may wrap in the cell if the cell is not wide enough to accommodate the new size.
   c. the row height increases automatically to accommodate the size of the text.
   d. the cell width increases automatically to accommodate the size of the text.

9. The option to rotate text in a cell is found
   a. on the Orientation page of the Format Cells dialog box.
   b. on the Format menu.
   c. on the Rotate button in the Formatting Toolbar.
   d. on the Alignment page of the Format Cells dialog box.

10. Excel stores a date as
   a. a number.
   b. a date.
   c. text.
   d. a mixture of text and numbers.

Short Answer

1. How are numbers aligned in a cell?

2. How can you enter 1–2-97 and make it appear as January 2, 1997?

3. How do you change the font of the text entered in a cell?

4. How do you change the color of the text entered in a cell?

5. Under what circumstances do you have to format a cell as text?

6. How do you merge cells?

7. How are dates aligned in a cell?

8. The entry 1.2E103 is an example of what number format?

9. What is a serial number?

10. What is the default alignment for text in a cell?

For Discussion

1. Describe the AutoFormat feature and discuss the advantages of using it.

2. How can you designate where the pages will break when the worksheet prints?

3. Compare the Page Break Preview with the Print Preview view.

4. Give examples of ways you could use borders.

Review Exercises

1. Enhancing the Restaurant Sales Worksheet

In this exercise, you will enhance the worksheet with border, shading, and number formats.

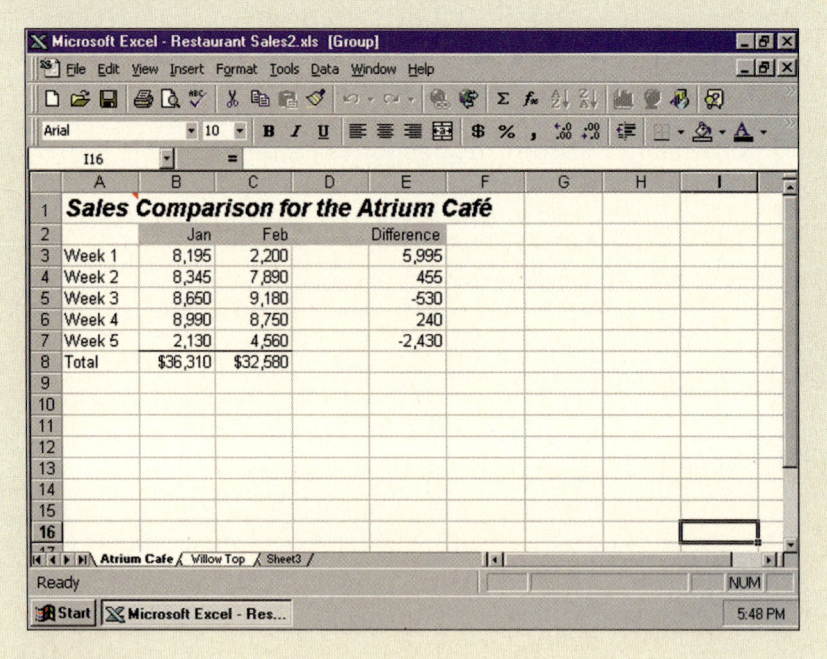

Figure 3.3

1. Open *Restaurant Sales.xls*, the file you saved at the end of Project 2.

2. Right align cells B2 and C2 on both worksheets.

3. Format all numbers on both worksheets (except for cells B8 and C8) with the Currency format, using no decimal places and no dollar sign. Format B8 and C8 on both worksheets with Currency, no decimal places, and a dollar sign.

4. Format cell A1 on both worksheets with bold, italic, 14 point.

5. Add a border to the bottom of cells B7 and C7 on both worksheets.

6. Add light gray fill to cells B2:E2 on both worksheets.

7. Save the file as *Restaurant Sales2.xls* and close it.

2. Creating a Concert List

In this exercise, you will create a workbook for a list of concerts and enhance the worksheet with formatting.

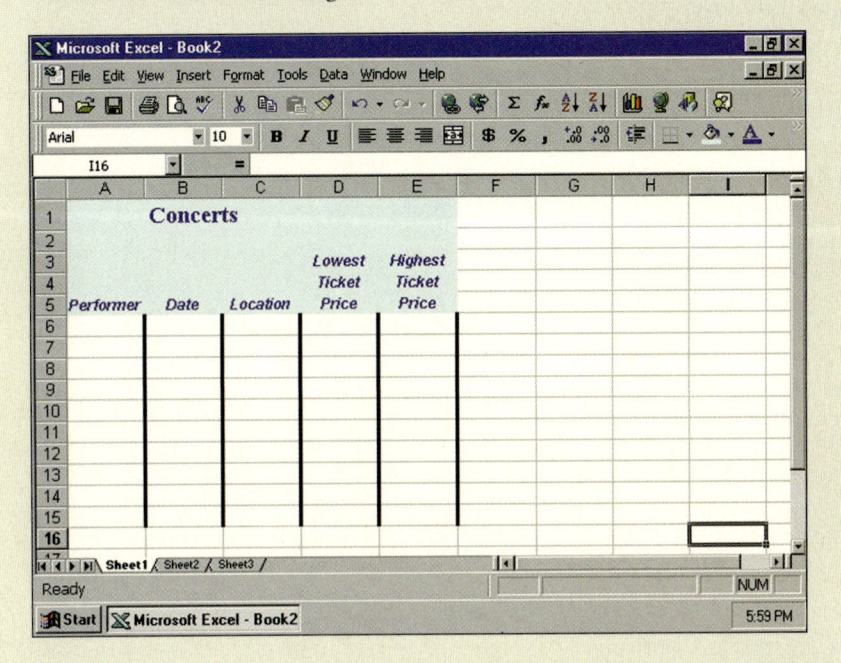

Figure 3.4

1. Go to http://www.ticketmaster.com and follow the link to the Box Office.

2. Search for at least 10 concerts by groups or performers that you like. Obtain information about when and where the concert will be and how much the tickets cost.

3. Create a worksheet with these column headings: Performer, Date, Location, Lowest Ticket Price, Highest Ticket Price.

4. Format the title with 14 point Times New Roman.

5. Format the column headings in bold, italic, 9 point and center them.

6. Use a thick border between each column.

7. Fill the range A1:E5 with light blue and change the color of the text in the range to dark blue.

8. Save the file as *Concerts.xls* and close it.

Assignments

1. Reformatting the *Income.xls* File

Open the Income.xls file. Move the data in cells B15:F22 to Sheet2. Format the data on Sheet1 using your own ideas for borders, shading, fonts, and so on. When finished, save the file as *Income 3.xls*.

2. Using AutoFormat

If you have Internet access, download *Revenues.xls* from www.awl.com/is/select/. If you are unable to download this file, ask your instructor how to obtain it. Experiment with different AutoFormats. Choose one of the formats you like and save the file as *Revenues2.xls*. Open *Revenues.xls* again and save it with another format that you like as *Revenues3.xls*. Open *Revenues.xls* and save it with another format that you like as *Revenues4.xls*.

Editing the Structure of a Worksheet and a Workbook

Think of yourself as an Excel architect. You design workbooks using the Excel "materials" — cells, columns, rows, and worksheets. When you want to edit the structure of a worksheet or a workbook, you have to request that materials be added to or removed from the file. Sometimes the design you want calls for different-sized materials or special materials — such as headers and footers. This project introduces you to the tools you'll need to modify the structure of a worksheet.

Objectives

After completing this project, you will be able to:

➤ **Insert, delete, and arrange worksheets**

➤ **Change the size of columns and rows**

➤ **Insert columns, rows, and cells**

➤ **Delete columns, rows, and cells**

➤ **Create headers and footers**

The Challenge

You have a workbook that contains March and April restaurant sales information that you have been preparing for the hotel manager, Mr. Gilmore.

You need to delete some information, add some information, make some adjustments in the columns and rows, and add a header and footer.

The Solution

You will begin your edits by deleting one of the worksheets, inserting a new worksheet, and rearranging worksheets. Then you will adjust the width of columns and the height of rows as needed. Next, you will insert and delete columns, rows, and cells, and, finally, you will add the headers and footers. Figure 4.1 shows the first worksheet in the workbook.

To obtain the files you need for this project, download them from the Addison Wesley Longman web site (http://www.awl.com/is/select/ or obtain them from your instructor.

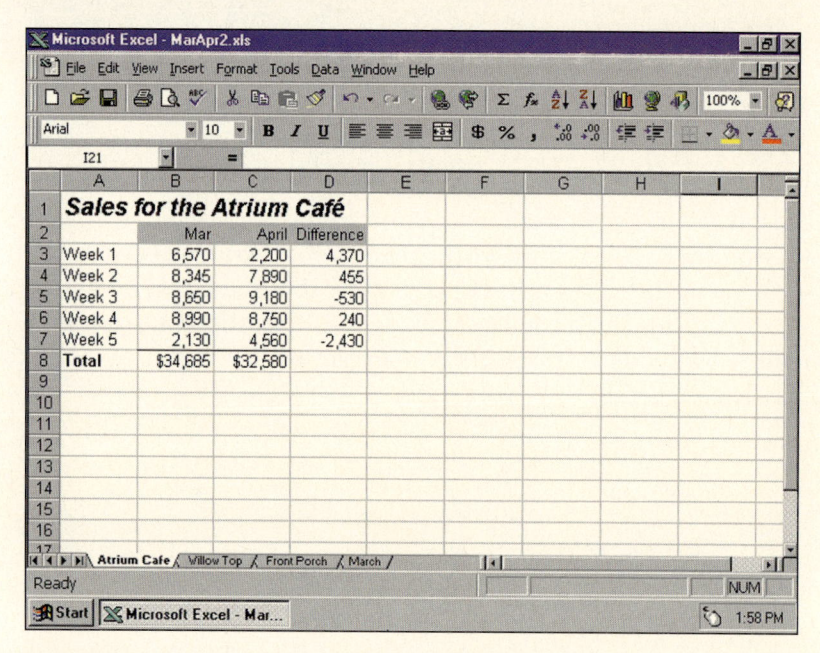

Figure 4.1

The Setup

So that your screen will match the illustrations and the tasks in this project will function as described, make sure that the Excel settings listed in Table 4.1 are selected on your computer. Because these are the default settings for the toolbars and view, you may not need to make any changes to your setup.

Table 4.1: Excel Settings

Location	Make these settings:
View, Toolbars	Deselect all toolbars except Standard and Formatting.
View	Use the Normal view and display the Formula Bar and Status Bar.

Inserting, Deleting, and Arranging Worksheets

As you remember (if you don't remember, just keep it to yourself and no one will be the wiser), a workbook starts out with three worksheets. You can add more worksheets or delete up to two of the three. You also can rearrange the order of worksheets.

TASK 1: TO INSERT AND DELETE PAGES:

1 Open *MarApr.xls.*

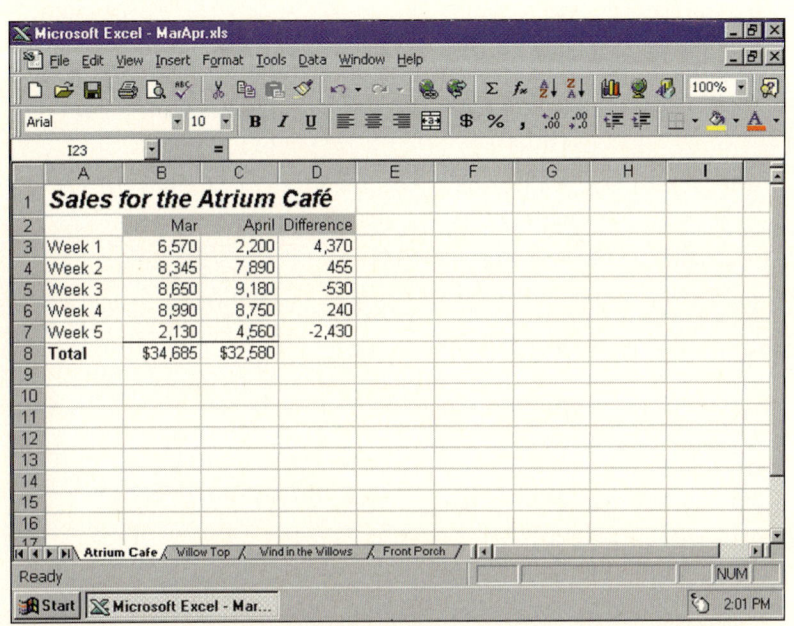

2 Click each worksheet tab to see each page of the workbook.

3 Right-click the tab for Wind in the Willows.

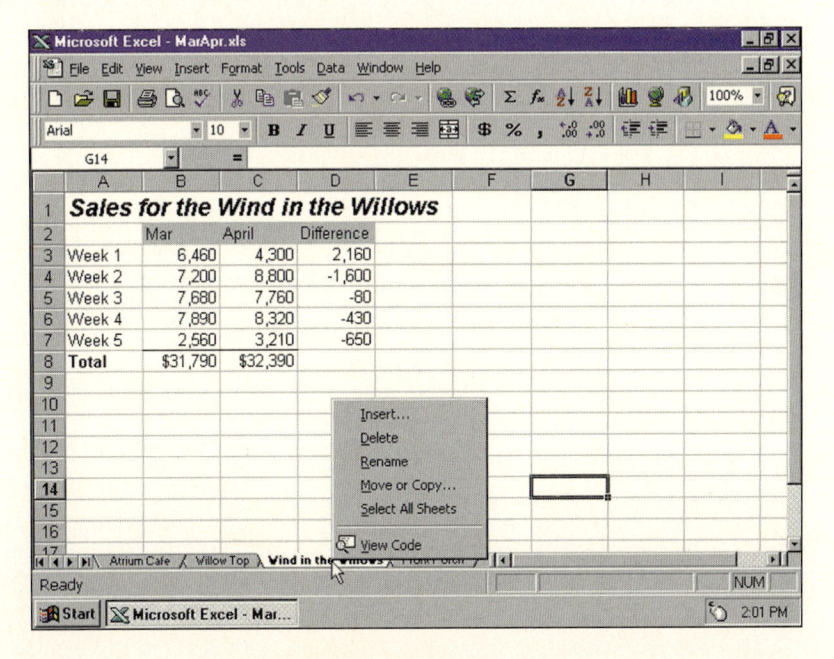

4 Choose Delete.

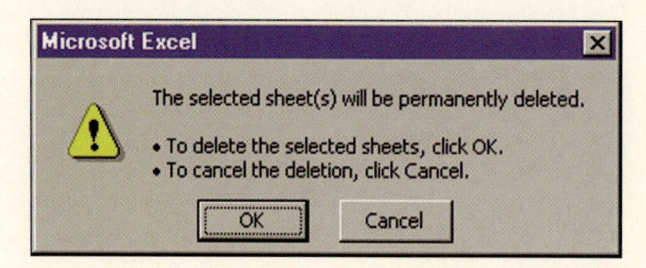

5 Click OK.

The worksheet is permanently deleted from the workbook, and no amount of clicking the Undo button will bring it back.

6 Right-click the Atrium Café tab and choose Insert.

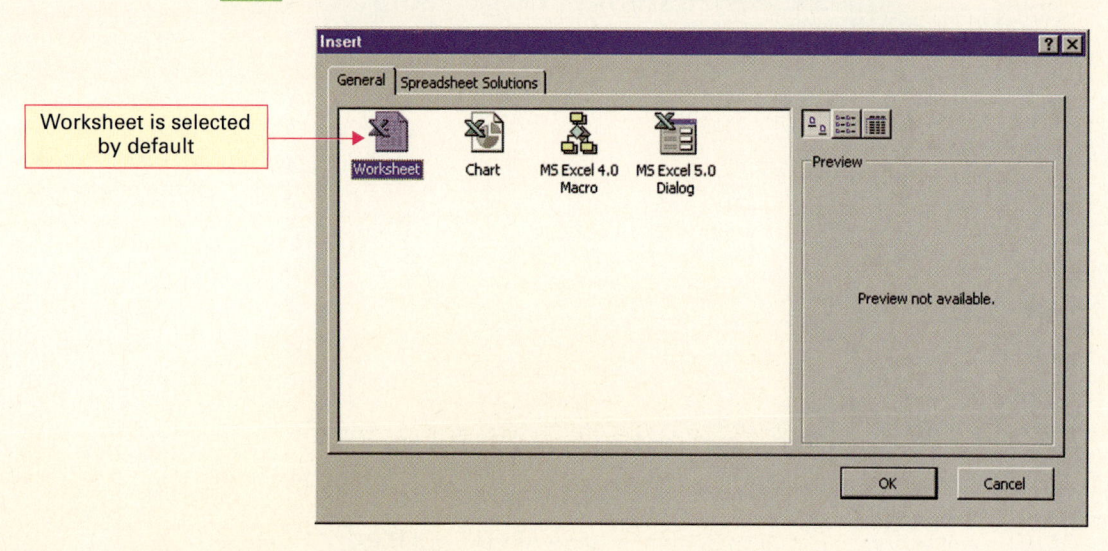

7 Click OK.

A new blank worksheet is inserted before the selected worksheet.

8 Rename the new worksheet **March**.

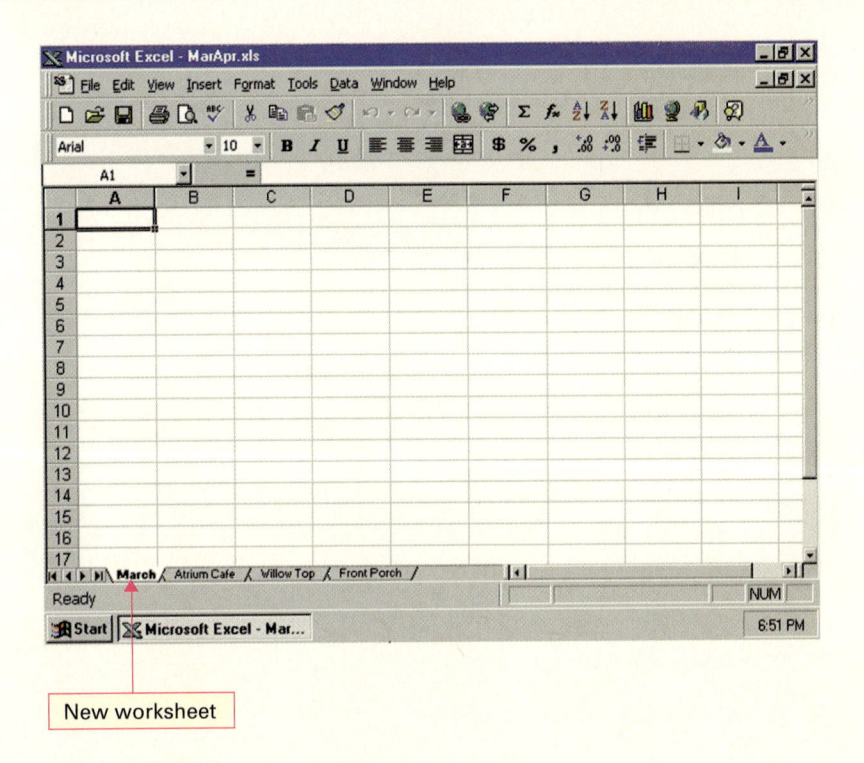

New worksheet

9 Drag the March tab to between the Atrium Café tab and the Willow Top tab, but don't release the mouse button yet.

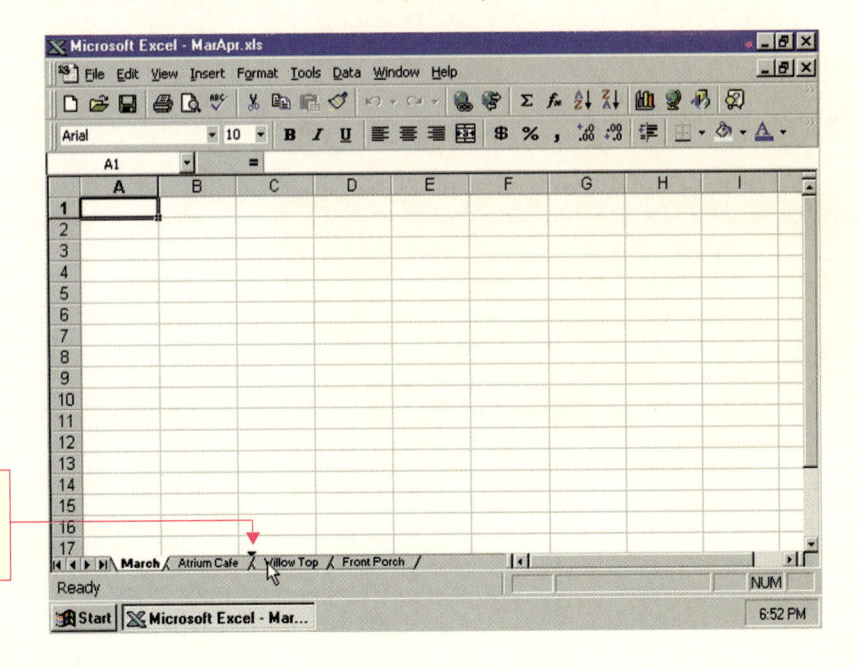

The black triangle marks the location where the new worksheet will be positioned

10 Continue dragging to the end of the tabs and then release the mouse button.

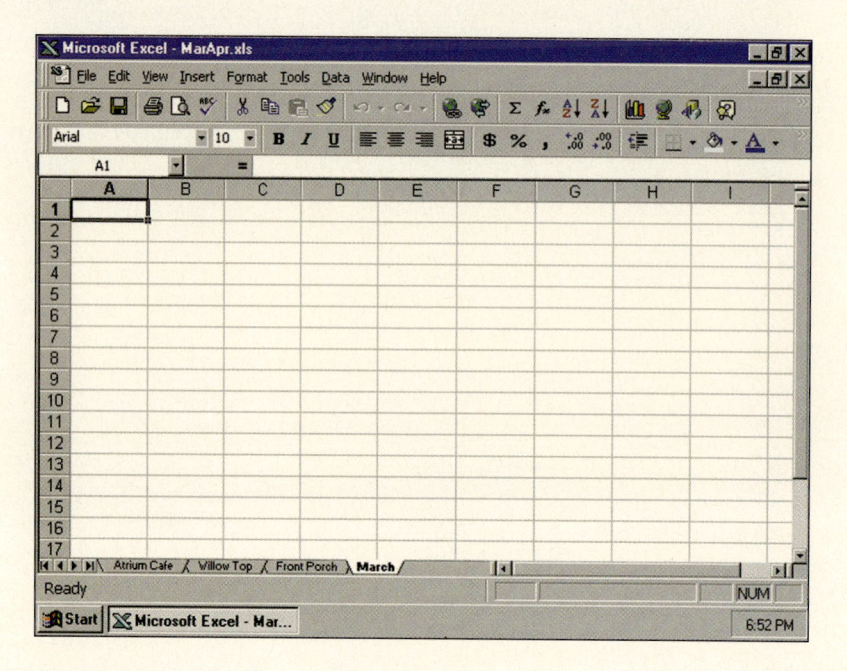

Changing the Size of Columns and Rows

When you create a new workbook, all the columns are the same width, and all the rows are the same height. When you add data to a worksheet, you often must change the row heights and column widths to accommodate the data. As you have already seen in a previous project, the height of a row increases or decreases automatically when you change the point size of the data; however, you may want to change the height of a row just to improve the spacing.

TASK 2: TO CHANGE THE WIDTH OF COLUMNS BY DRAGGING:

1 Type the following in the designated cells of the March worksheet:
A1: **March Sales**
A2: **Atrium Café**

> **Note** Excel will add the accent to the "e" in "café" automatically.

A3: **Willow Top Restaurant**
A4: **Front Porch Restaurant**

2   Point to the line that divides column letters A and B in the Column heading row.

The pointer changes to a double-headed arrow

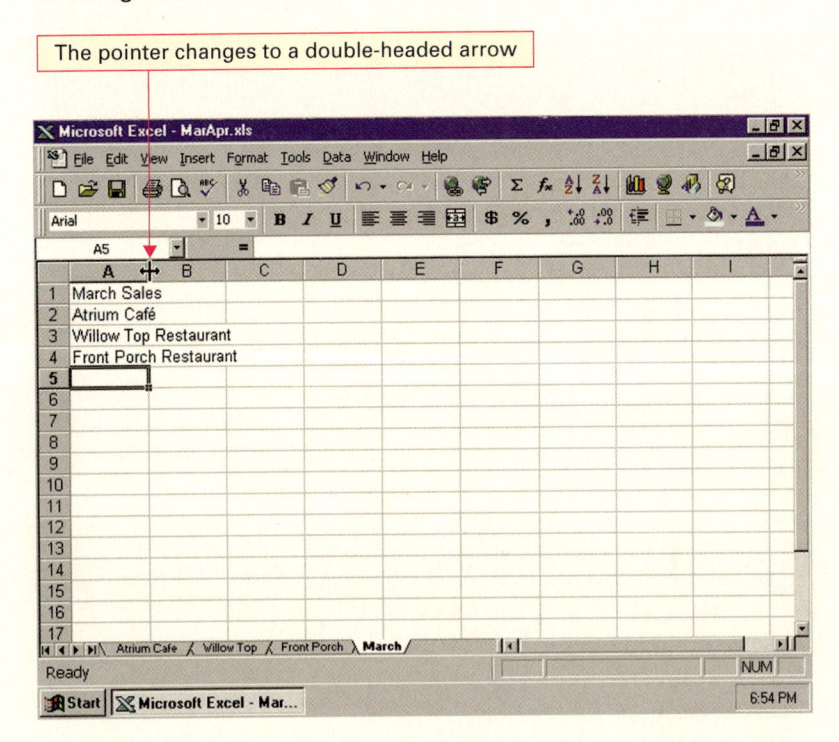

3   Drag the line to the right until the column is wide enough to hold the text.

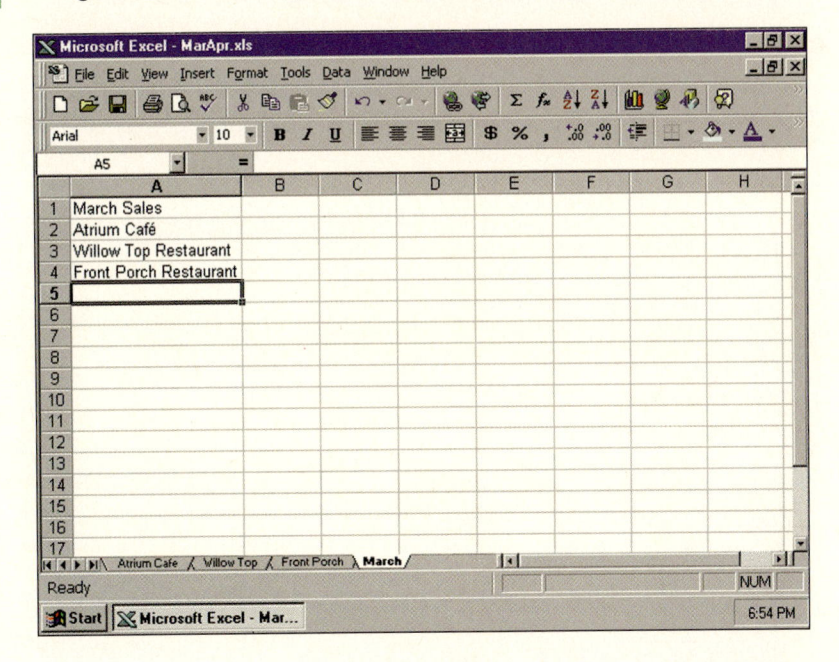

4 Drag the column until it is too wide as shown:

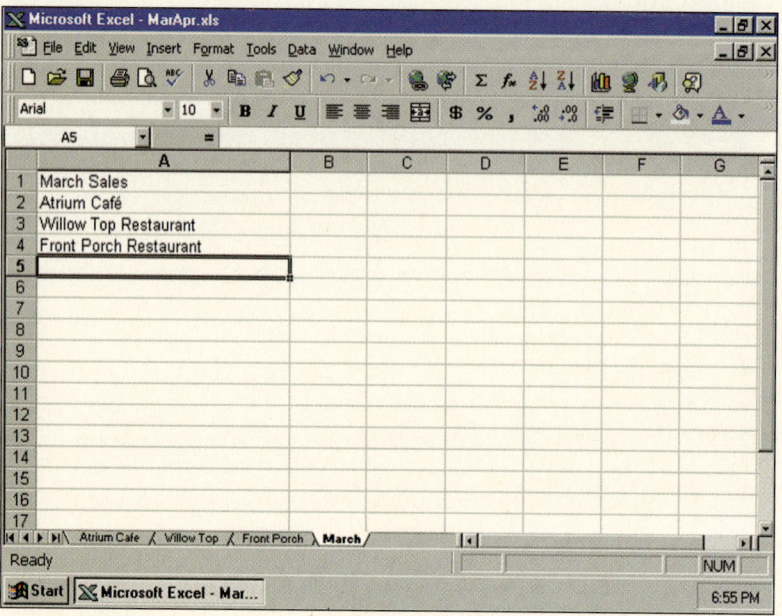

5 Type the following in the designated cells:
B2: **34685**
B3: **45240**
B4: **30835**

6 Drag the line between column letters B and C until column B is too wide as shown:

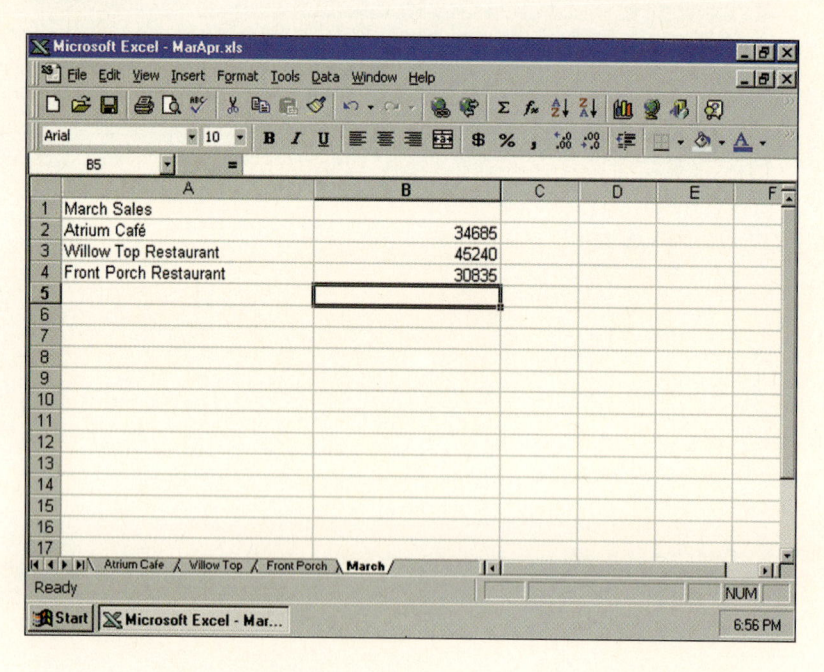

Using AutoFit

Another way to change the width of a column is to use AutoFit. ***AutoFit*** automatically adjusts columns to be just wide enough to accommodate the widest entry and can adjust the widths of several columns at once.

TASK 3: TO CHANGE THE WIDTH OF COLUMNS BY USING AUTOFIT:

1 Select columns A and B by dragging the mouse pointer through A and B at the top of the columns.
The columns are highlighted.

2 Choose Format, Column.

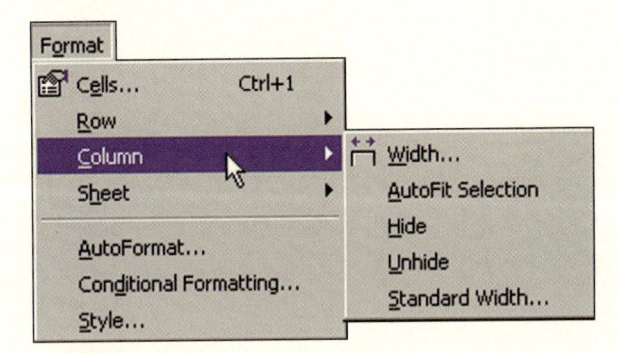

3 Choose AutoFit Selection.

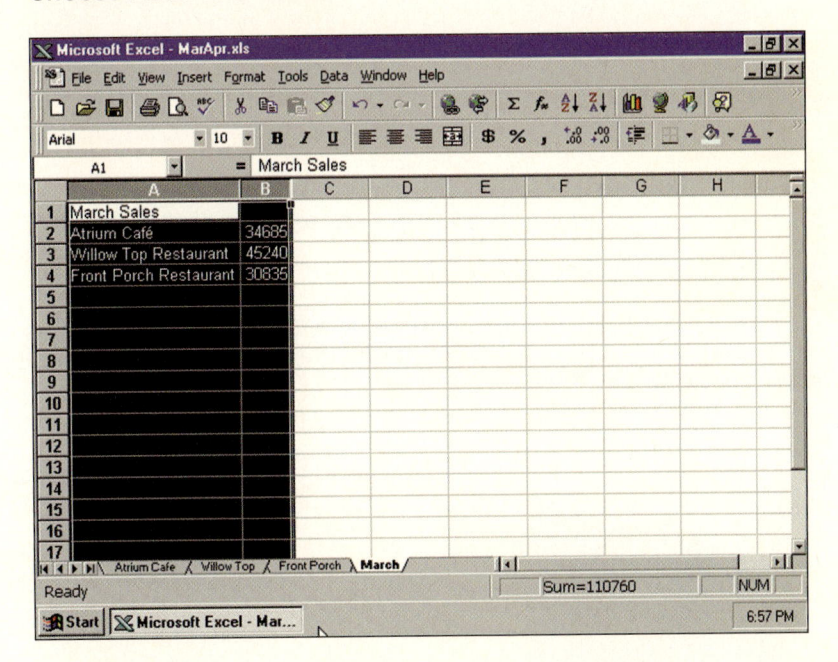

> **Tip** You can select multiple columns and double-click a line between the column letters to AutoFit the selections.

Adjusting Row Height

If you want to control the spacing in a worksheet, you can make rows taller or shorter by dragging them to the desired height.

TASK 4: TO CHANGE THE HEIGHT OF ROWS:

1 Point to the line that divides row numbers 1 and 2 in the row indicators column.

The pointer changes to a double-headed arrow →

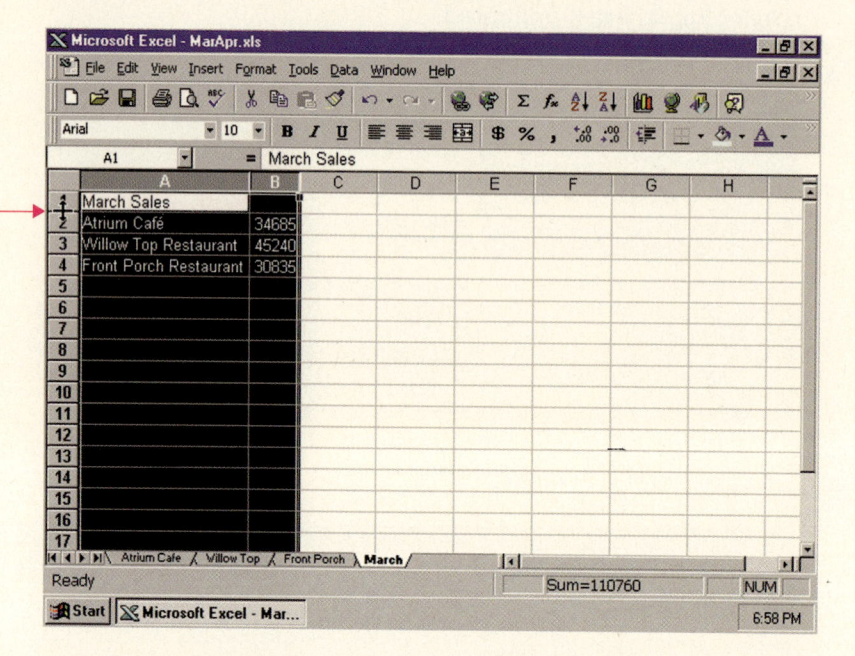

It doesn't matter if columns are selected when you change the row height because you don't have to select anything to change the height.

2 Drag down to make the row taller.

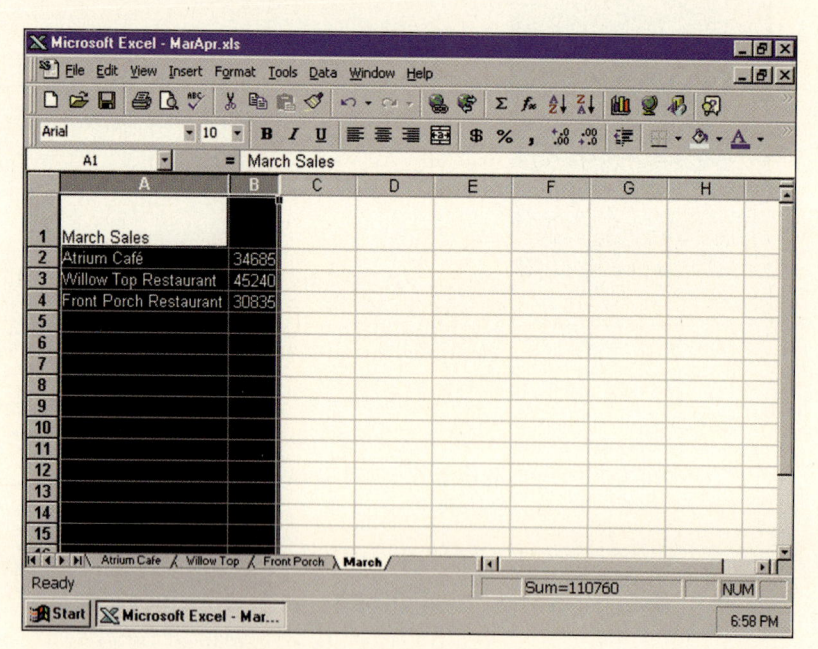

Tip You also can size rows with AutoFit. As you probably can guess, the command is under Format, Row or you can select the rows and double-click the line between the row numbers.

Inserting Columns, Rows, and Cells

When you insert a column, all the other columns move to the right to give the new column room. When you insert rows, all the other rows move down, and when you insert cells, the other cells move to the right or move down. Excel is so polite!

TASK 5: TO INSERT A COLUMN, A ROW, AND A CELL:

1   Click anywhere in column A.
The cell is selected.

2   Choose Insert.

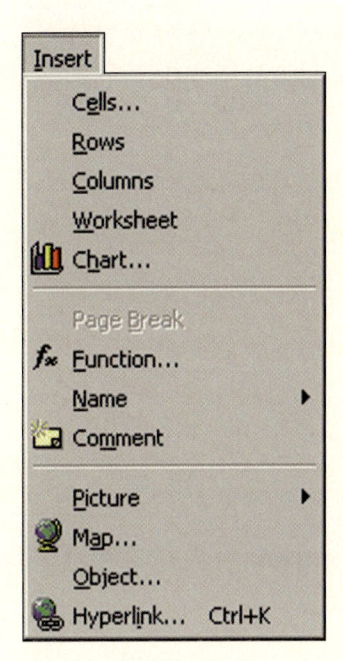

3   Choose Columns.

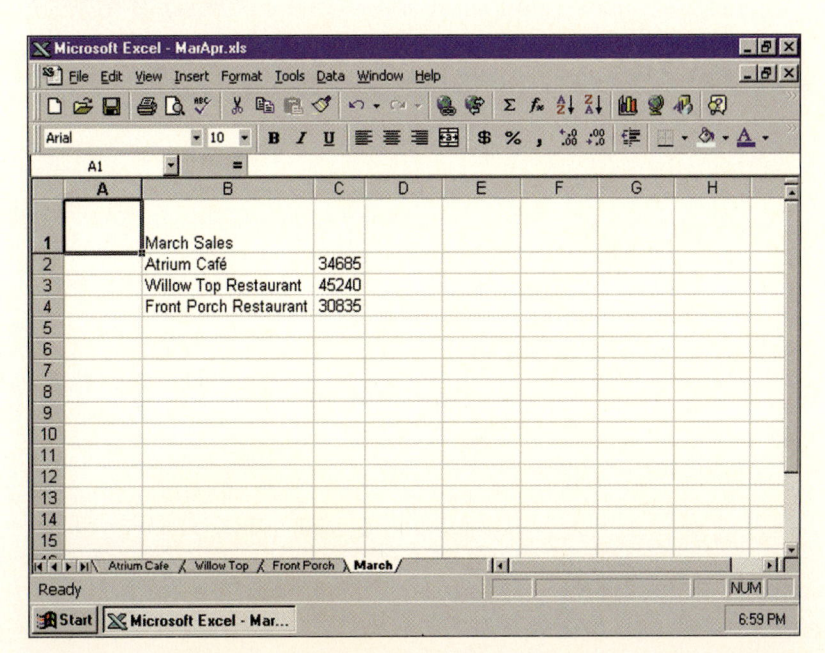

> **Tip** To insert multiple columns, select the number of columns you want to insert in the location where you want to insert them, and then choose Insert, Columns.

4 Click anywhere in row 2.
The cell is selected.

5 Choose Insert, Rows. (The new rows take on the dimensions of the row above.)

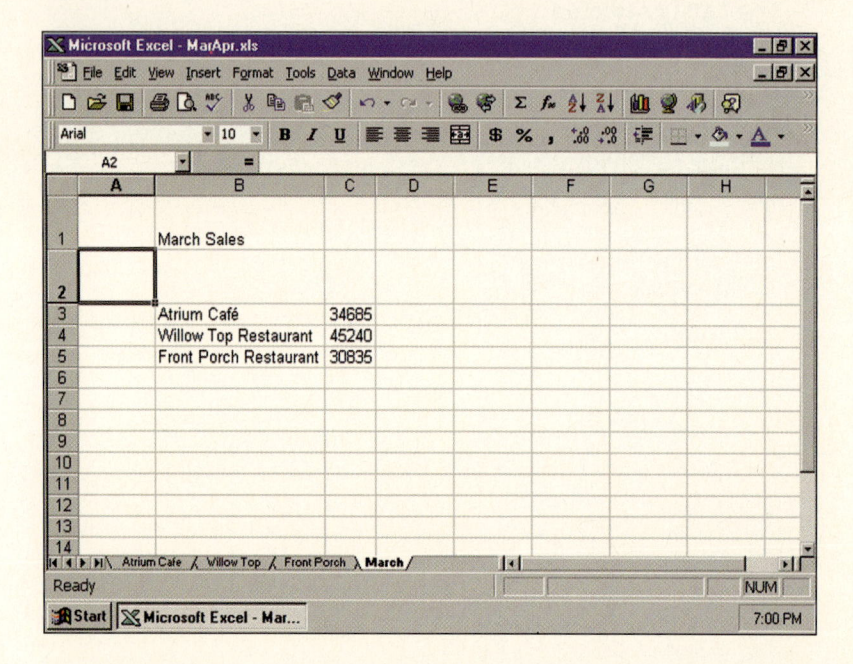

> **Tip** To insert multiple rows, select the number of rows you want to insert in the location where you want to insert them, and then choose Insert, Rows.

6 Type the following in the designated cells:
D1: **March Banquets**
D3: **D.A.R.**
D4: **L.W.V.**
D5: **B.S.A**
E3: **2560**
E4: **1500**
E5: **900**

7 Select cells D4 and E4.

8 Choose Insert, Cells.

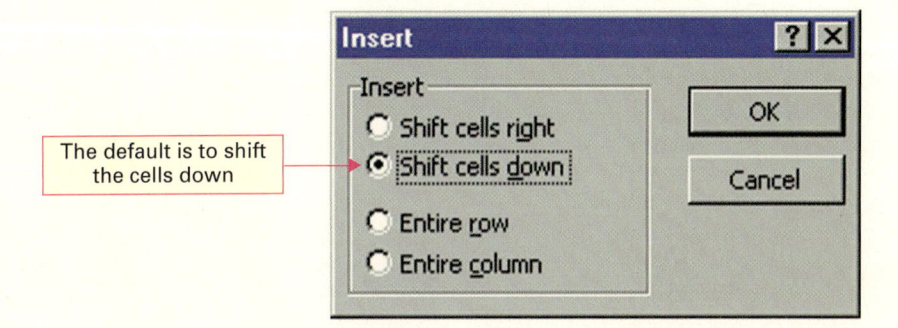

The default is to shift the cells down

9 Click OK.

If you had inserted a row instead of a cell, cells B4 and C4 would be blank

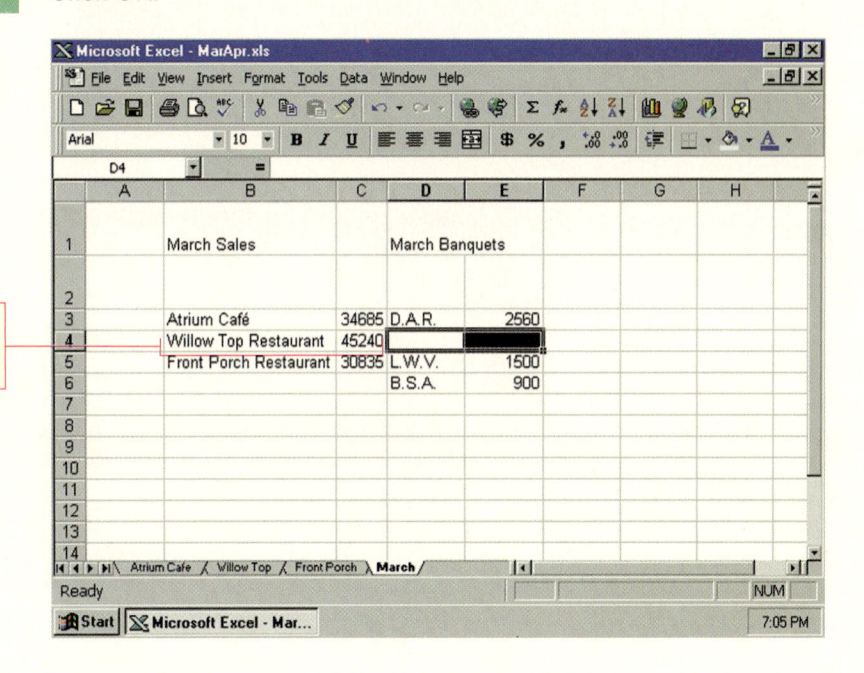

10   Type **G.S.A.** in cell D4, press ⊝, type **950**, and press ⟨ENTER⟩.

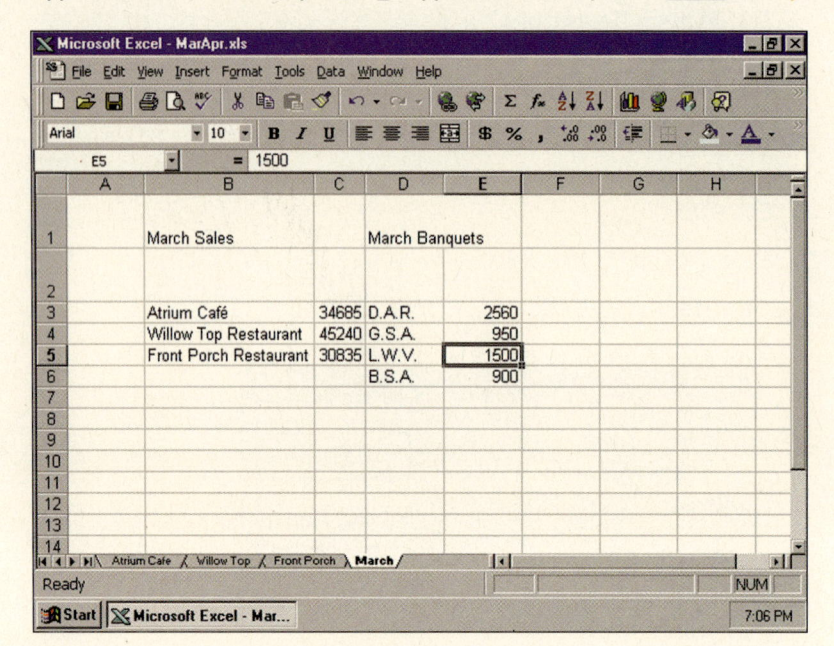

Deleting Columns, Rows, and Cells

When you delete columns, rows, or cells, you actually cut the space they occupy out of the worksheet. You don't just delete the data they contain.

> **Caution** When you delete a column or row, the entire column or the entire row is deleted. Before deleting, be sure that the column or row doesn't contain data in a location that is off screen.

TASK 6: TO DELETE A COLUMN, A ROW, AND A CELL:

1   Select row 2 by clicking the row 2 button — at the left of the row. The row is highlighted.

2   Choose Edit, Delete.

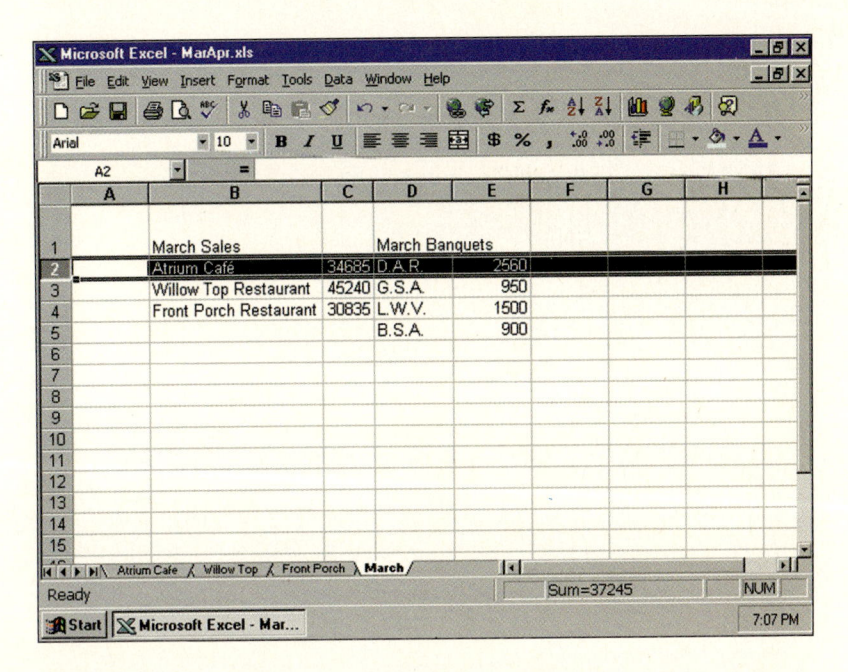

3 Select column A by clicking the column button A above the column. The column is highlighted.

4 Choose Edit, Delete.

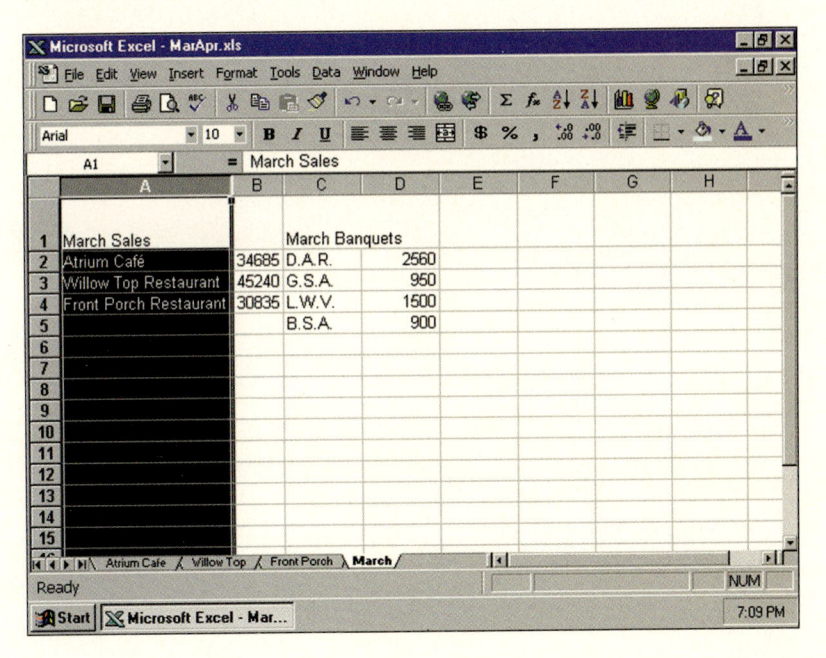

5 Select cells C2 and D2 and choose Edit, Delete.

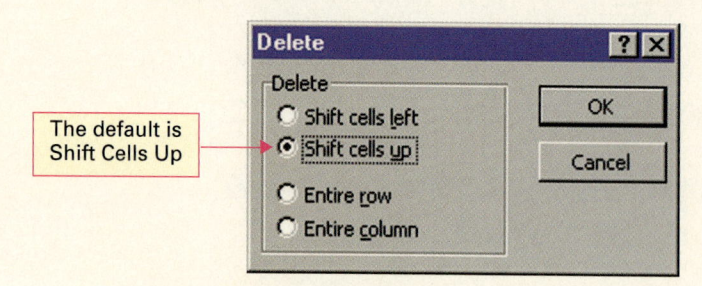

The default is Shift Cells Up

6 Click OK.

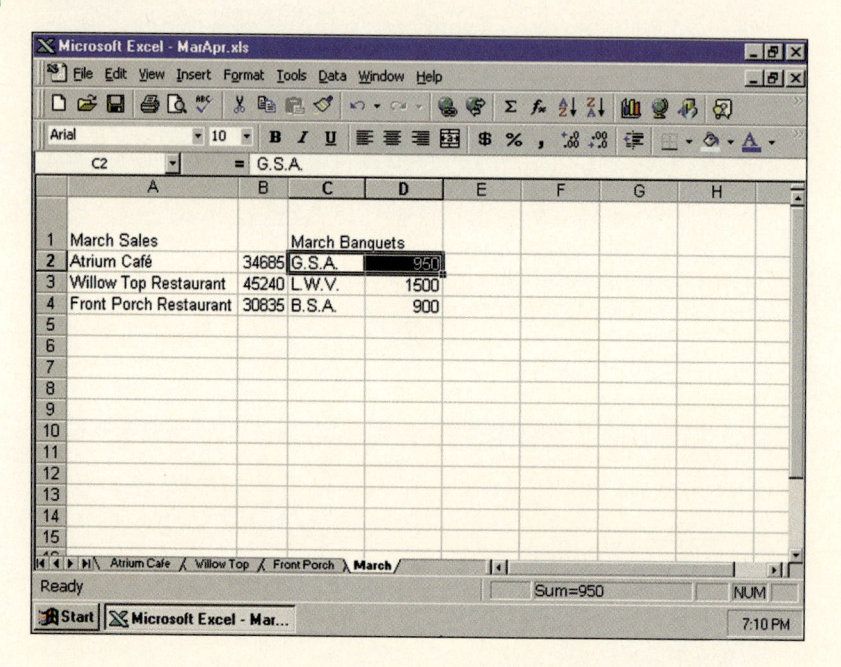

Creating Headers and Footers

A *header* prints at the top of every page of a worksheet, and a *footer* prints (you guessed it) at the bottom of every page. If the workbook has multiple worksheets, you can create headers and footers for each worksheet. A header or footer created for one worksheet doesn't print on any other worksheets in the same workbook.

TASK 7: TO CREATE A SIMPLE HEADER AND A FOOTER:

1   Choose View.

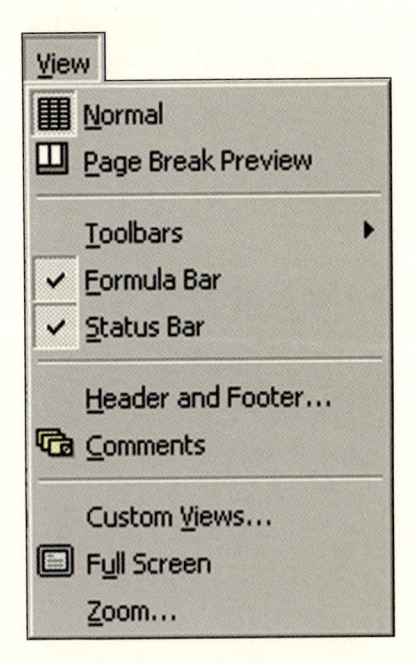

2   Choose Header and Footer.

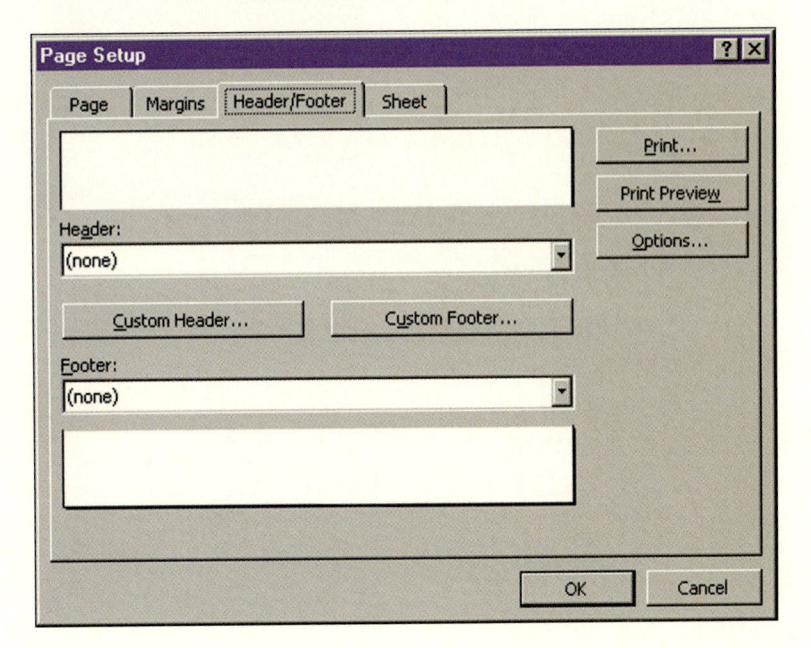

3 Click the down arrow for the Header list and choose Page 1.

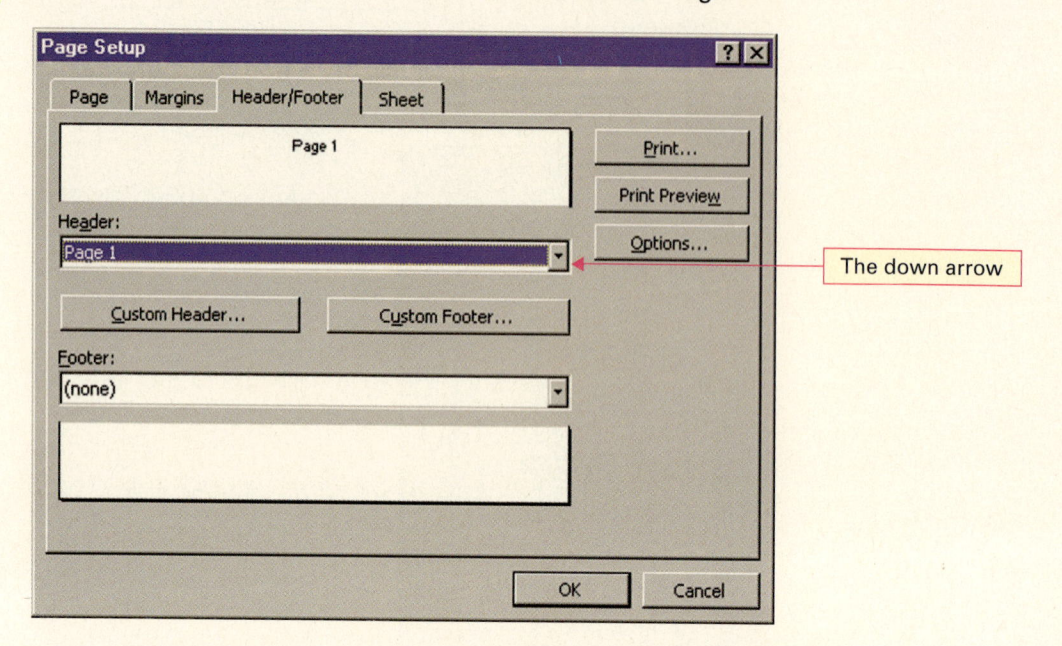

The down arrow

4 Click the down arrow for the Footer list and choose MarApr.xls.

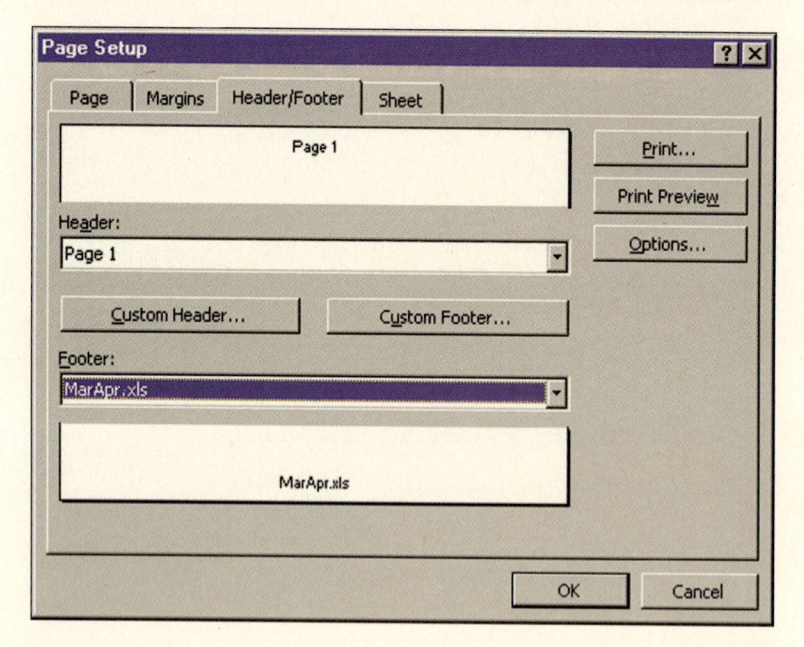

5 Click Print Preview.

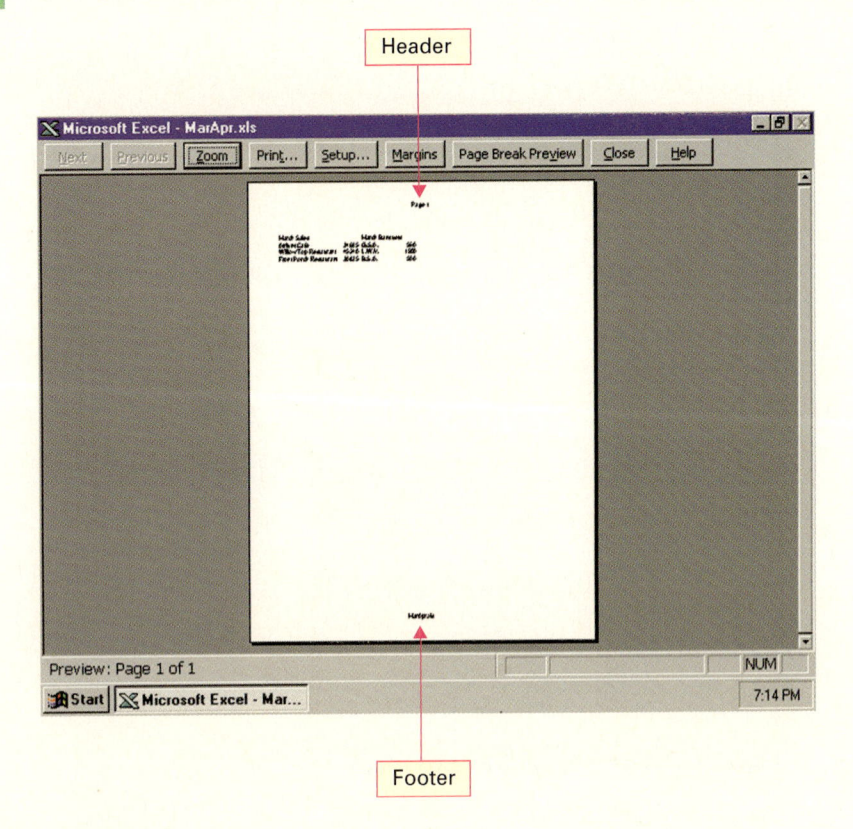

Header

Footer

6 Click Close.
The preview closes, and the worksheet displays in Normal view.

Creating a Custom Header and Footer

If you don't want to use the text supplied for a simple header or footer, you can create a custom header or footer and type the text that you want. Custom headers and footers are divided into three typing areas. The area on the left is left-justified, the area in the middle is centered, and the area on the right is right-justified.

TASK 8: TO CREATE A CUSTOM HEADER AND FOOTER:

1 Click the Atrium Café tab.
The Atrium Café worksheet displays.

2 Choose View, Headers and Footers. The Page Setup dialog box displays.

3 Click Custom Header.

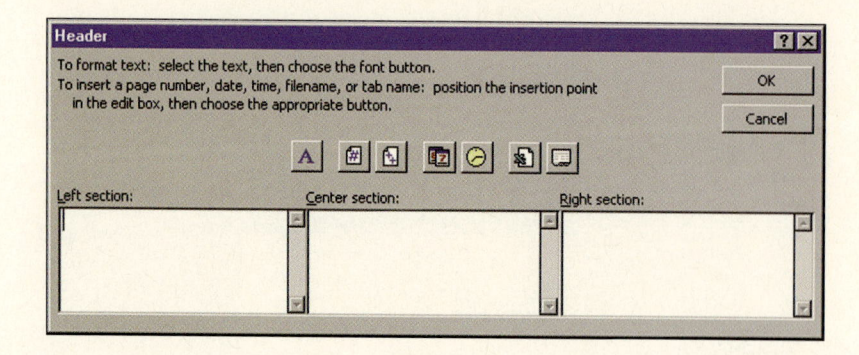

4 Type **Sales Report**, press (TAB) twice, and click the Date 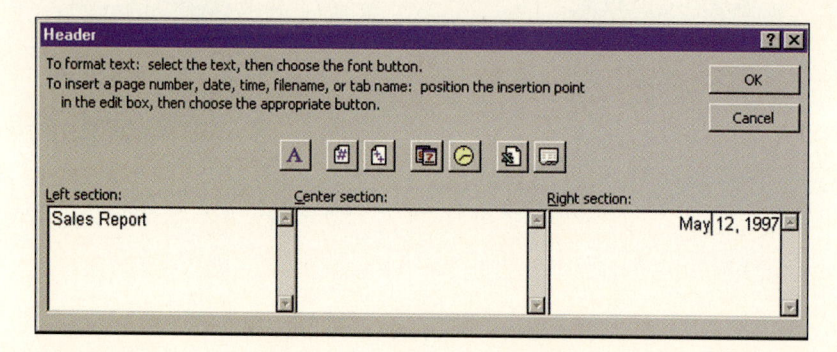 button. (When you click the Date button instead of typing the date, Excel adjusts the date to the current date each time the workbook is used.)

5 Click OK.
The Header dialog box closes and the Page Setup dialog box reappears.

6 Click Custom Footer.

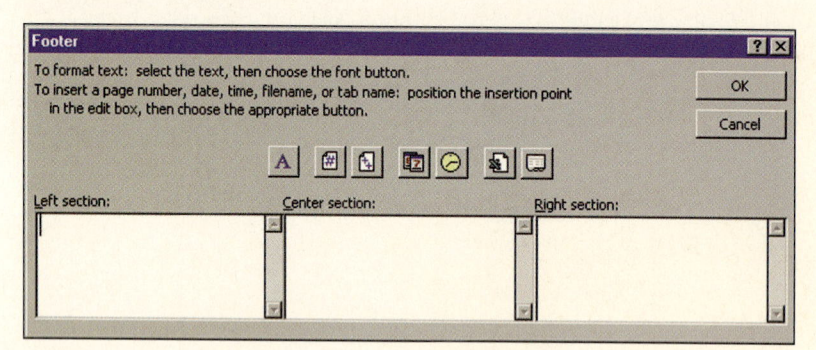

7 Press (TAB) and type **Prepared by Accounting**.

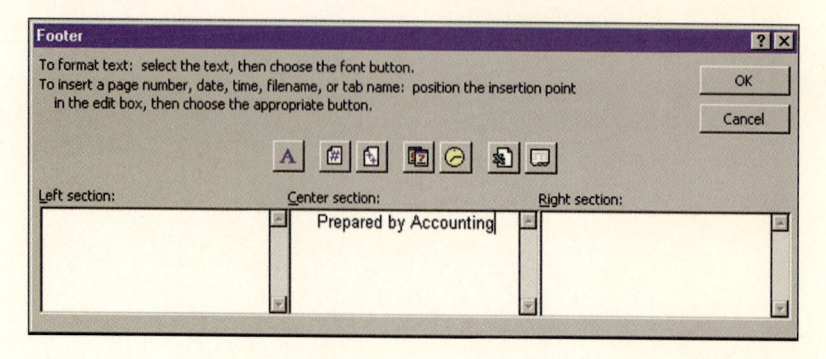

8 Click OK.
The Footer dialog box closes.

9 Click Print Preview.

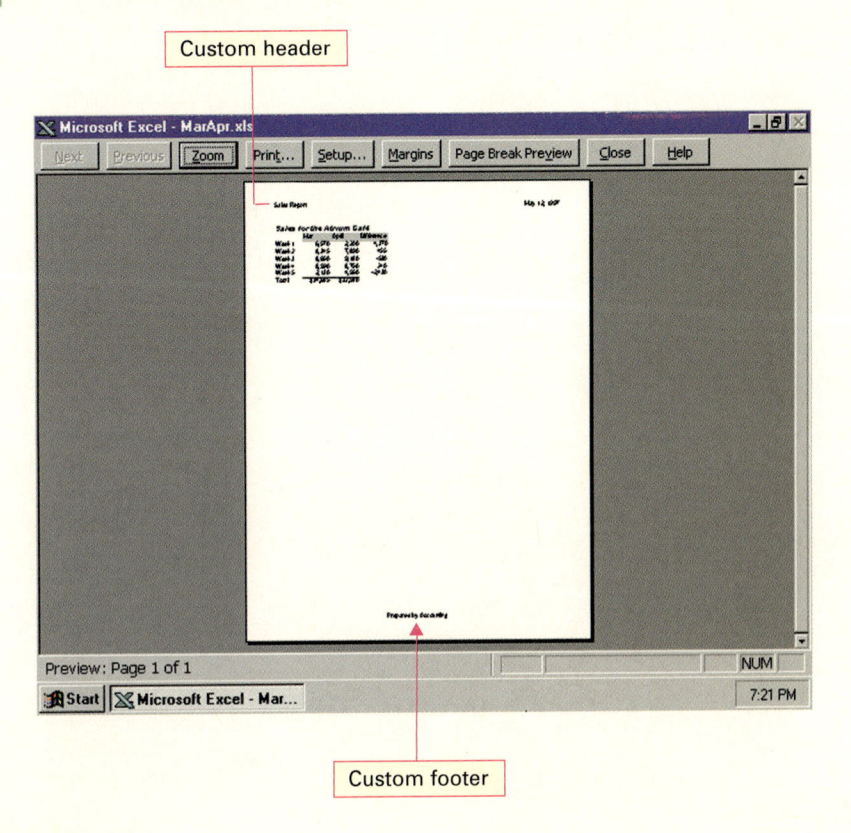

Custom header

Custom footer

10 Click Close.
The Print Preview closes, and the worksheet displays in Normal view.

The Conclusion

Save the worksheet as *MarApr2.xls* and close the file.

Summary and Exercises

Summary

- You can insert and delete worksheets, as well as rearrange them.
- You can change the width of columns and the height of rows.
- You can insert columns, rows, and cells.
- You can delete columns, rows, and cells.
- You can create a header that prints at the top of the page and a footer that prints at the bottom of a page. Headers and footers do not appear on screen in Normal view.

Key Terms and Operations

Key Terms	Operations
AutoFit	change the height of a row
footer	change the width of a column
header	create a footer
	create a header
	delete a cell
	delete a column
	delete a row
	delete a worksheet
	insert a cell
	insert a column
	insert a row
	insert a worksheet
	move a worksheet

Study Questions

Multiple Choice

1. A header prints at the
   a. top of every page in a workbook.
   b. bottom of every page in a workbook.
   c. top of every page in a worksheet.
   d. bottom of every page in a worksheet.

2. When you delete a column,
   a. the data in the column is deleted but the cells remain in the worksheet.
   b. the data in the column is deleted and so are the cells.
   c. the column is really just hidden.
   d. the column is moved to the end of the worksheet.

3. When you insert a cell, the other cells move
   a. down.
   b. to the left.
   c. to the right.
   d. down or to the right, as specified by the user.

4. A footer prints at the
   a. top of every page in a workbook.
   b. bottom of every page in a workbook.
   c. top of every page in a worksheet.
   d. bottom of every page in a worksheet.

5. AutoFit can adjust the width of
   a. only one column at a time.
   b. only a row.
   c. columns or rows.
   d. the page.

6. A custom header
   a. is divided into three typing areas.
   b. is created by choosing Format, Header and Footer.
   c. isn't visible in Print Preview mode.
   d. uses default data, such as the page number or the name of the file.

7. If you delete a cell,
   a. the data is deleted.
   b. the cell is deleted and the data displays in the next cell.
   c. the data and the cell are deleted.
   d. None of the above.

8. When you delete a cell, the other cells move
   a. up.
   b. down.
   c. to the left.
   d. up or to the left, as specified by the user.

9. When you drag to change the column width, the pointer displays as
   a. a four-headed arrow.
   b. an arrow.
   c. a two-headed arrow.
   d. a hand.

10. To insert a column, first
    a. select the column where you want the new column to go.
    b. click in the column where you want the new column to go.
    c. A or B
    d. None of the above.

Short Answer

1. How do you insert multiple rows?

2. How do you insert multiple columns?

3. What is a custom header?

4. How do you delete a worksheet?

5. How do you delete a row?

6. How do you delete a cell?

7. How do you create a header with the filename in the center?

8. If the row height adjusts automatically, why would you need to change the height of a row?

9. How do you move a worksheet?

10. How do you see a header or footer without actually printing the worksheet?

For Discussion

1. When would it be an advantage to use AutoFit instead of dragging columns to change the width?

2. Discuss the advantages of using a custom header or footer.

3. Describe a circumstance in which it would be preferable to insert a cell instead of a row.

4. What precautions should you take before deleting a column or a row?

Review Exercises

1. Editing the MarApr2 Workbook
In this exercise you will enhance the worksheet and create a footer.

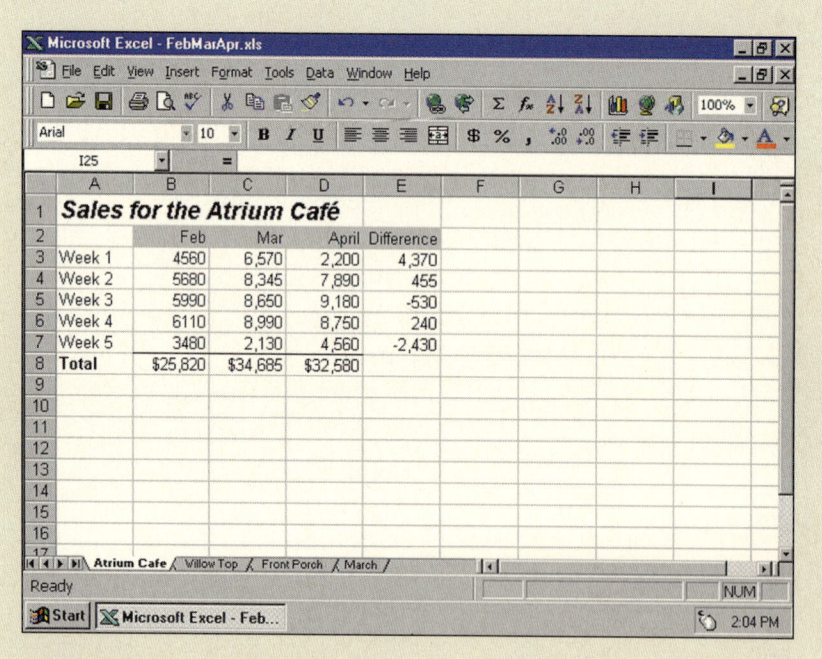

Figure 4.2

1. Open *MarApr2.xls* and click the Atrium Café tab, if necessary.

2. Insert a column before column B and type this information:

   B2: **Feb**

   B3: **4560**

   B4: **5680**

   B5: **5990**

   B6: **6110**

   B7: **3480**

   B8: **=SUM(B3:B7)**

3. Apply a gray fill to cell B2, apply a border to the bottom of cell B7, and format cell B8 with a Currency format (no decimal places) and remove the bold.

4. Create a footer for the Willow Top worksheet that says "Located in The Grande Hotel" and center the footer.

5. Save the file as *FebMarApr.xls* and close it.

2. Creating a Sales Workbook for the Sandwich Shops and Snack Bars

In this exercise, you will create a workbook that can be used to track the sales of all the sandwich shops and snack bars at The Willows Resort.

1. Download the file *Willows.doc* from the Addison Wesley Longman web site (http://www.aw.com./is/select), or ask your instructor for this file. Open the file and find the list of sandwich shops and snack bars.

2. Create a workbook with a worksheet for each of the nine shops and name each worksheet with the name of the shop.

3. Type a title on each worksheet that says "Sales for *xxx*," where *xxx* is the name of the sandwich shop or snack bar. In column A, starting in cell A3, list the weeks in the month (Week 1, Week 2, and so on) and the word "Total" (as in Figure 4.2). In cells B2, C2, and D2, list the first three months of the year (Jan, Feb, and Mar).

4. Create a footer with a centered page number for each worksheet.

5. Save the file as *ShopSales.xls*.

Assignments

1. Creating a Banquet Workbook

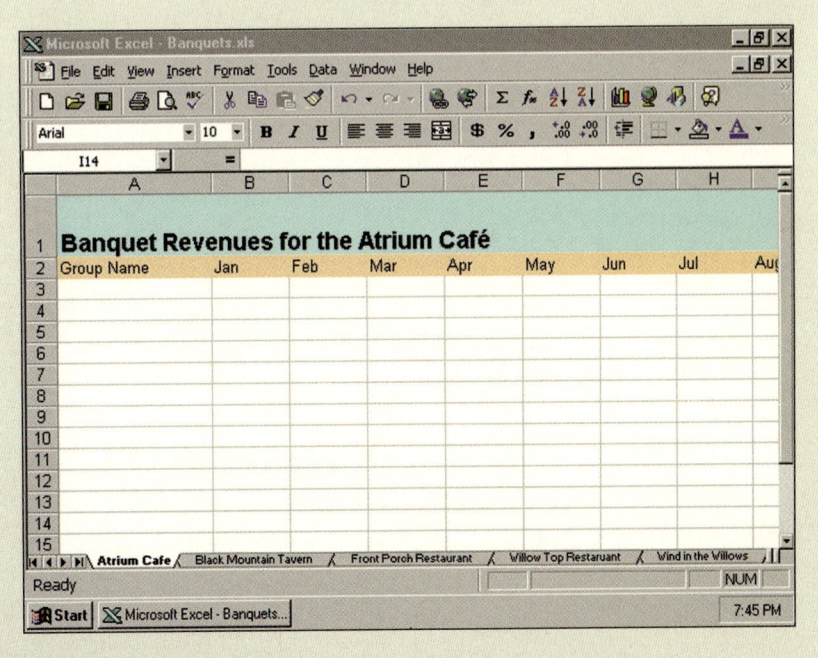

Figure 4.3

Create a workbook with five worksheets and name each worksheet as follows: Atrium Café, Willow Top Restaurant, Wind in the Willows, Front Porch Restaurant, and Black Mountain Tavern. Arrange the worksheets in alphabetical order. Add the text and formatting shown in Figure 4.3 to all the worksheets. (Remember, you can enter the same data on multiple worksheets at the same time.) Save the file as *Banquets.xls* and close it.

2. Creating a Shopping List (Optional Exercise)

Take an international shopping trip via the Planet Shopping Network (http://www.planetshopping.com). Create a workbook that lists the items you would like to buy, their prices (including any shipping, handling, taxes, and duties), and their Web addresses. Use the SUM formula to total the prices and other costs. Create a worksheet for each shopping category (apparel, books, music, jewelry, automobiles, and so on). Save the workbook as *ShopTilYouDrop.xls*.

Creating a More Complex Workbook

Well, you're getting pretty good at this, so you're probably ready for something more challenging. This project provides both challenge and fun.

Objectives

After completing this project, you will be able to:

➤ **Copy data from another workbook**

➤ **Sort data**

➤ **Enter formulas with relative references**

➤ **Use headings in formulas**

➤ **Enter formulas with absolute references**

➤ **Create and modify a chart**

The Challenge

Ruth Lindsey, the manager of most of the gift shops at The Willows Resort, would like for you to work on an inventory of the ten top selling items and create some charts for the first quarter sales.

The Solution

You will copy data from an existing workbook into the inventory workbook, enter new data, and create formulas to calculate the number of items that you need to order and the wholesale prices of the items. Additionally, you will create a chart for the first quarter sales and a chart for the January sales. Figure 5.1 shows the results.

You can download the files needed for this project form the Addison Wesley Longman web site (http://www.aw.com./is/select) or you can obtain them from your instructor.

The Setup

So that your screen will match the illustrations in this chapter and to ensure that all the tasks in this project will function as described, you should set up Excel as described in Table 5.1. Because these are the default settings for the toolbars and view, you may not need to make any changes to your setup.

Table 5.1: Excel Settings

Location	Make these settings:
View, Toolbars	Deselect all toolbars except Standard and Formatting.
View	Use the Normal view and display the Formula Bar and Status Bar.

Copying Data from Another Workbook

You have copied data from one range to another on the same worksheet, and you have copied data from one worksheet to another in the same workbook. Now you will copy data from one workbook to another. The procedure is very similar to what you have already learned.

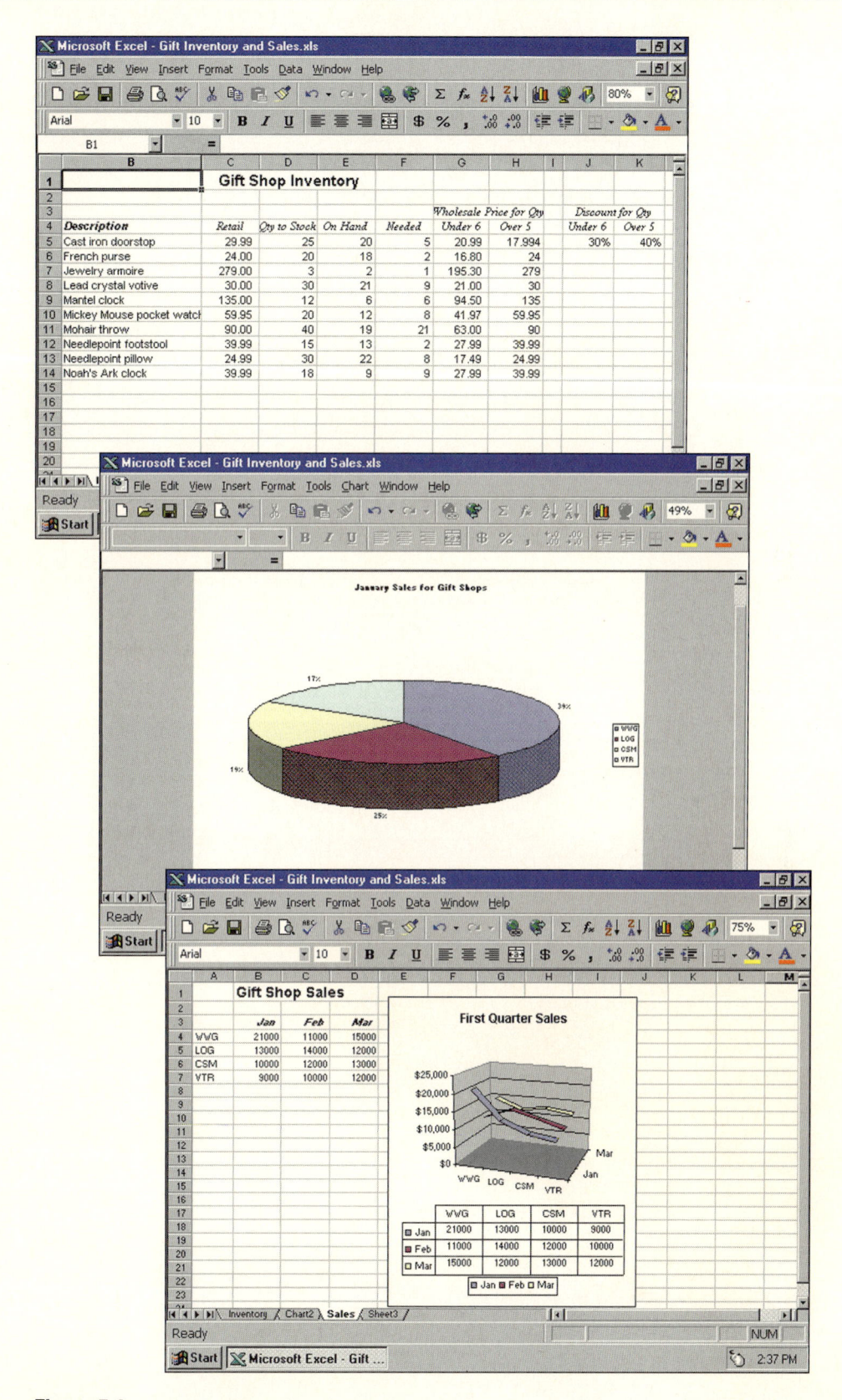

Figure 5.1

TASK 1: TO COPY DATA FROM ANOTHER WORKBOOK:

1 Open *Giftinv.xls.*

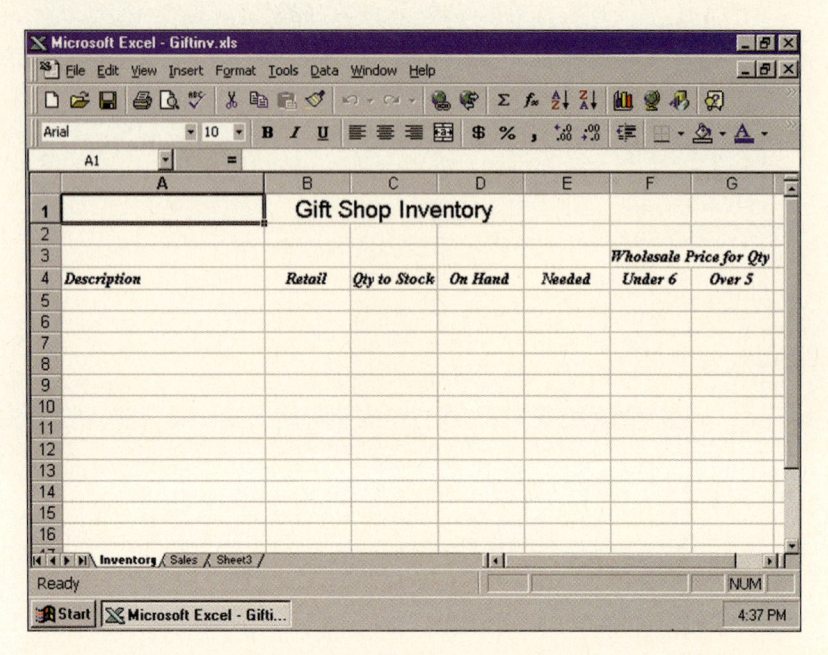

2 Open *TopTen.xls* and select the range A4:B13.

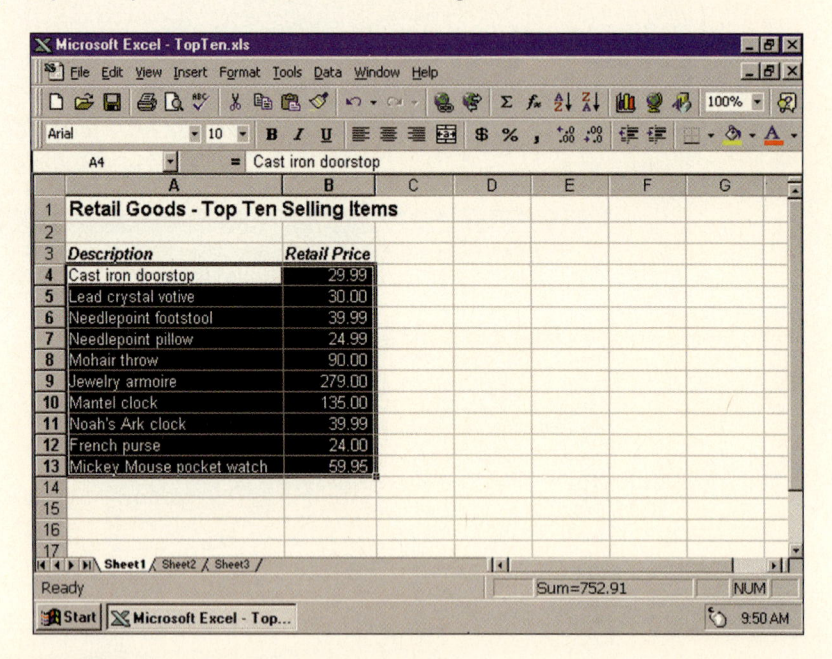

3 Click [icon].
The data is copied to the Clipboard.

4 Choose Window, Giftinv.xls.
The *Giftinv.xls* workbook displays.

5   Click in cell A5 and click 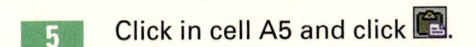.

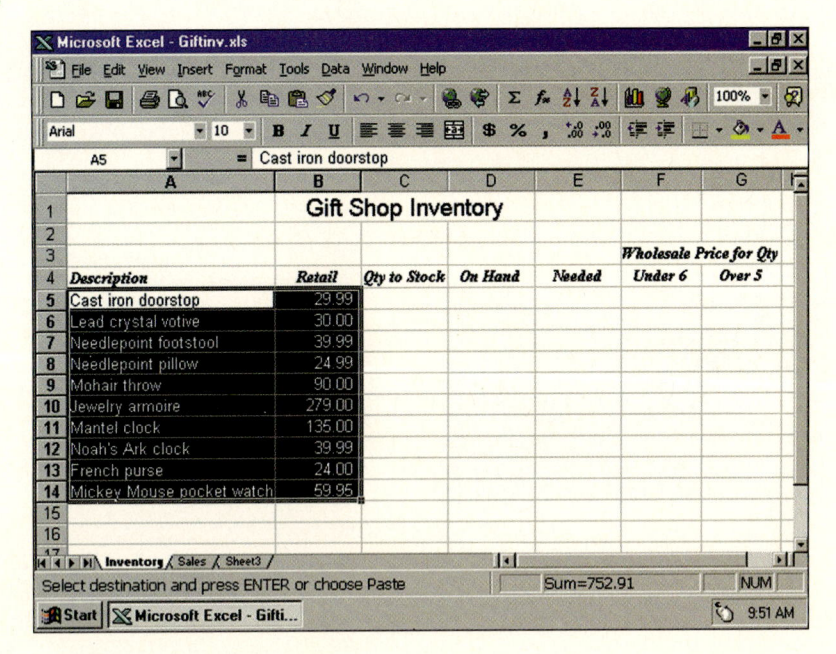

6   Choose Window, TopTen.xls.
The *TopTen.xls* workbook displays.

7   Click ☒ in the menu bar.
The *TopTen.xls* workbook closes, and the Giftinv.xls workbook displays.

Sorting Data

You can sort columns of data in an Excel worksheet in ascending order or descending order. The Standard toolbar has a button for each function.

TASK 2: TO SORT DATA:

1   Make sure that the range A5:B14 is still selected.
When you sort data, you must be careful to select all the columns that should be included in the sort. When selecting the rows to include, don't include the row with the column headings.

2 Click the Sort Ascending 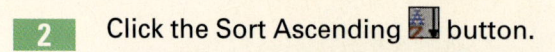 button.

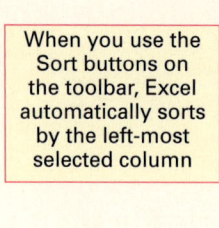

When you use the Sort buttons on the toolbar, Excel automatically sorts by the left-most selected column

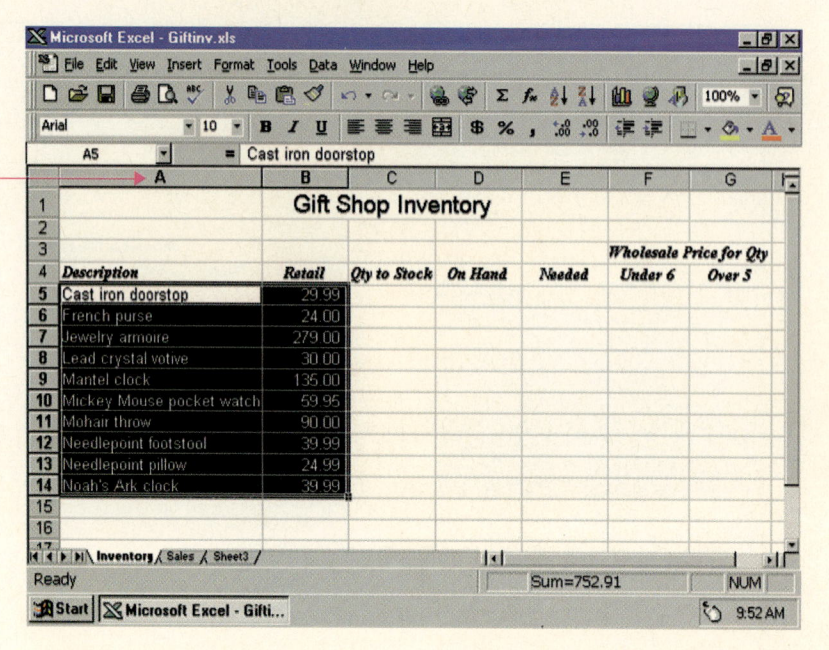

Tip If you want to sort a range by any column other than the first column, you must use the Sort command on the Data menu. This command displays a dialog box that allows you to specify the column you want to sort on and the order of the sort. You also can specify two other columns to sort on after the first column is sorted. Check it out. Choose Data, Sort to see the dialog box.

Entering Formulas with Relative References

All the formulas you have used so far have included cell addresses that are relative references. A *relative reference* is an address that Excel automatically changes when the formula is copied to another location. For example, if the formula =A1+A2 is in cell A3 and you copy it to cell B3, Excel changes the formula in column B to refer to the cells in column B, and the formula becomes =B1+B2. Generally, this is precisely what you want, and you are happy that Excel can make such intelligent decisions on its own.

Perhaps you are wondering how this works. Here's the scoop: Excel doesn't interpret a relative cell address in a formula as the actual cell address but rather as a location relative to the location of the formula. For example, Excel interprets the formula =A1+A2 in cell A3 as "Add the cell that is two rows above the formula in the same column to the cell that is one row above the formula in the same column." Therefore, when you copy the formula to any other column, the formula will add the cells that are two rows and one row above the location of the formula.

TASK 3: TO ENTER AND COPY A FORMULA WITH RELATIVE ADDRESSES:

1 Enter the following data in the *Qty to Stock* column and the *On Hand* column so that you can write a formula to calculate the value for the *Needed* column.

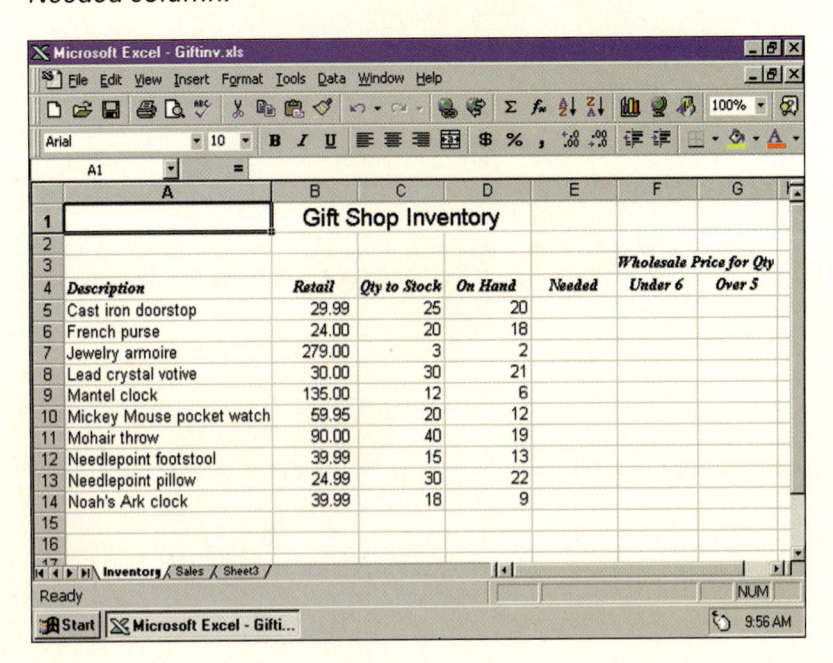

2 Click in cell E5, type **=C5−D5**, and press ⟨ENTER⟩.

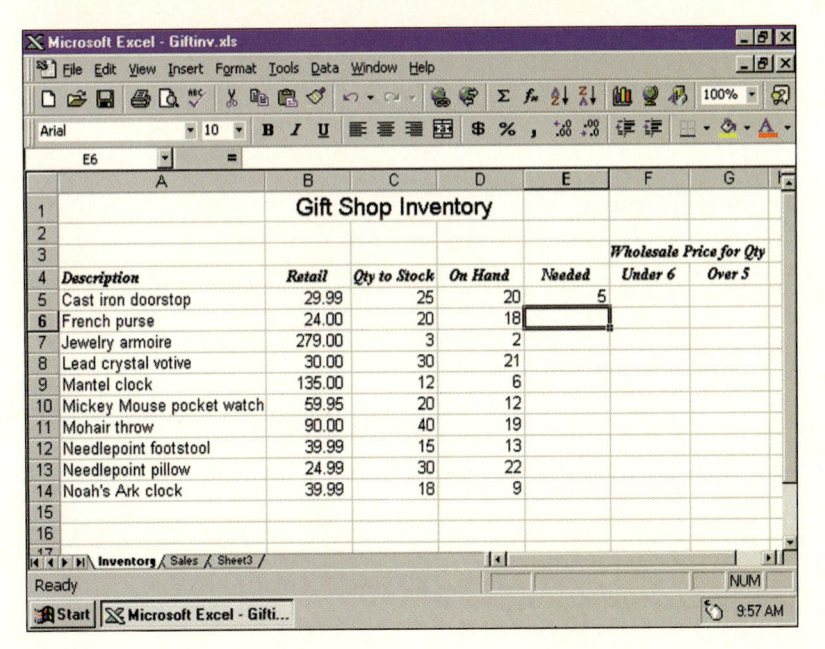

3 Copy cell E5 to the range E6:E8.

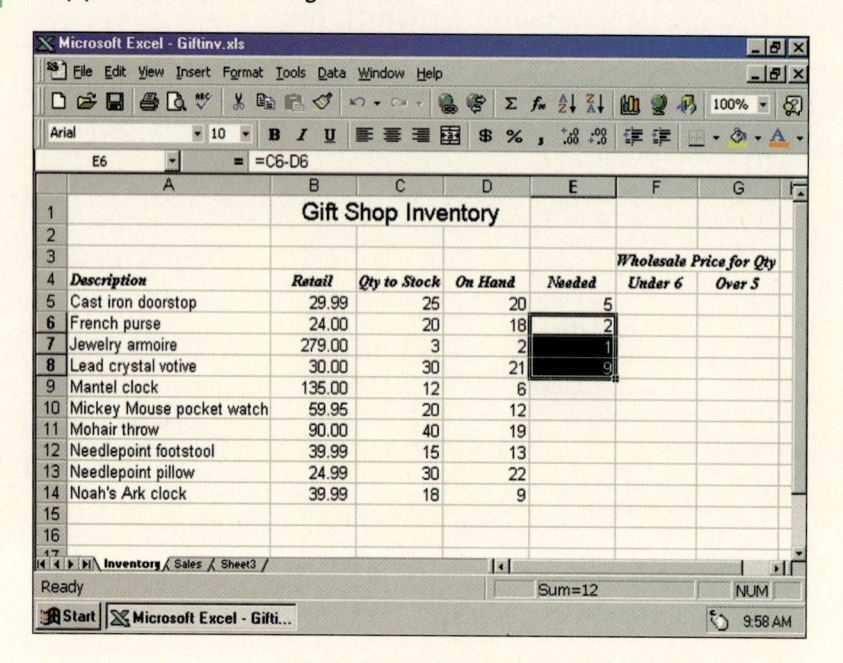

4 Click in cell E6 and notice the formula in the formula bar.

Excel changed the formula from =C5−D5 to =C6−D6

Using Headings in Formulas

Using headings in formulas instead of cell addresses is a new feature in Excel 97. The *headings* feature is helpful in two ways: when you create a formula, you can think in logical terms (such as "quantity times cost") and you can easily recognize the purpose of the formula. When you see the formula "Quantity*Cost," you know immediately what it does, but the formula A1*B1 gives you very little information.

TASK 4: TO ENTER A FORMULA THAT USES HEADINGS:

1 Click in cell E9, type **=qty to stock−on hand**, and press ⏎ENTER.
The cell displays the correct calculation.

> **Tip** You do not have to capitalize the headings in formulas.

2 Copy cell E9 to the range E10:E14.
The range also displays the correct calculations relative to the rows.

3 Click in cell E10 and look at the formula in the formula bar.
The formula in cell E10 is the same as in E9.

Entering Formulas with Absolute References

As you have already seen, when formulas with relative references are copied, the cell addresses change appropriately; however, sometimes formulas refer to a cell or range that should never be changed when the formula is copied. To prevent the cell or range address from changing, you must make the address an *absolute reference*. An absolute reference is denoted with the dollar sign symbol, as in A1.

TASK 5: TO ENTER AND COPY A FORMULA WITH AN ABSOLUTE REFERENCE:

1 Scroll the worksheet so that columns B through J are visible.

2 Click in cell F5, type **=B5−(B5*I5)**, and press ⏎ENTER.
This formula calculates the wholesale price of the item using the discount that applies if you are ordering a quantity of less than six. The wholesale price is the retail price minus the discount (which is determined by multiplying the retail price by 30%).

3 Copy cell F5 to F6.
The answer is obviously not correct.

4 Click in cell F6 and look at the formula in the formula bar.

> Excel changed the formula to =B6−(B6*I6).
> The reference to B6 is correct, but the reference to I6 isn't.

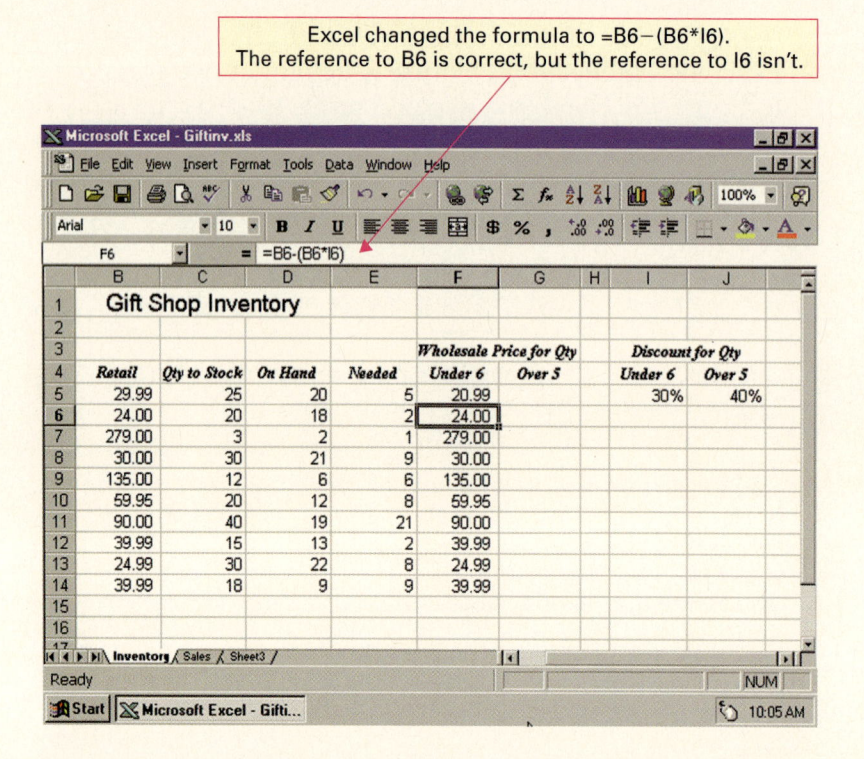

5 Edit the contents of cell F5 and insert dollar signs before and after "I" so the formula looks like **=B5−(B5*I5)** and press (ENTER).
The result in cell F5 is the same as before, but watch what happens when you copy it.

6 Copy cell F5 to the range F6:F13.

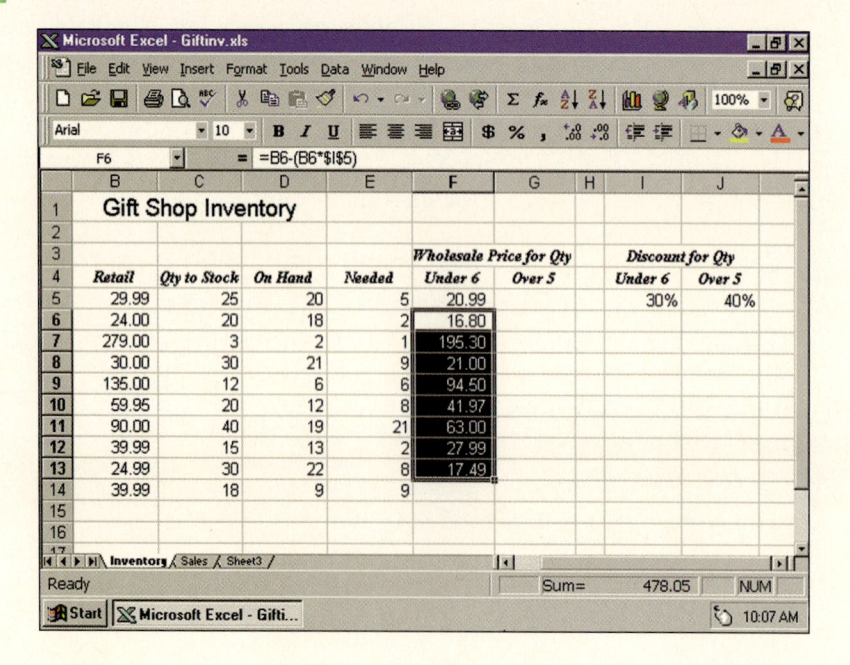

Pointing to Enter Absolute References

In the previous task, you typed the complete formula in the cell, but, as you have seen in other projects, you can enter a formula with the pointing method. When you use this method, you can designate an absolute reference with the F4 key.

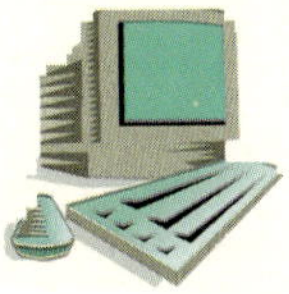

TASK 6: TO ENTER A FORMULA WITH AN ABSOLUTE REFERENCE USING THE POINTING METHOD:

1 Click in cell F14, type an equal sign (=), move to cell B14 using ←, and then type a minus sign followed by an open parenthesis.

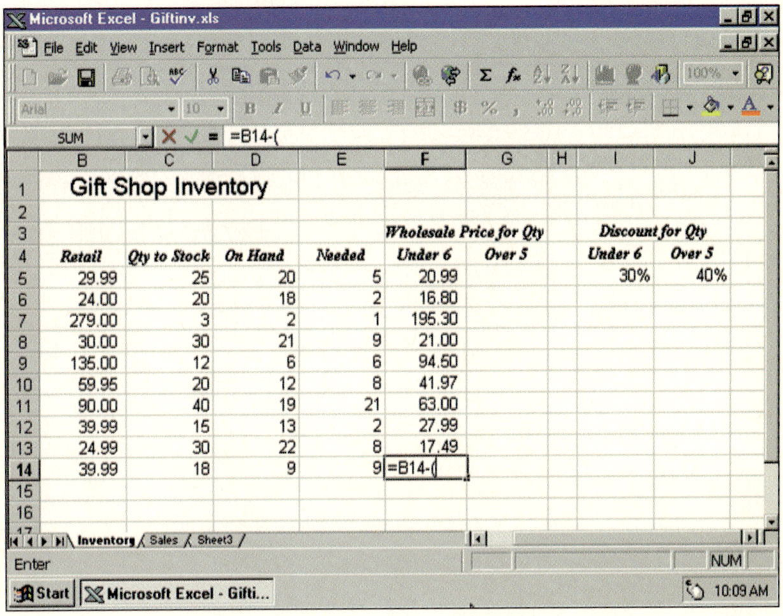

	B	C	D	E	F	G	H	I	J
1	Gift Shop Inventory								
2									
3					Wholesale Price for Qty			Discount for Qty	
4	Retail	Qty to Stock	On Hand	Needed	Under 6	Over 5		Under 6	Over 5
5	29.99	25	20	5	20.99			30%	40%
6	24.00	20	18	2	16.80				
7	279.00	3	2	1	195.30				
8	30.00	30	21	9	21.00				
9	135.00	12	6	6	94.50				
10	59.95	20	12	8	41.97				
11	90.00	40	19	21	63.00				
12	39.99	15	13	2	27.99				
13	24.99	30	22	8	17.49				
14	39.99	18	9	9	=B14-(				
15									
16									

2 Move to cell B14 again, type an asterisk (*),move to cell I5, and then press F4.

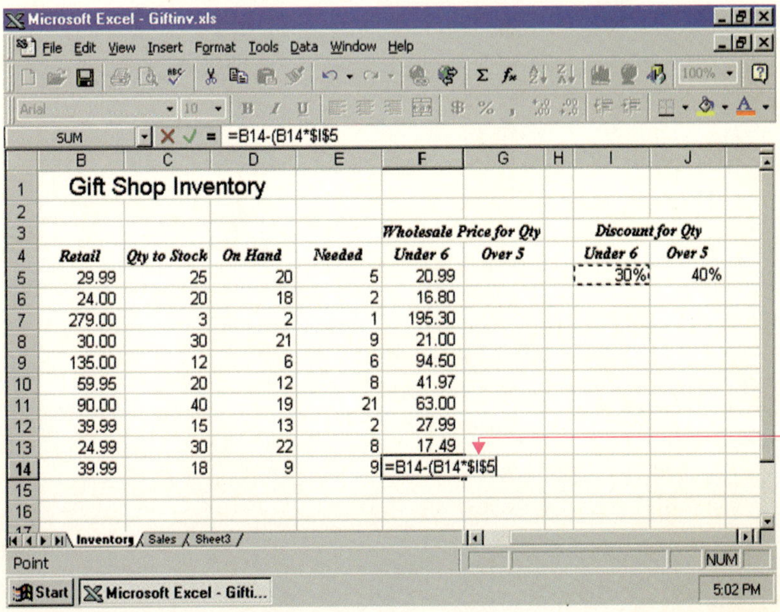

	B	C	D	E	F	G	H	I	J
1	Gift Shop Inventory								
2									
3					Wholesale Price for Qty			Discount for Qty	
4	Retail	Qty to Stock	On Hand	Needed	Under 6	Over 5		Under 6	Over 5
5	29.99	25	20	5	20.99			30%	40%
6	24.00	20	18	2	16.80				
7	279.00	3	2	1	195.30				
8	30.00	30	21	9	21.00				
9	135.00	12	6	6	94.50				
10	59.95	20	12	8	41.97				
11	90.00	40	19	21	63.00				
12	39.99	15	13	2	27.99				
13	24.99	30	22	8	17.49				
14	39.99	18	9	9	=B14-(B14*I5				
15									
16									

The F4 key makes the reference absolute when you use the pointing method

3 Type a closing parenthesis and press ENTER.
The correct calculation (27.99) displays in the cell.

Using Headings with Absolute References

The heading feature in Excel 97 also works with absolute references. When designating an absolute reference for a heading, only one dollar sign is used, and it precedes the heading.

TASK 7: TO ENTER AND COPY A FORMULA WITH AN ABSOLUTE REFERENCE USING HEADINGS:

1 Click in cell G5, type **=retail−(retail*$over 5)**, and press ENTER.

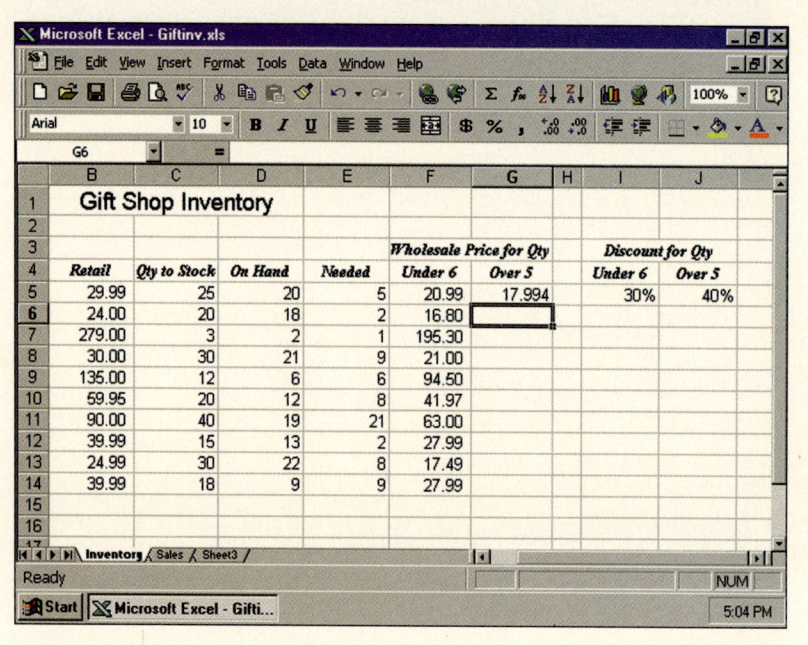

2 Copy cell G5 to the range G6:G14.
The cells display the correct computations.

Creating and Modifying a Chart

Charts present data in a worksheet in a way that numbers never can — visually. Seeing trends and data relationships is so much easier when you look at a chart than when you read numbers. To put a new spin on a tired, old saying, you might say, "A chart is worth 16,777,216 cells." The *Chart Wizard* helps you create charts in Excel.

TASK 8: TO CREATE A COLUMN CHART:

1   Click the Sales tab.

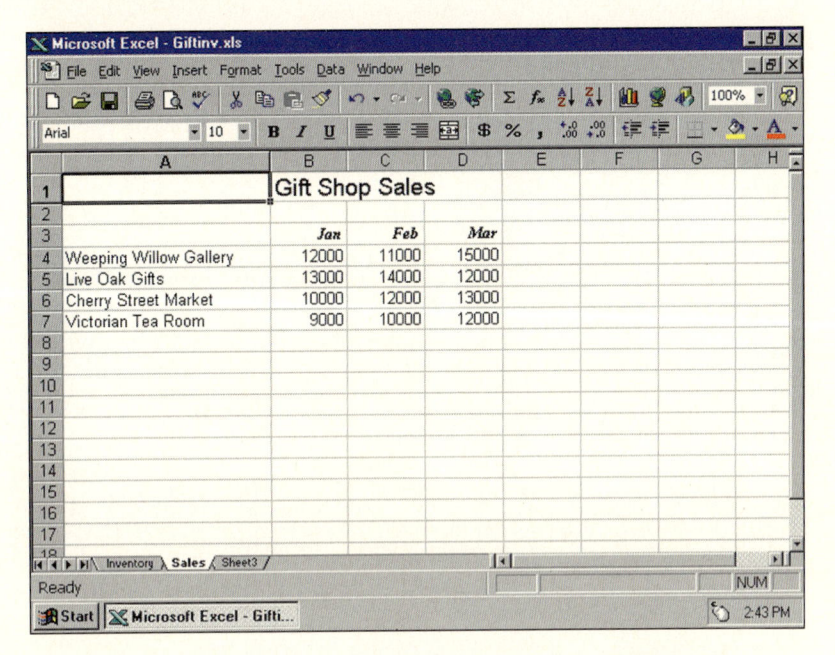

2   Select the range A3:D7 and click the Chart Wizard button.

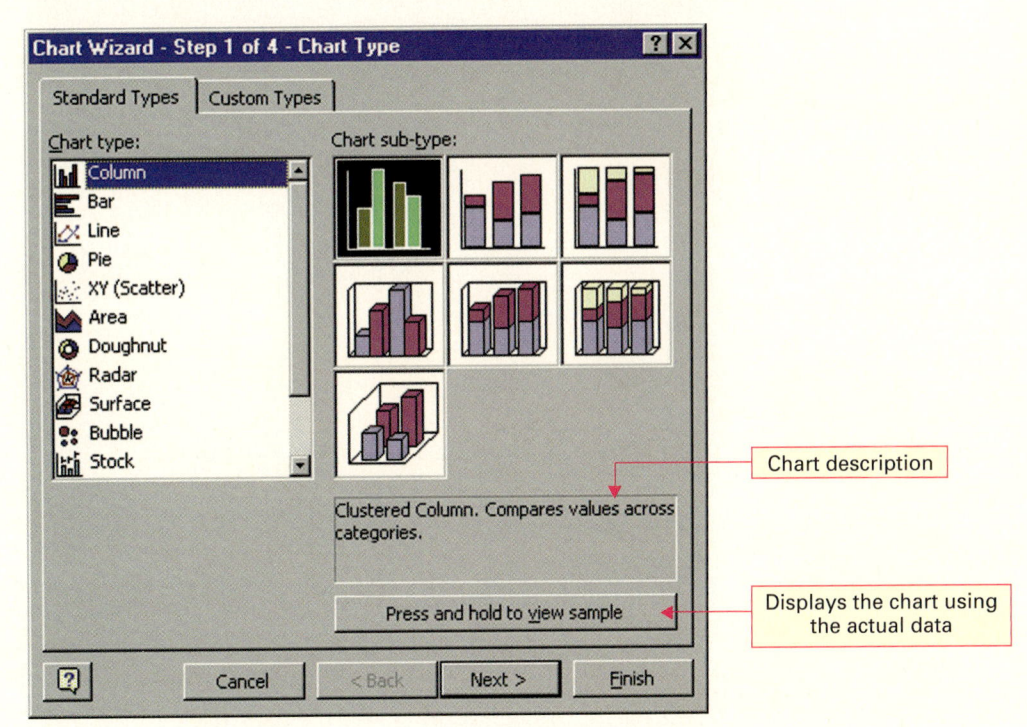

3 Click Next to accept the chart type.

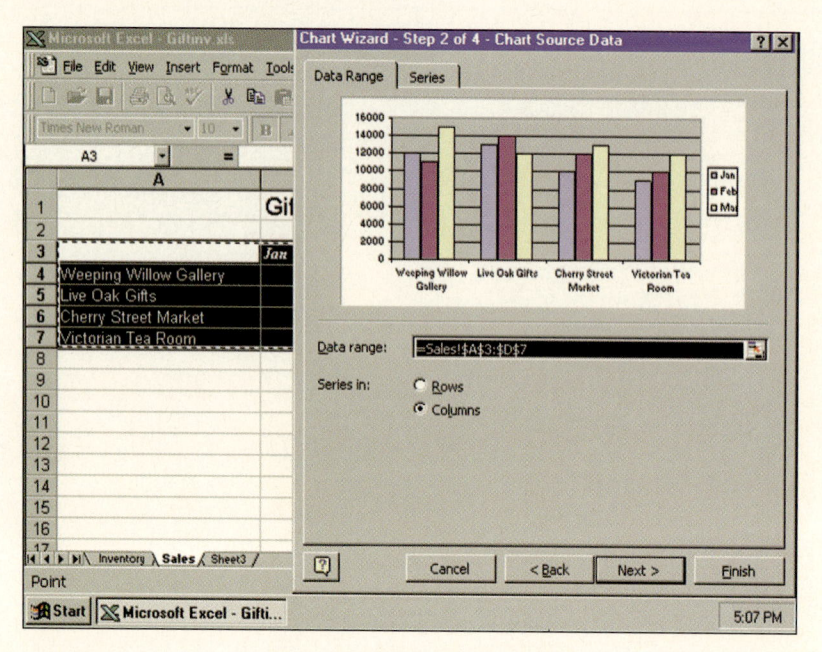

4 Click Next to accept the data range.

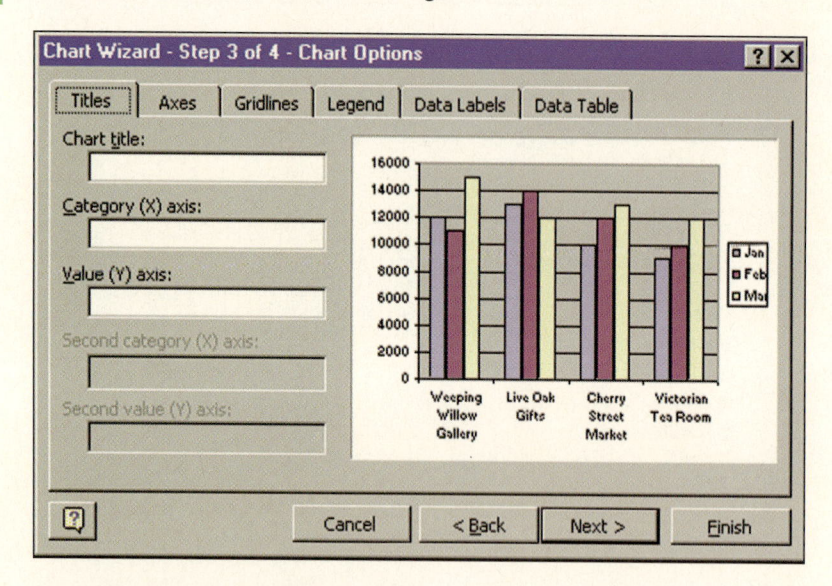

5 Type **First Quarter Sales** for the Chart title and click Next.

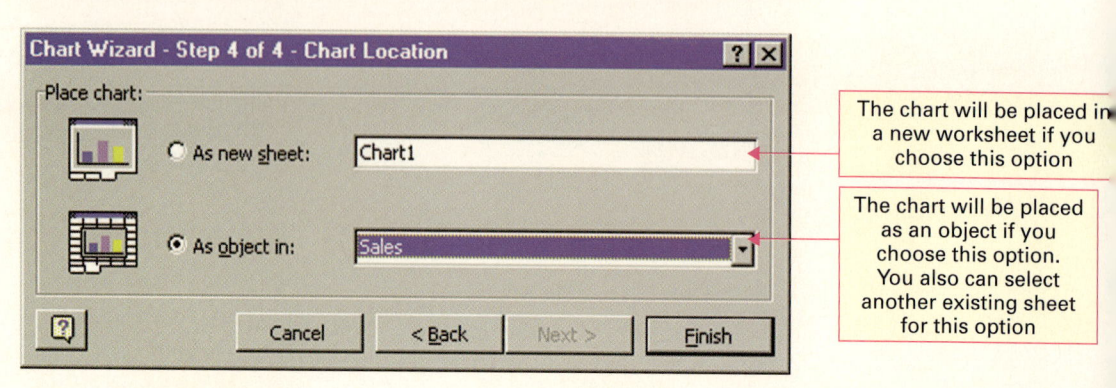

The chart will be placed in a new worksheet if you choose this option

The chart will be placed as an object if you choose this option. You also can select another existing sheet for this option

6   Click Finish.
The chart displays in the current worksheet with *selection handles*. You may want to close the Chart toolbar to see the complete chart.

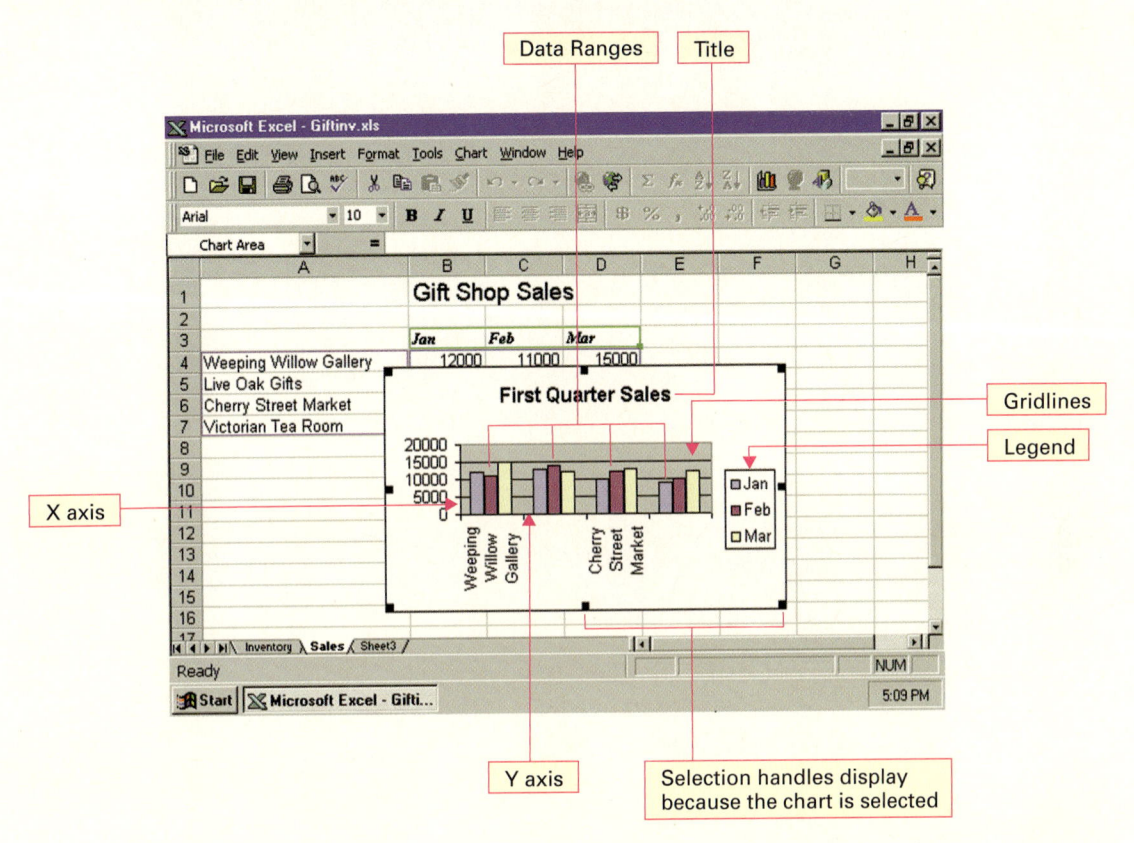

Note The Chart Wizard arbitrarily displays every other data label (in this example, Weeping Willow Gallery and Cherry Street Market), because there is too much text to show all the labels.

Moving and Sizing a Chart

When you place a chart on the same page as the worksheet, the Chart Wizard may place the chart in a location that obscures the data in the worksheet, and it may make the chart too small. Because the chart is an object, you can move it and size it however you want.

TASK 9: TO MOVE AND SIZE THE CHART:

1   Point to a blank area of the chart and drag the chart to the right of the data that created the chart.
The chart moves to the new location.

2 Point to a handle at the bottom of the chart and drag the handle down to make the chart about three rows taller.

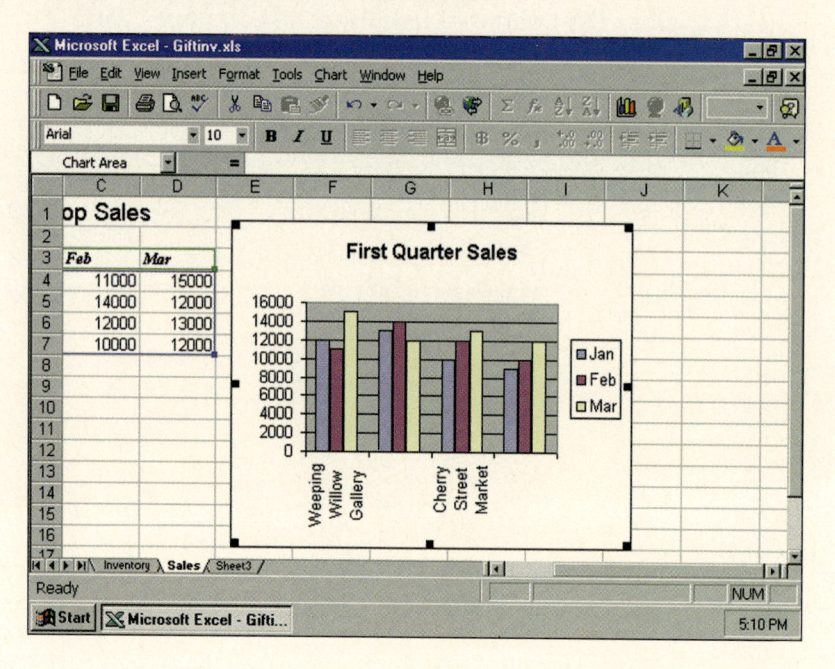

Changing Chart Data

The chart is linked to the data in the worksheet; when you change the data in the worksheet, the chart reflects the change. By the same token, when you change a value in a *data range* in the chart, the data in the worksheet reflects the change.

TASK 10: TO CHANGE CHART DATA:

1 In the worksheet, change the names of the gift shops to abbreviations as follows:
Weeping Willow Gallery: **WWG**;
Live Oak Gifts: **LOG**;
Cherry Street Market: **CSM**;
Victorian Tea Room: **VTR**.
After changing the names, make column A narrower.

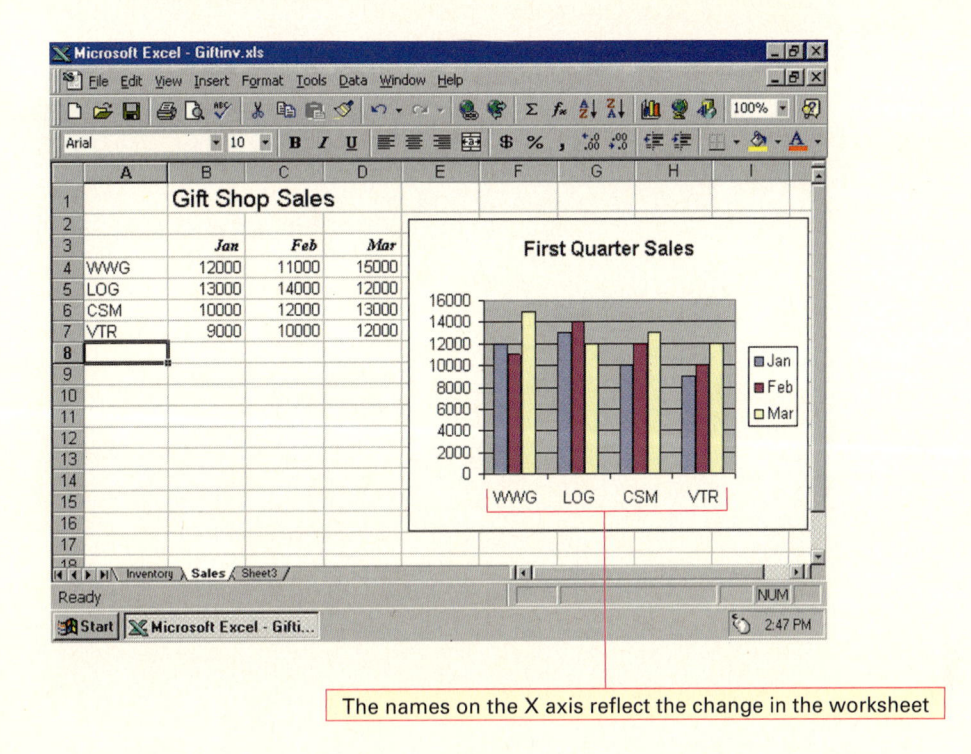

The names on the X axis reflect the change in the worksheet

2 Change the value in cell B4 to 18000 and notice the change in the chart. The height of the first column increases when you change the value.

3 Click the first column in the chart to select the data range for January.

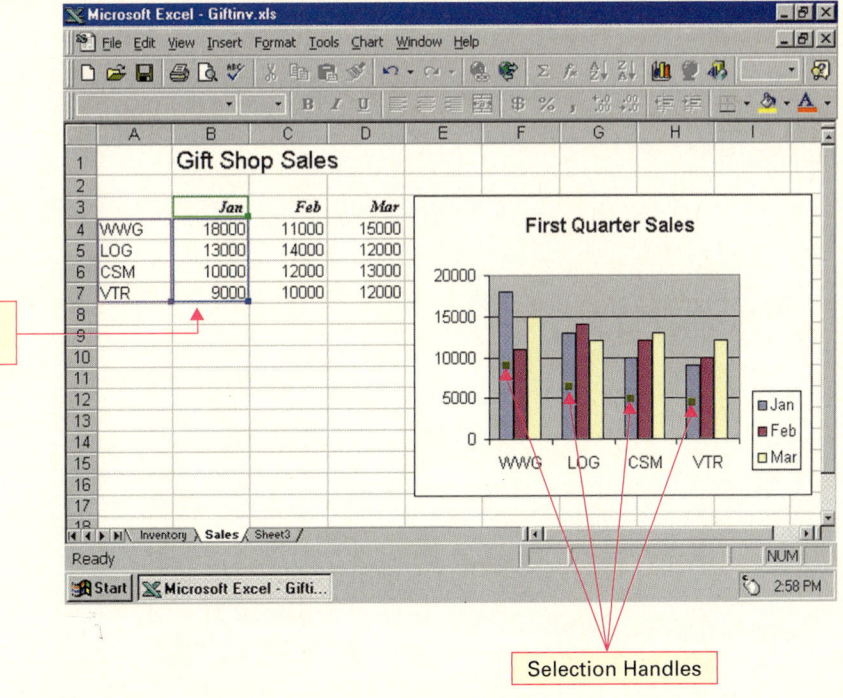

Excel outlines the data that the range refers to

Selection Handles

4 Click the first column again.

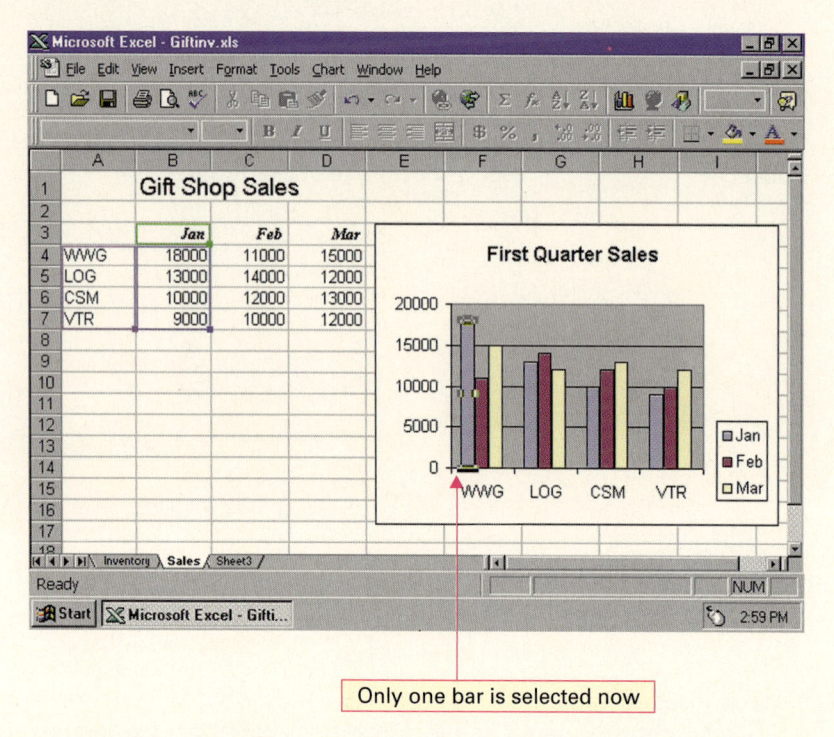

Only one bar is selected now

5 Drag the top of the column up until the value is 21000.

The data in cell B4 changes

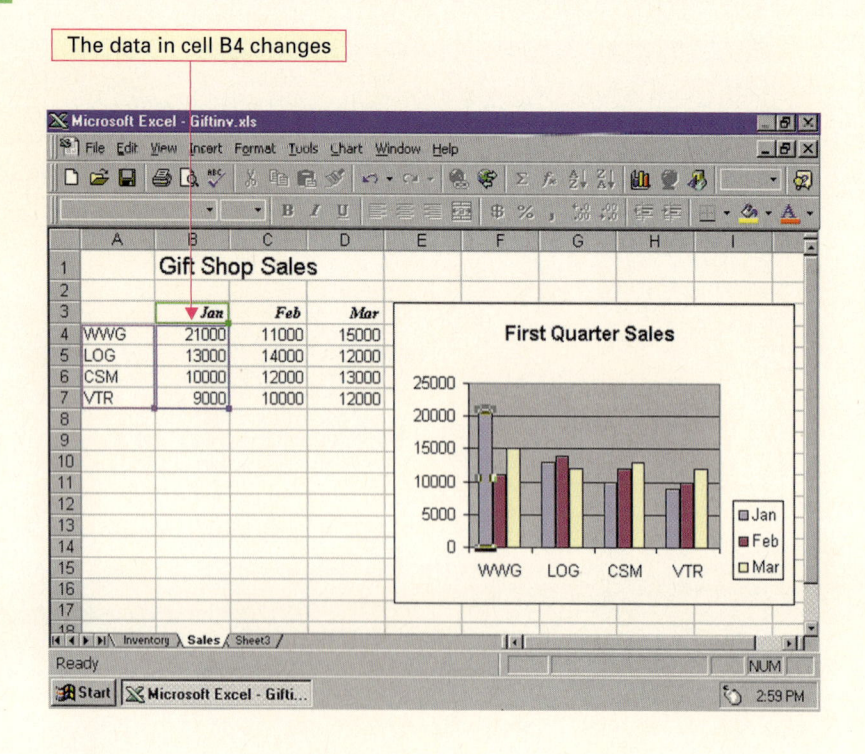

Formatting Chart Elements

When you create a chart with the Chart Wizard, the Chart Wizard decides how the chart elements will look. For example, the Chart Wizard uses the General number format for the scale on the Y axis. After the chart is created, you can format each element of a chart and use the settings that you want.

TASK 11: TO FORMAT CHART ELEMENTS:

1   Right-click the legend, choose Format Legend, and click the Placement tab.

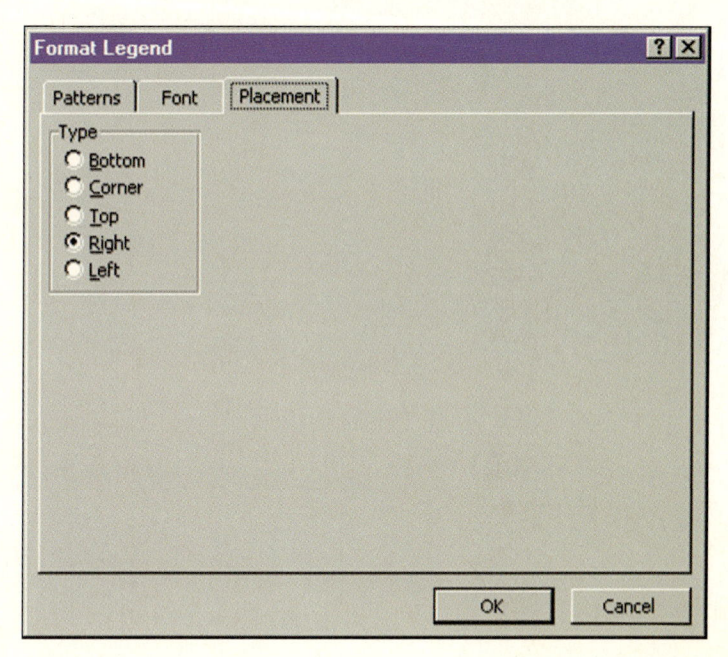

2   Select Bottom and click OK.

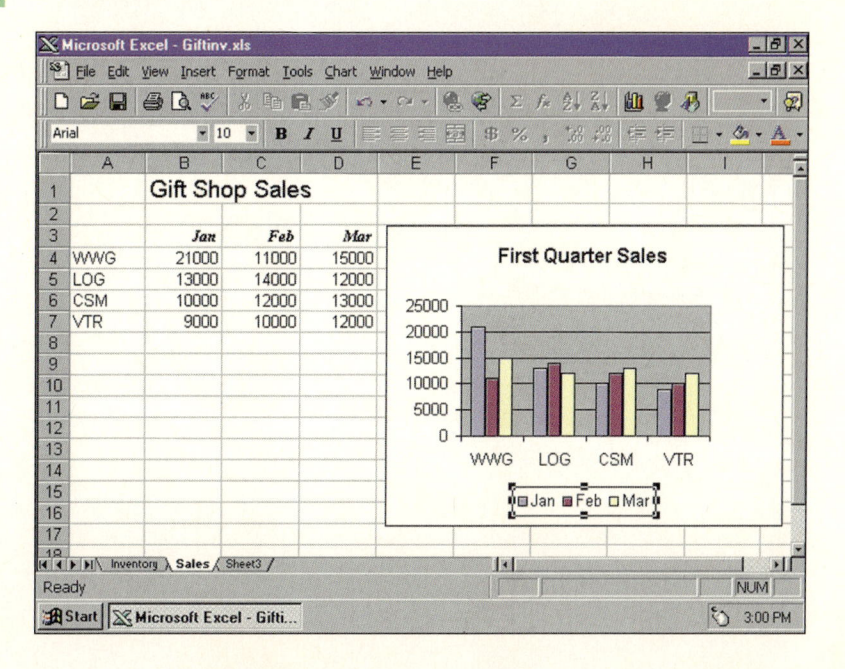

3 Right-click the numbers on the Value axis (Y axis), choose Format Axis, and click the Number tab.

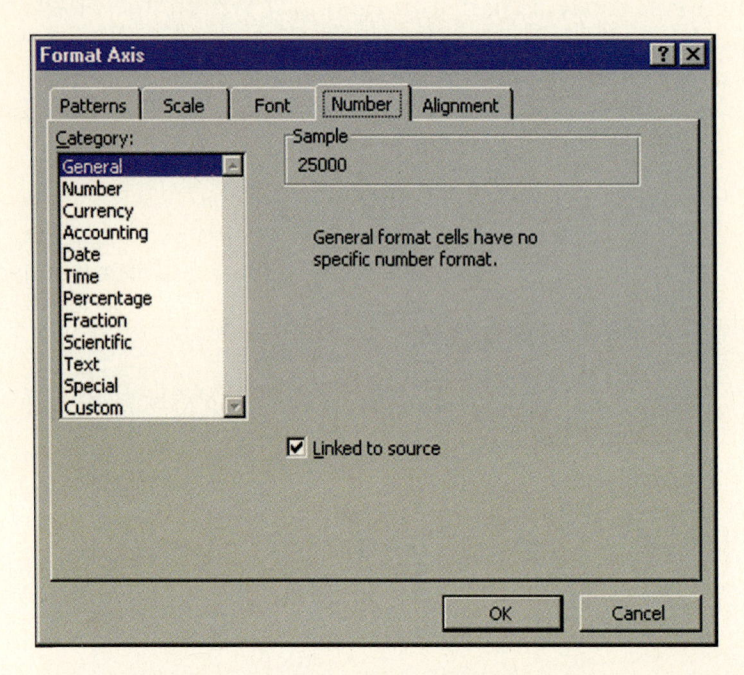

4 Select Currency, 0 decimal places, and click OK.

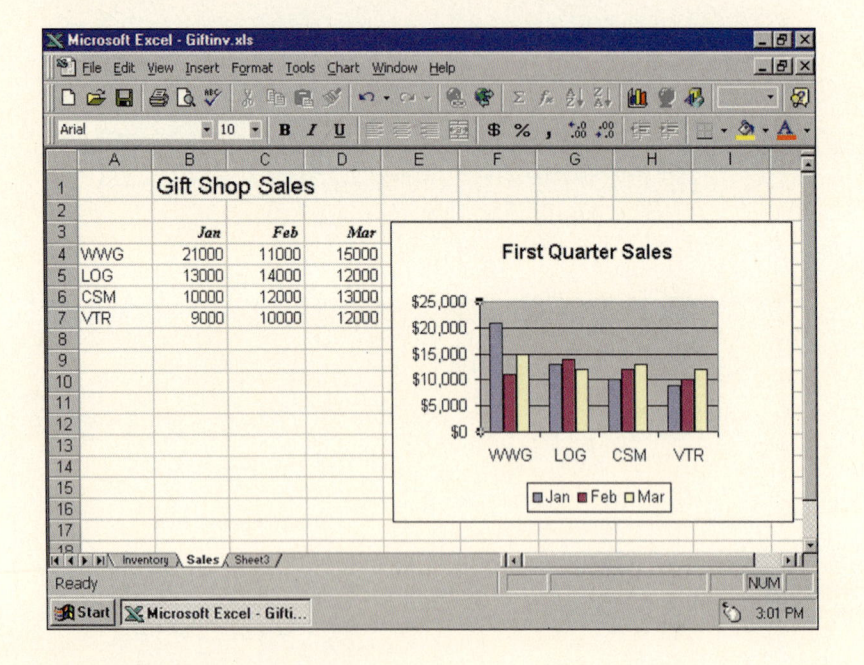

5 Right-click the text on the Category axis (X axis), choose Format Axis, and click the Font tab.

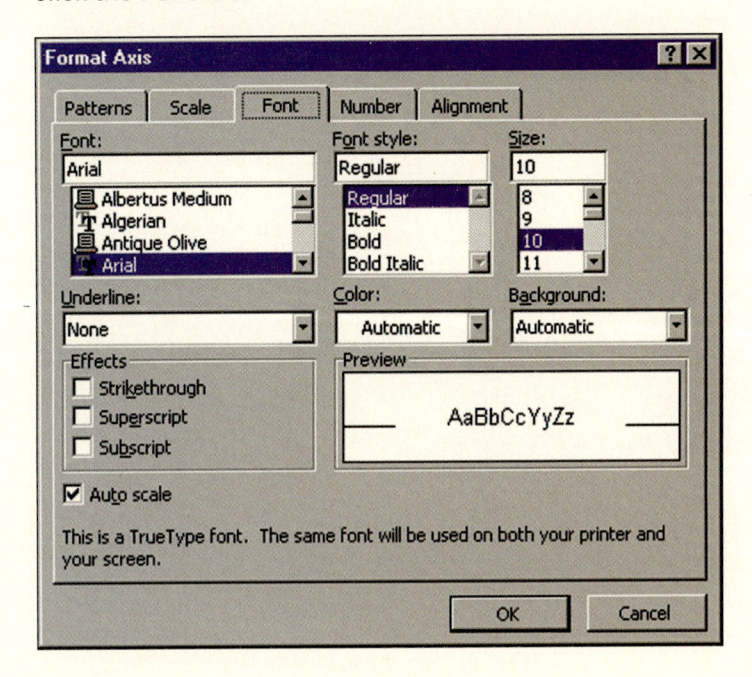

6 Select 8 for the Size and click OK.
The font size of the text is decreased.

Changing the Chart Type

Excel 97 provides many *chart types* and *chart sub-types*. Not all chart types are appropriate for the data in a workbook. Some charts are designed especially for certain types of data. For example, the Stock chart requires three series of data which must be arranged in a specific order: high, low, and close (a stock's high and low values for the day and the closing price of the stock).

TASK 12: TO CHANGE THE CHART TYPE:

1 Right-click a blank area of the chart and choose Chart type.

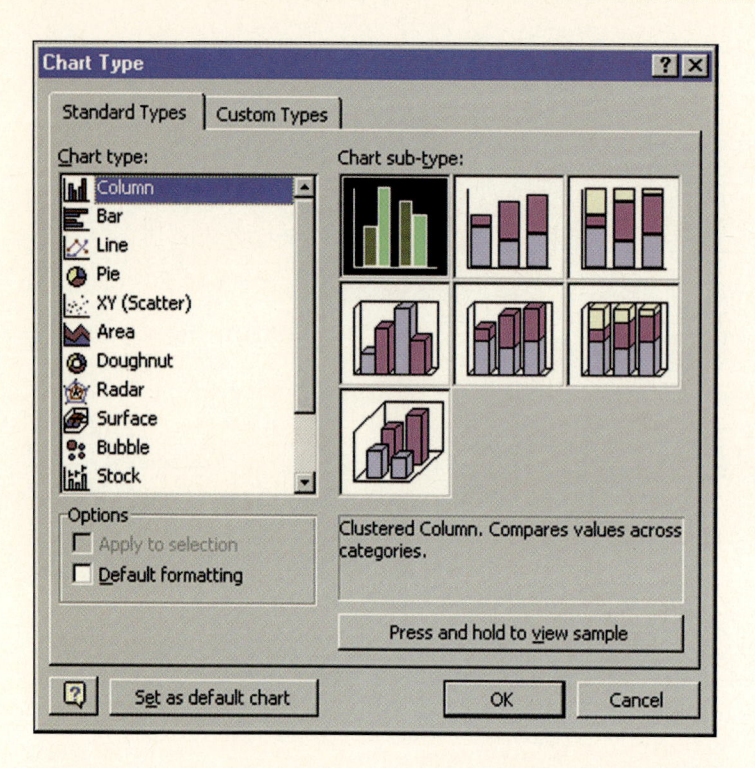

2 Select Line for Chart Type, select the 3-D line sub-type, and click OK.

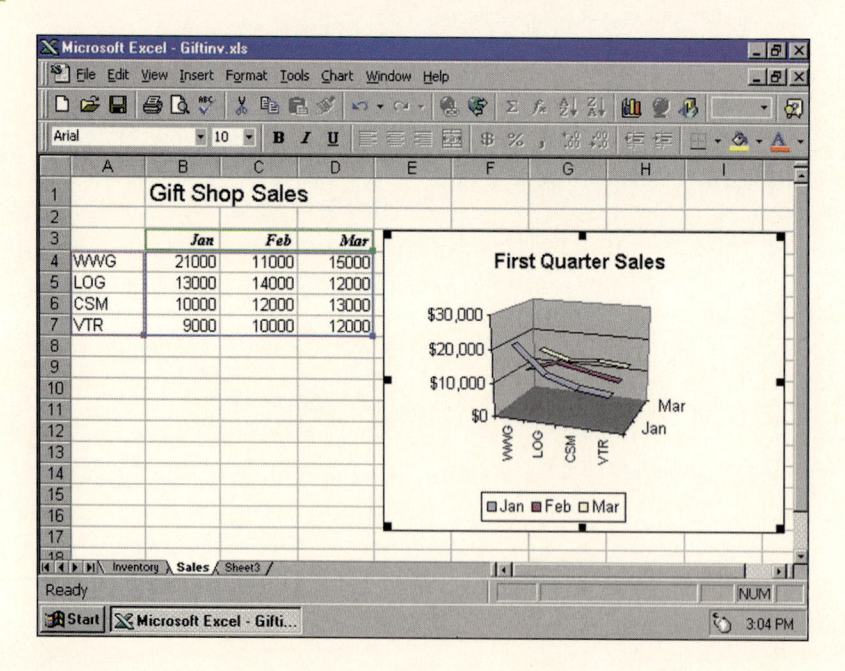

Changing the Chart Options

Settings for the chart **titles**, **X axis**, **Y axis**, **gridlines**, **legend**, **data labels**, and **data table** are all contained in the Chart Options dialog box. After you have created a chart, you can select the options that you want.

TASK 13: TO CHANGE THE CHART OPTIONS:

1 Right-click a blank area of the chart, choose Chart Options, and click the Data Table tab.

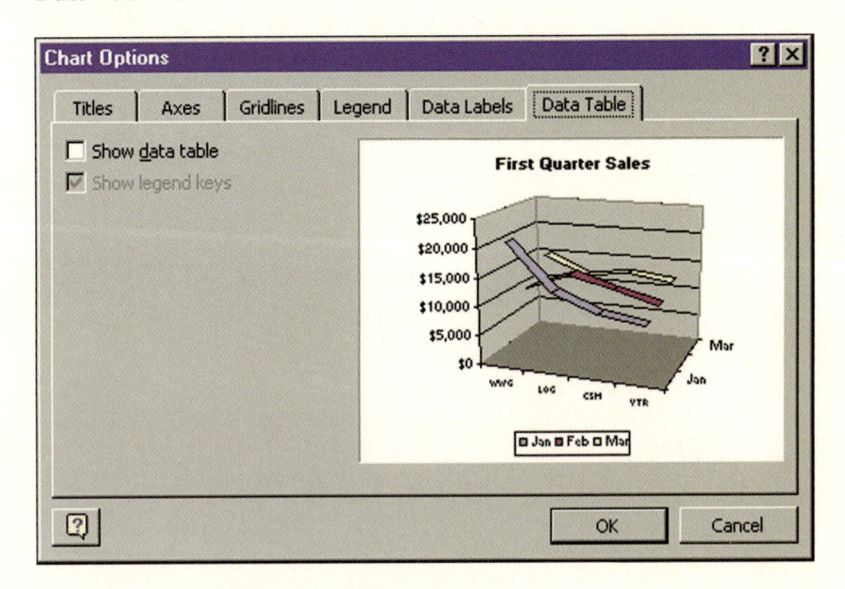

2 Select Show data table and click OK.

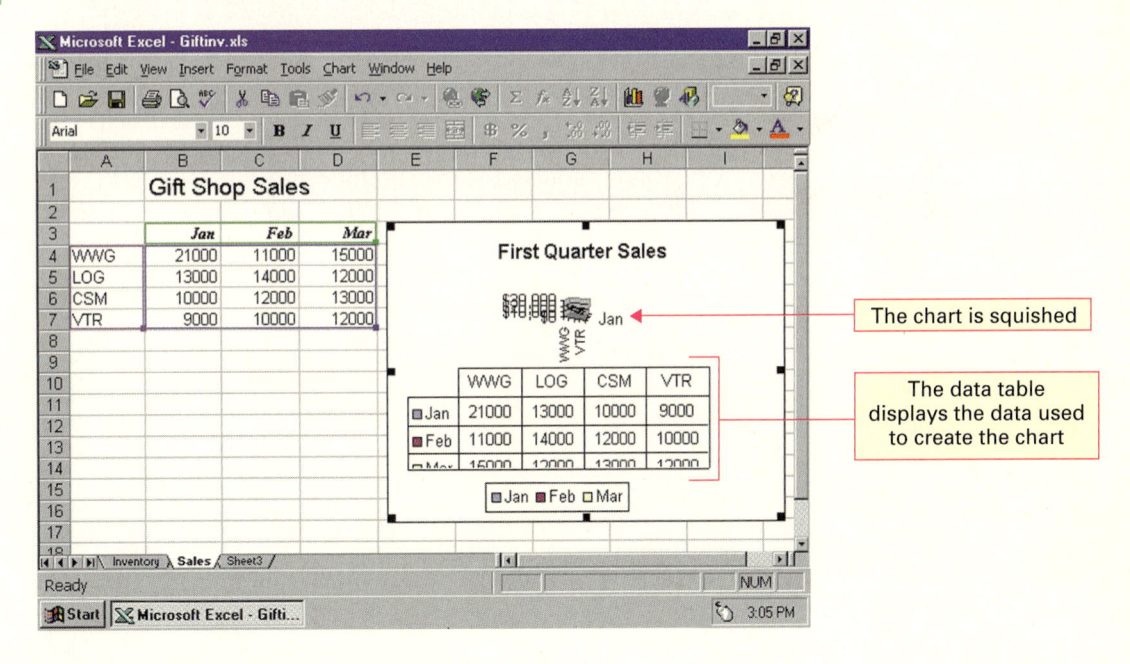

The chart is squished

The data table displays the data used to create the chart

3 Make the chart about 9 rows taller.
The graph returns to its former size.

Creating a Pie Chart

A pie chart is a popular type of chart that shows the relationship of parts to the whole. When selecting data for a pie chart, you will select only one data range.

TASK 14: TO CREATE A PIE CHART:

1 Select the range A4:B7, click ▥, and select Pie as the Chart type and Exploded pie as the sub-type. (A description of the selected chart sub-type shows below the chart sub-type pictures.)

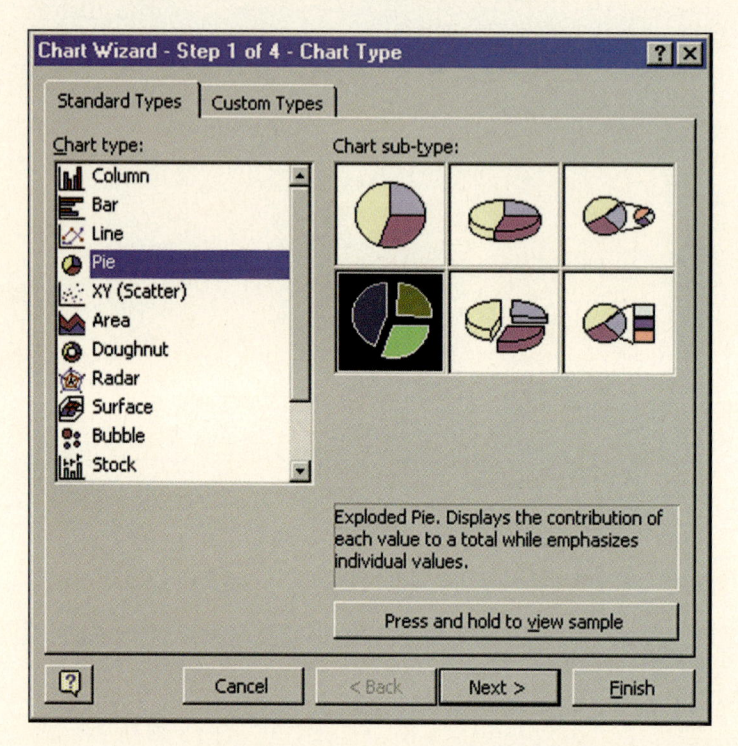

2 Click but don't release the button named Press and hold to view sample. A preview of the chart using your data displays in a Sample box.

3 Release the mouse button and click Next.

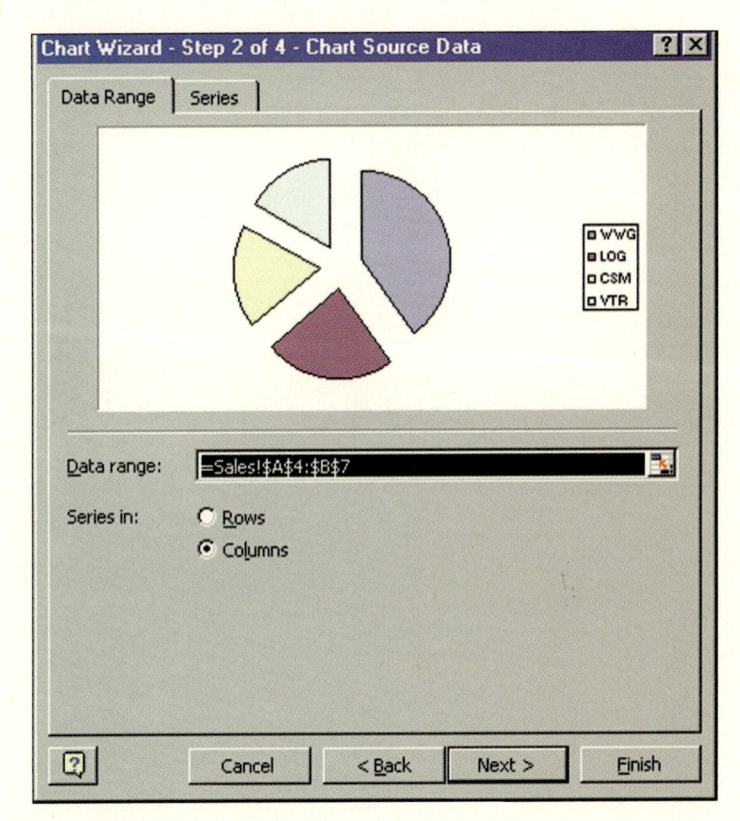

4 Click Next.

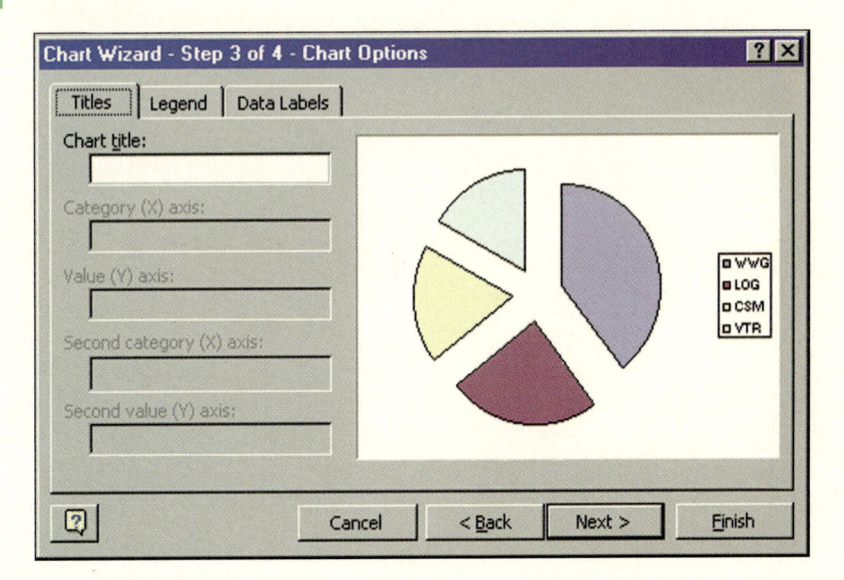

5 Type **January Sales for Gift Shops** for Chart title and click Next.

6 Select As new sheet and click Finish.

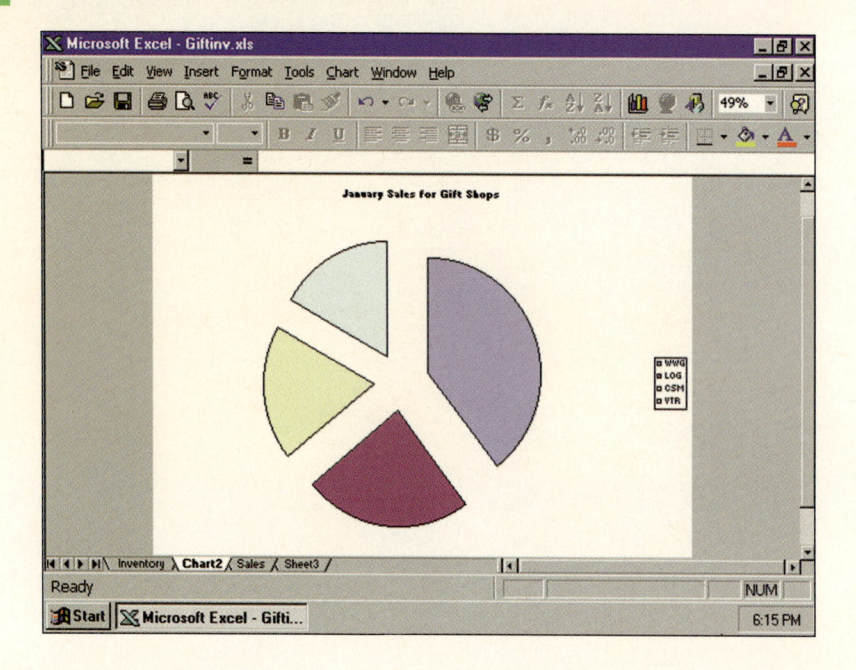

7   Change the chart sub-type to Pie with a 3-D visual effect.

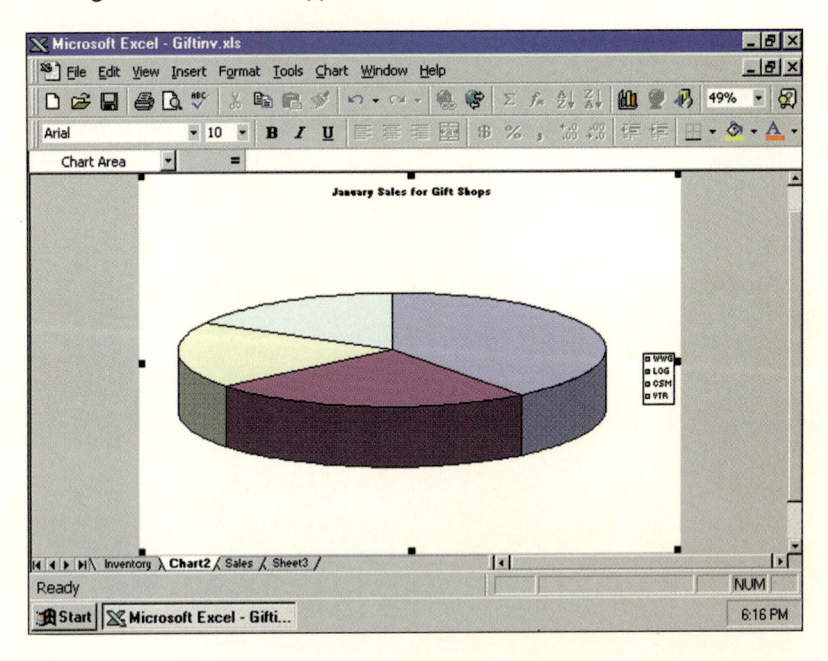

8   Right-click the pie, choose Format Data Series, and click the Data Labels tab.

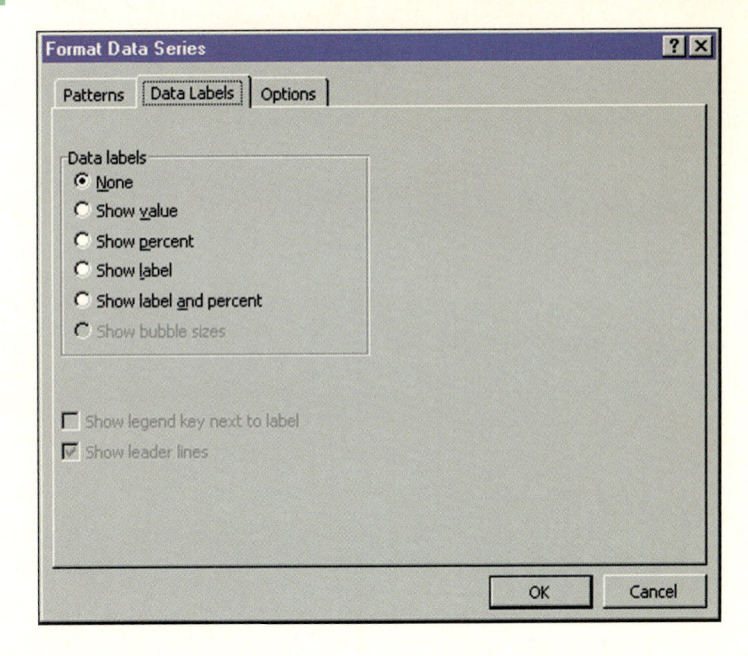

9 Select Show percent and click OK.

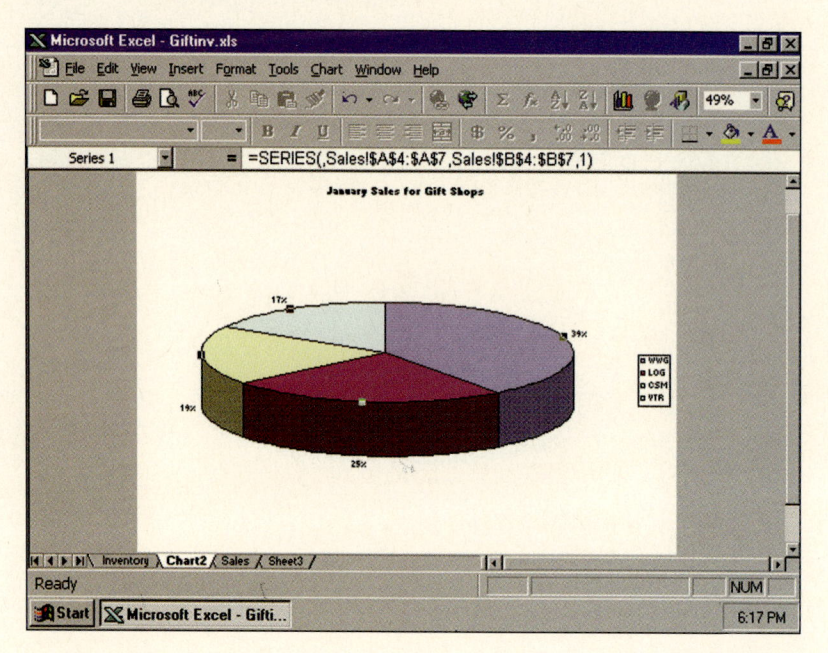

The Conclusion

Save the file as Gift Inventory and Sales.xls. Preview each page of the workbook and print each page if you have access to a printer. Close the file.

Summary and Exercises

Summary

- You can copy data from one workbook to another.
- You can sort data in ascending or descending order.
- Formulas use relative references, headings, and absolute references to refer to particular cells on the worksheet.
- Excel can change the address of relative references when a formula is copied, but it cannot change the address of an absolute reference.
- Charts represent the data in a worksheet visually.
- Charts can be displayed on any worksheet in a workbook.
- Once a chart has been created you can change the type, format the elements, or choose different chart options.

Key Terms and Operations

Key Terms
absolute reference
chart
chart sub-type
chart type
Chart Wizard
data labels
data range
data table
gridlines
heading
legend
relative reference
selection handles
title
X axis
Y axis

Operations
change the chart type
copy data from another workbook
create a chart
enter formulas with relative or absolute addresses
format a chart
move a chart
size a chart
sort data

Study Questions

Multiple Choice

1. Which of the following categories isn't included in the Chart Options dialog box?
   a. Data Labels
   b. Data Table
   c. Axes
   d. Pattern

2. When you sort by using the Sort Ascending button on the Standard toolbar,
   a. columns are sorted individually.
   b. you can sort on only one row.
   c. the first column must be the key column.
   d. you can sort by as many as three columns.

3. Which of the following statements about the Chart Wizard is false?
   a. The Chart Wizard creates charts by guiding you through a step-by-step process.
   b. The Chart Wizard can create only a limited number of charts that are available in Excel 97.
   c. The Chart Wizard is launched by a button on the Standard toolbar.
   d. The Chart Wizard doesn't give you an opportunity to format the chart before it is created.

4. Which of the following formulas is written in incorrect form?
   a. =A1/A10
   b. =A1/A1
   c. =quantity*retail
   d. =quantity*$retail$

5. A relative reference
   a. is the actual address of a cell.
   b. is the range that contains the data labels for a chart.
   c. can be changed by Excel when the formula that contains it is copied to another location.
   d. is denoted by a dollar sign.

6. When a chart is selected,
   a. it has selection handles.
   b. the outline of the chart is blue.
   c. it opens in a separate window.
   d. None of the above.

7. An exploded pie chart is a chart
   a. type.
   b. sub-type.
   c. option.
   d. element.

8. To designate a cell address as an absolute reference when entering a formula using the pointing method, press
   a. F2.
   b. F3.
   c. F4.
   d. F5.

9. If you want to show the relationship of individual values to a total, which chart type would you use?
   a. column
   b. stock
   c. line
   d. pie

10. To prevent a cell address from changing when the formula that contains it is copied to a new location,
    a. use a relative address for the cell.
    b. use an absolute address for the cell.
    c. use the value of the cell instead of the address.
    d. copy the formula with the Edit, Copy command.

Short Answer

1. When you create a chart, what are the two locations where you can place the chart?

2. What is a data table?

3. Where can a legend be placed on a chart?

4. What command do you use if you want to sort on more than one column?

5. How do you move a chart?

6. How do you size a chart?

7. What is the difference between a relative and an absolute reference?

8. Can you use an absolute reference in a formula that uses headings instead of cell addresses?

9. What happens if you change the data in a worksheet after you have created a chart that uses the data?

10. What happens in the worksheet when you select the data ranges in a chart?

For Discussion

1. Discuss the advantages of using headings in formulas.

2. Discuss the advantages of presenting information in charts as opposed to numbers.

3. Name and describe the elements of a chart.

4. Explain how Excel interprets the following formula if it were located in cell H10: =I5+I6*A1.

Review Exercises

1. Revising the Gift Inventory and Sales Workbook

In this exercise, you will make changes to an existing chart.

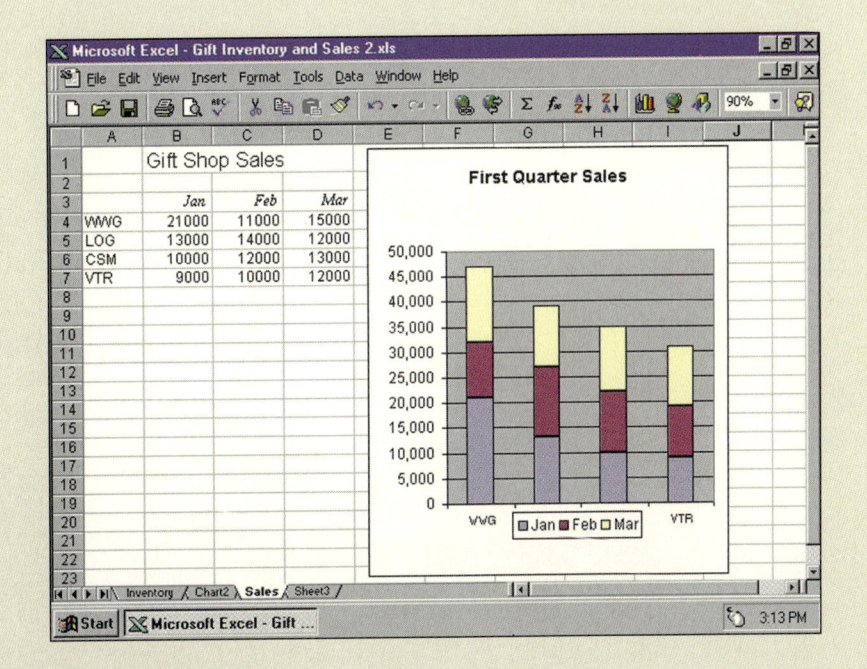

1. Open *Gift Inventory and Sales.xls*.

2. Click the Sales tab if necessary.

3. Change the chart type to a stacked column.

4. Remove the data table.

5. Remove the dollar sign from the numbers on the Y axis.

6. Save the file as Gift Inventory and Sales 2.xls and close the file.

2. Creating a New Items Workbook

In this exercise, you will create a workbook that lists five possible new items and computes the discount on the items.

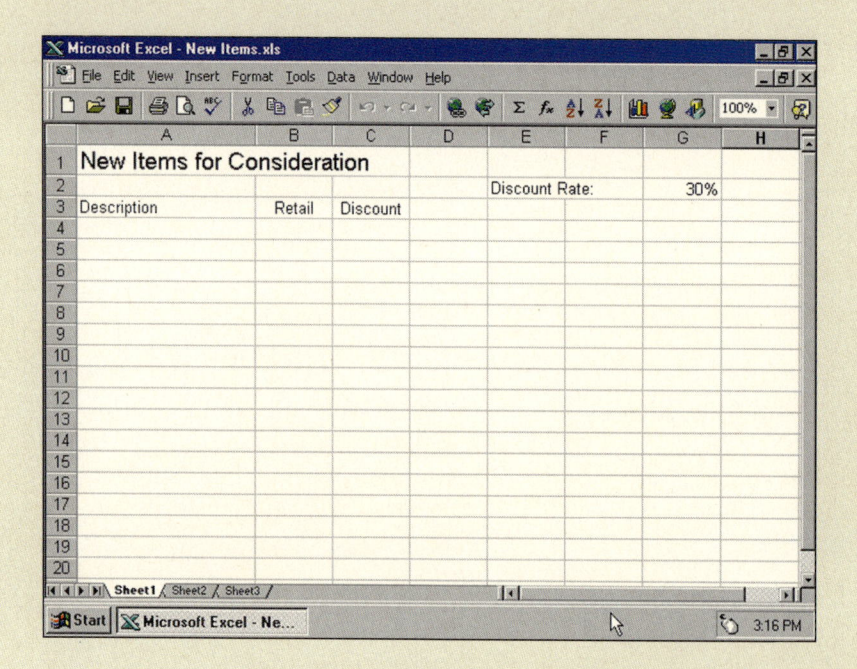

1. Create the workbook shown above.

2. Find five items on the Web that you can suggest as new items for the gift shops to carry. Enter the descriptions of the items and their retail prices in the worksheet in the appropriate columns.

3. In cell C4, enter the formula that multiplies the discount rate in cell G2 times the retail price in cell B4. Copy the formula to the range C5:C8.

4. Save the file as *New Items.xls* and close the file.

Assignments

1. Creating a Chart of Expenditures

Create a workbook that lists your expenditures for the past month. Create a pie chart for the data. Are you spending too much on pizza?

2. Completing a Vacation Package Workbook

Download the workbook *Vacation.xls* from the Addison Wesley Longman web site (http://www.awl.com/is/select/) or ask your instructor for this workbook file. Sort the data in ascending order in the range A4:C8. Enter a formula in cell D4 that multiplies the Price/Person times the appropriate discount rate (cell H4). Copy the formula to the other cells in the column. Enter appropriate formulas for the Travel Agency discounts and the Resort Club discounts. Use headings in the formulas for the Resort Club discounts.

Notes

Notes

Notes

Glossary

Absolute reference An address you use to reference a specific cell or range of cells in a worksheet; this reference, which doesn't change, is denoted with the dollar sign symbol, as in A1.

Active cell The cell in which you can enter data or perform calculations. You make the cell active by clicking in the cell or by moving to the cell with keystrokes. This cell is outlined with a black border.

Arithmetic operators The operators you use to perform calculations in formulas and functions: + (addition), − (subtraction), * (multiplication), / (division), % (percent), and ^ (exponentiation).

AutoCalculate A feature that displays a calculation in the status bar when you select a range with values.

AutoFit A feature that automatically adjusts the column or row to be just wide enough to accommodate the widest or tallest entry.

Border A line that displays on any side of a cell or group of cells. You can use borders to draw rectangles around cells, to create dividers between columns, to create a total line under a column of numbers, and so on.

Cell The intersection of a column and a row in a worksheet.

Chart A visual representation of data in a worksheet.

Chart sub-type A variation on a Chart type. For example, the column type chart has these sub-types in both 2-D and 3-D: Clustered Column, Stacked Column, and 100% Stacked Column.

Chart type A chart that represents data in a specific format, such as columns, a pie, scatter points, etc.

Chart Wizard An Excel feature you use to create charts. When you create a chart with the Chart Wizard, the Chart Wizard decides how the chart elements will look.

Clipboard A memory area in which data that has been cut or copied is stored.

Column A vertical block of cells in a worksheet that extends from row 1 to row 65,536.

Column indicators The letters associated with the columns on a worksheet.

Comment Text that you can attach to cells in a worksheet to provide additional information.

Data labels The names you attach to different types of data in a chart. You define this setting in the Chart Options dialog box.

Data range A block of cells used to create an element in a chart.

Data table A table showing the data that is used to create a chart.

Edit mode The mode in which you edit the contents of a cell.

Enter mode The mode in which you enter data in a worksheet.

Error mode The mode Excel switches to if you make an error when entering data in a cell.

Fill A color or a shade of gray that you apply to the background of a cell. Also called *shading* or *patterns*.

Footer Text that prints at the bottom of every page of a worksheet.

Formatting toolbar Contains buttons and controls for formatting. To use the toolbar, click a button to perform a command or view a dialog box.

Formula A mathematical statement that performs calculations. You create and enter formulas to perform the specific calculations needed.

Formula bar The area at the top of the window that displays the cell address and the contents of the active cell. You can use it to enter and edit data and formulas.

Function A mathematical statement that performs calculations. Functions are formulas that have already been created by Excel. They perform calculations that are commonly used such as calculating a sum or an average.

Gridlines The vertical and horizontal lines in a chart that mark the values.

Header Text that prints at the top of every page of a worksheet.

Legend The description of elements in a chart. You define this setting in the Chart Options dialog box.

Menu bar The bar at the top of the window that contains menu options. To use the menu, click an option to display a drop-down menu, and then click an option on the drop-down menu to perform a command, view another menu, or view a dialog box.

Mode indicator A feature displayed on the far left side of the status bar. It shows a word that describes the current working condition of the program. For example, the word *Ready* means that the worksheet is ready to receive data or execute a command. Other modes include *Edit, Enter, Point, Error,* and *Wait.*

Office Assistant The new Help feature that offers help on the task you're performing, often referred to as context-sensitive help.

Order of precedence   The sequence in which each operation should be performed when a formula has more than one operation. The Excel order of precedence is as follows: exponentiation, then multiplication or division (from left to right), and finally addition or subtraction (from left to right). If the formula has parentheses, the operation(s) in the parentheses are performed first.

Page break   A mark that indicates where one page ends and another one begins.

Page Break Preview   The view in which you can see where the pages will break when the worksheet prints.

Pattern   A color or a shade of gray that you apply to the background of a cell. Also called *fill* or *shading*.

Point mode   The mode in which you're pointing to cells to build a formula or function in a worksheet.

Print Preview mode   The mode that shows the full page view of the current page of the current worksheet. In this mode you can view additional pages of the worksheet, or you can zoom in on the page so that you can actually read the data, if necessary.

Range   A block of cells selected as a group.

Ready mode   The mode in which the worksheet is ready to receive data or execute a command.

Relative reference   A worksheet address that Excel automatically changes when a formula is copied to another location.

Row   A horizontal block of cells in a worksheet that extends from column A to column IV.

Row indicators   The numbers associated with the rows on a worksheet.

Scientific notation   A number format used for very large numbers and very small decimal numbers. For example, the scientific notation for 1,000,000,000 is 1E+09 which means 1 times 10 to the ninth power. If you enter a number that won't fit in a cell, Excel either converts the number to scientific notation or displays pound signs (#) in the cell.

Scroll bars   The bars on the side or the bottom of the window that enable you to scroll the screen vertically and horizontally.

Selection handles   The black squares that appear when a chart is selected. You use them to size the chart.

Shading   A color or a shade of gray that you apply to the background of a cell. Also called *fill* or *pattern*.

Standard toolbar   Contains buttons and controls used to the most common perform commands. To use the toolbar, click a button to perform a command or view a dialog box.

Status bar   The bar at the bottom of the window that displays information about the current workbook.

Title   The name of the chart. You define this setting in the Chart Options dialog box.

Title bar   The bar at the top of a window that displays the Minimize, Maximize/Restore, and Close buttons.

Toolbar   A bar that contains buttons for performing commands. To use the toolbar, click a button to perform a command or view a dialog box.

Wait mode   The mode in effect when the worksheet is busy and cannot accept data or commands.

Web toolbar   The toolbar containing buttons for Internet use. To display the Web toolbar, click the Web Toolbar button in the Standard toolbar. To hide the Web toolbar, click the Web Toolbar button again.

Workbook   A file that contains Excel worksheets. By default, a new workbook file has three worksheets.

Worksheet   A page in a workbook file.

Worksheet scroll buttons   The buttons you use on the scroll bar to scroll the tabs for the worksheets.

Worksheet tab   A part of the window that displays the names of worksheets in the current workbook. Clicking a tab displays the worksheet.

X axis   The horizontal axis in a chart. You define this setting in the Chart Options dialog box.

Y axis   The vertical axis in a chart. You define this setting in the Chart Options dialog box.

Index

Notes

Notes

Notes

Notes

Notes

Notes